INCLUSION, PARTICIPATION AND DEMOCRACY:
WHAT IS THE PURPOSE?

Inclusive Education: Cross Cultural Perspectives

VOLUME 2

Series Editors:
Len Barton, *Institute of Education, University of London, United Kingdom*
Marcia Rioux, *School of Health, Policy & Management, Atkinson Faculty of Liberal & Professional Studies, York University, Toronto, Ontario, Canada*

Editorial Board:
Mithu Alur, *National Resource Centre for Inclusion, Bandra (West), Mumbia, India*
Susan Peters, *College of Education, Michigan State University, East Lansing, MI, U.S.A.*
Roger Slee, *Education Queensland, Brisbane, Queensland, Australia*
Ronald G. Sultana, *Euro-Mediterranean Centre for Educational Research, University of Malta, Msida, Malta*

SCOPE OF THE SERIES

This series is concerned with exploring the meaning and function of inclusive education in a world characterised by rapid social, economic and political change. The question of inclusion and exclusion will be viewed as a human rights issue, in which concerns over issues of equity, social justice and participation will be of central significance. The series will provide an inter-disciplinary approach and draw on research and ideas that will contribute to an awareness and understanding of cross-cultural insights and questions. Dominant assumptions and practices will be critically analysed thereby encouraging debate and dialogue over such fundamentally important values and concerns.

Inclusion, Participation and Democracy: What is the Purpose?

Edited by

JULIE ALLAN
University of Stirling, U.K.

KLUWER ACADEMIC PUBLISHERS
DORDRECHT / BOSTON / LONDON

A C.I.P. Catalogue record for this book is available from the Library of Congress.

ISBN 1-4020-1264-0 (HB)
ISBN 1-4020-1265-9 (PB)

Published by Kluwer Academic Publishers,
P.O. Box 17, 3300 AA Dordrecht, The Netherlands.

Sold and distributed in North, Central and South America
by Kluwer Academic Publishers,
101 Philip Drive, Norwell, MA 02061, U.S.A.

In all other countries, sold and distributed
by Kluwer Academic Publishers,
P.O. Box 322, 3300 AH Dordrecht, The Netherlands.

Printed on acid-free paper

Printed in the Netherlands.

TABLE OF CONTENTS

Part Three: Pressing for Change

NOTES ON CONTRIBUTORS

Mel Ainscow is Professor of Education at the University of Manchester. He is a former headteacher and LEA inspector, and has recently advised Ministers on policies related to achievement and inclusion, particularly in respect of performance league tables. He has also been a consultant to UNESCO, UNICEF and Save the Children and directed the UNESCO Teacher Education Project, Special Needs in the Classroom, involving activities in more than 80 countries.

Julie Allan is Professor of Education in the Institute of Education, University of Stirling and Director of the Participation, Inclusion and Equity Research (PIER) Network. Her research interests are in inclusion, children's rights and new community schools and she has recently been Advisor to the Scottish Parliament. Her book, Actively seeking inclusion, is published by Falmer.

Fernando Almeida Diniz has recently retired after over thirty years as a teacher and researcher in education. He has held senior posts in the Universities of Edinburgh and Greenwich (London) and led a number of national projects to promote social justice perspectives in education policy and practice.

Keith Ballard is a Professor in the Department of Education at the University of Otago, New Zealand. His research interests are in inclusive education, action research with families of disabled children, qualitative methodologies and culture. He edited the collection, Inclusive education: International voices on disability and justice, published by Falmer.

Dora S. Bjarnason is an Associate Professor at the Iceland University of Education. She has worked within inclusive education, and disability studies for almost two decades as a researcher and a lecturer in Iceland, the USA, Australia, New Zealand, Japan and Denmark, at various Universities and research institutes. She is the mother of a young man with significant Impairments and the author of several books and articles on inclusion.

Alison Closs is Senior Lecturer in Inclusive Education at Edinburgh University. She has known former Yugoslavia since 1960, receiving the Order of the Yugoslav Flag with Gold Star in 1984 for services to Yugoslav Youth. Her edited book, The Education of Children with Medical Conditions (published by David Fulton), was runner-up for the NASEN Academic Book Award in 2000.

Colleen Cummings is a researcher in the School of Education, University of Newcastle. Her research interests include social and educational exclusion. She has been involved in research on the social exclusion of young mothers, the role of schools in community generation and youth transitions.

Alan Dyson is Professor of Education at the University of Newcastle. He is the Director of the Special Needs Research Centre and his research interests encompass special educational needs policy at school, local and national level and the relationship between social disadvantage and educational difficulty. He is currently working with UNESCO to develop an Open File on Inclusive Education which will support policymakers internationally.

Gwynned Lloyd works in the School of Education, University of Edinburgh. Her research interests include inclusion/exclusion, gender and deviance and she has published widely in these areas. She has recently been involved in a study of alternatives to exclusion.

Alan Millward is based in the School of Education, University of Newcastle. His research interests encompass special and inclusive education and social disadvantage, and he has been involved in numerous research projects in these areas, at local, national and international levels.

Kari Nes is an Associate Professor in Education at Hedmark University College in Norway. She is involved in international collaboration on inclusion research and on the development of European master studies in inclusive education. She is presently engaged in a national evaluation of inclusion.

Roger Slee is currently Deputy Director General in the Queensland Government, seconded from his post as Professor and Dean in the University of Western Australia. He is the editor of the International Journal of Inclusive Education and the author of numerous books and articles on inclusion.

Marit Strømstad is an Assistant Professor at the department of education, Hedmark college, Norway. She is engaged in teacher education, pre-service and postgraduate. In recent years she has been engaged in a project aimed at evaluating the inclusiveness of Norwegian schools. She is co-editor of a forthcoming book on inclusion in teacher education.

Linda Ware has published extensively on educational inclusion and curriculum development for inclusive classrooms. Most recently her publications have addressed disability studies in education. She is a Visiting Professor in the Department of Disability Studies and Human Development at the University of Illinois, Chicago and concurrently holds the position of Visiting Scholar in the Disability Studies Program and the Center on Human Policy at the Syracuse University School of Education.

SERIES EDITOR'S FOREWORD

The question of inclusive education is one which many societies are attempting to address. It is a fundamentally serious and complex issue raising challenges that cover conceptual, organizational, pedagogical, curricular and socio-economic concerns and questions. In this edited collection of papers the reader is confronted with these challenges through, on the one hand, a critical informative analysis of some of the key existing ideas and, on the other, a series of alternative insights and questions requiring further exploration and debate. Adding to the overall quality of the book is the much needed cross-cultural dimension in terms of insights, knowledge, understanding and difficult questions.

This is an important book in which new research and interpretations are reported on and discussed. Overall, the papers provide a serious critique of such factors as: the limitations of existing definitions of inclusive education; the narrowness of the focus within which inclusive issues are too often presented; the negative impacts of marketisation, performativity and the standards agenda on the realisation of inclusive values and practice and the constraints of significant socio-economic inequalities and disadvantages within and between communities and schools. These raise serious questions concerning the extent to which schools can make a positive difference in the lives of many pupils.

The papers explore a range of significant issues and recurring themes. Firstly, the ambiguity, contradictory and fragmentary nature of official policy development and implementation is carefully identified and critically explored. This provides the context for examining and understanding some of the powerful barriers to inclusive planning and practice. Secondly, existing definitions of inclusive education are highlighted and critiqued. Alternative definitions are developed thereby broadening the framework within which the complexity of the wider socio-economic contexts and the position and role of schools can be understood and pursued. Thirdly, the extent and quality of the reflective thinking in these papers is most vividly demonstrated in the number of difficult questions they raise, thereby providing a wealth of issues for investigation and debate. For example:

- What, precisely, is the link between inclusive schools and an inclusive society?
- How far does much of the existing knowledge and practice of special education constitute one of the major barriers to inclusion?
- To what extent is the support that some children and their families receive based on an inappropriate medicalised approach?
- What form will teacher education for inclusion take?

Finally, the cross-cultural insights within the book provide further stimulus for reflecting on our own values, priorities and practices. The reinforce the importance of understanding these complex ideas and issues in relation to particular historical, cultural and social contexts. Trying to understand the distinctiveness and connections between different societies in relation to these developments is a challenge of immense importance. One issue which we all need to address concerns the extent to which war, or the threat of war, is a serious barrier to the pursuit of inclusive practices and values? This crucial issue certainly moves the thinking from any narrow and single dimension approach to the question of inclusion.

We are therefore delighted to include this book in our series. The papers are readable, informative and will contribute to encouraging further critical interest, debate and research into these exciting, crucial and difficult questions.

Len Barton
Marcia Rioux
January 2003

JULIE ALLAN

1 INTRODUCTION

Posing the question 'what is the purpose?' in respect of inclusion, participation, and democracy might seem like a futile gesture. For those of us involved in inclusion, as teachers, teacher educators or researchers, the purpose appears to have been clear: to maximise the participation of young people in mainstream schools. There has been increasing recognition that this is a complex process and that in order to understand inclusion, it is necessary also to attend to the exclusionary pressures within institutions (Booth & Ainscow, 1995). Furthermore, there is widespread acceptance of the need to undergo radical school change (Barton, 1997) and to pathologise schools as the source of exclusion and failure, rather than the young people within them (Slee, 1996). Yet, in spite of this more sophisticated understanding of what needs to be done to achieve inclusion, questions about what young people are being included 'in' and for what purpose remain.

Education policies, including policies of inclusion, operate within a regime of accountability which is inefficient, ineffective and socially unjust (Salter and Tapper, 2000; Vidovitch and Slee, 2001) and which is described by Strathearn (1999) as a 'tyranny of transparancy' (p. 309). Schools and education authorities are forced to concentrate on 'proving' rather than improving and as Ball (2000) points out, these performative frameworks create an imperative for fabrication by those under scrutiny. Blackmore (cited in Vidovitch and Slee, 2001) contends that if accountability frameworks are not problematised, they could become the 'midwives of globalization ... which deliver market ideologies uncritically around the globe' (p. 451), while McNeil (2002) asks if whether the language of accountability will eliminate democratic discussions about the purpose of schooling. These warnings, however, appear to have gone unheeded and the obsession with standards has 'shut down the civic imagination, constrained curriculum and attenuated pedagogy' (Rose, cited in Slee, 1997, p. 307).

The quest for indicators and outcomes within the quality assurance genre has extended to inclusion; however, the views of disabled youngsters and their parents, regarding what the desirable consequences of inclusion should be have been disregarded. Consequently, institutions concerned with teacher education have been forced to search for 'inclusivity indicators' (Nunan et al, 2000, p. 75), which reduce inclusion to a contrived cultural performance by professionals. These symbolic displays of values, for example that teachers should 'recognise the cultural and social embeddedness of problems with respect to both their conceptualisation and solution' (ibid, p. 80), surely cannot be taken as 'evidence' of their existence. Alternatively, attempts have been made to produce indicators

1

J. Allan (ed.), Inclusion, Participation and Democracy: What is the Purpose?, 1-8.
© 2003 *Kluwer Academic Publishers. Printed in the Netherlands.*

which specify increases in the numbers of children 'present' in mainstream schools (DfEE, 1997) or even a reduction in the number of children formally assessed as having special educational needs (Scottish Executive, 1999). These are quite simply inept.

The desire for certainty within education more generally creates closure in practices and profound injustices for particular individuals. Derrida (1997) suggests that injustice is a product of the pressure to reach a just decision, and the instant when this occurs is a 'madness' (Derrida, 1990, p. 967). Furthermore, he argues that the certainty with which recommendations, for example about what constitutes good practice, need to be made allows for the evasion of responsibility. This irresponsibility extends to the kind of guarantees and assurances (of quality, 'value added,' or enhancement) required within education, which Derrida (2001) suggests, sets up an inertia from which it is impossible to break away:

> Any presumption of guarantee and of non-contradiction in so paroxystic a situation ... is an optimistic gesticulation, an act of good conscience and irresponsibility, and therefore indecision and profound inactivity under the guise of activism (p. 71).

In order to grasp the problems created by this will to certainty, we need to understand the role of misunderstanding (Biesta, 2001) within educational processes and to allow much of what we think we know to be unravelled. So, far from being futile, asking 'what is the purpose of inclusion, participation and democracy?' is an attempt to create, in Derrida's (1992) terms, an 'epic gesture ... a call towards that which is given at the same time as contradictory or impossible' (p. 30).

THE STIRLING COLLOQUIUM MEETING

This book has emerged from a meeting of an International Colloquium on inclusion, held at the University of Stirling, Scotland, in June 2001. The group comprises international scholars in the field of inclusive education, who have met regularly since 1994. The first publication to emerge from the Colloquium's first meeting in Newcastle, edited by Catherine Clark, Alan Dyson and Alan Millward (1995), attempted to map the field of inclusion and in so doing, demonstrated the huge diversity of meanings, policies and practices, within as well as between, countries. Tony Booth and Mel Ainscow (1998), in the second book to emerge from our deliberations, this time in Cambridge, concluded that the only way to succeed in understanding inclusion was to look simultaneously at exclusion. Keith Ballard (1999) foregrounded 'voice' in the meeting in Aukland, New Zealand and in response to our collections of 'stories' from young people, parents and professionals, he urged us to accept John Ralston Saul's (1997) notion of participation as 'the very expression of permanent discomfort' (p. 195). Forthcoming publications from a meeting in Rochester, USA (edited by Linda Ware) will address ideology and inclusion and Tony Booth, Kari Nes and Marit Strømstad consider inclusive teacher education in the book arising from a meeting in Hamar, Norway.

At the Stirling Colloquium meeting, participants set out to address the following questions:

- What are the goals/ambitions for inclusion and what forms of participation are necessary to achieve these? What changes in culture and politics are implied?
- What is the nature of the interaction between inclusion and identity (both individual and collective)?
- Is it possible to specify an ethical framework for inclusion?
- What kinds of consequences can be specified in relation to inclusion?

The authors have considered these questions either implicitly or explicitly in their chapters, but in posing them, I was not expecting definitive answers. Rather, I was looking to broaden our dialogue and to move out, even if only for a short time, from narrow frameworks of outcomes, indicators and notions of 'what works.' The book, then, seeks to broaden the arena in which inclusion is debated, to help to navigate around the contradictory and fragmentary policies which push and pull professionals in different directions, and to articulate a framework which works within, rather than against, these tensions to achieve consequences that are acceptable to children and families.

This collection addresses inclusion in relation to the kinds of educational goals which are appropriate for individuals and their communities. It seeks to articulate the nature of participation and democracy which might be achieved in inclusive settings and the consequences for all concerned. These consequences relate to the kinds of educational, social and personal experiences which are acceptable, and are distinctively different from the narrowly defined performative 'outcomes.'

The authors share a common concern for challenging the tautological discourses of inclusion, participation and democracy and interrupting the fixation on schooling, techniques and resources. They offer a broader vision of what might be possible and analyses of what stands in the way of this in practice. The Colloquium members would all characterise themselves as 'pro-inclusion,' and the majority of the chapters contain some powerful reflexive commentary of individuals' political and personal engagement with the inclusion project.

As the host of the Colloquium, I felt obliged to provide the participants with some authentically Scottish experiences. One event stood out from the usual garish emblems of nationhood and the inevitable Castle visit and I mention this here, not in an effort to imply that I was a classy host, but because it seemed to provide an illustration to the Colloquium participants of 'real' inclusion in practice. I invited my head of department, Peter Cope, to bring his group of young fiddle players to perform and the impact on the participants was electrifying. The Blackford Fiddle Group consists of youngsters and adults of all ages who play traditional Scottish fiddle music. The Group is explicitly inclusive, in that there is no entry selection and tuition is deliberately 'non-scholastic,' (for example by teaching in groups and using colour coded notation) in an effort to be as accessible as possible and in contrast with approaches to formal music learning. During public performances, such as the one witnessed by the Colloquium participants, individuals elect when and what to play, according to their familiarity with particular tunes and their skill level. Linda Ware said of the performance: 'We've been sitting around all day discussion how to do inclusion and these guys have just done it, right before our eyes.' Subsequently Peter Cope and I have been working with the young fiddlers in an attempt to understand, from their perspective, what it means to be included. We see is value in stepping outside conventional school frameworks in order to understand the processes of inclusion and participation. The contributors to this volume also underline the importance of addressing the 'bigger picture.'

INTRODUCING THE CHAPTERS

Part One of the book goes beyond schooling to consider the nature of individuals' engagement with communities and society. In the first chapter, *Including ourselves: teaching, trust, identity and community,* Keith Ballard takes as his starting point the premise that ideological contexts and practices are in conflict with notions of trust and community. Ballard uses the idea of 'stories to live by' to examine how our own stories as researchers and teachers may interact with the stories of others in and beyond our communities and society. He asks: if the dominant story in our various societies is one of individualism and of distrust, then what is it that we are to be included in? Ballard examines the extent to which the 'sociality of identity' (James, 1994, p. 3) is being lost through challenges to the concept of society and the disengagement of individuals. His account of technicist and reductionist approaches to teaching (in which the teacher's role is to manage learning outcomes), accountability, and 'performance management' in education shows how it takes the very soul away from individual teachers and learners. Ballard's analysis elucidates the nature of participation as concerned with a sense of belonging and developing identity through relationships. Inclusion, he contends, is about ourselves.

Marit Strømstad offers a critique of the emphasis within Norway on school reform to achieve inclusion, arguing that the technicist, practice oriented, approach has sidestepped the major societal changes required. She analyses the ways in which inclusion appeared within Norway's Reform 97 and demonstrates the ways in which its impact is limited by its narrow focus and by the ways in which the participation of students is confined to practical, rather than pedagogical, matters. Strømstad presents findings from research on participation which highlights stark differences in perceptions of students and their teachers about the level of students' participation in decision-making. Inclusion, according to Strømstad, is political work which needs to be undertaken by all concerned.

In chapter three, *Participation and democracy: what's inclusion got to do with it?*, Colleen Cummings, Alan Dyson and Alan Millward unpack some of the assumptions behind notions of inclusion, participation and democracy and explore the relationship between them. Their research on the role of schools in area regeneration highlights the struggles faced by schools in particular areas to manage children's behaviour, improve educational attainment and meet the wider social and learning needs in the context of a strong accountability regime. The authors report on the different conceptualisations of the role of schools arising within different social and economic contexts and in response to the 'standards agenda' and the education market place. They call for a more sophisticated understanding of the relationship between educational processes and outcomes and subsequent life chances than has hitherto been evident and ask whether the term 'inclusive education' has outlived its usefulness.

Kari Nes, in her chapter *Why does education for all have to be inclusive education? From Jomtien to Salamanca and beyond*, considers what the principle of education for all means in practice. She traces the impact of the Salamanca and Jomtien statements alongside Kisanji's (1998) analysis of indigenous customary education in North and South African villages. She uses this analytical framework to scrutinise the *Index for Inclusion* (Booth et al, 2000) and the Norwegian National Curriculum and argues for an social anthropological approach to curriculum planning which analyses culture and addresses the basic needs of people.

Each of the chapters contained in Part Two offer a challenge to the way in which inclusion is understood. Dora Bjarnsson explores the question of adult status for disabled people, drawing on a study of young Icelandics. She illustrates how the choices made by parents on behalf of their sons or daughters may restrict entry into adulthood and portrays the youngsters as travellers, moving along a either a main road or a special road. A further group of young people were characterised as nomads, travelling in the wasteland, and failing to acquire adult status.

Gwynned Lloyd examines the case of Attention Deficit Hyperactivity Disorder (ADHD) in the context of inclusion. She analyses the media's portrayal of the enthusiastic oversimplification and normalisation of this complex 'disorder' and contrasts this with the more cautious tone adopted in the medical and psychological literature. Her analysis also focuses on the opposing views of two exponents of different positions (Baldwin & Cooper, 2000) and, in a context in which parents can escape blame through the acceptance of the validity of the concept and the diagnostic procedures of ADHD, she questions the motivations and interests of individuals who appear to promote the medication of children with an ADHD diagnosis without an adequate research base. Lloyd considers ways of informing parents and teachers so that they may develop a critical awareness of the broader context of this condition and of the implications for inclusion.

In *Working past pity: problematising disability in the secondary curriculum*, Linda Ware describes her research with secondary school teachers in which she introduced them to humanities-based disability studies and helped them to integrate disability-related topics in their curriculum. Her project also included a lecture series and a number of 'collaborative inquiry dialogues' for University and secondary teachers. Ware analyses the teachers' knowledge shifts and their accompanying frustration the students who experienced this innovative curriculum describe how it altered how they understood both disability and themselves. Ware's goal of giving voice to unspoken questions that challenge the received narratives of disability represents a radical reworking of the inclusion project which goes beyond pity and which traverses the traditional curriculum and the conventional sites of knowledge production.

Alison Closs offers *An outsider's perspective on the reality of educational inclusion within former Yugoslavia*. These complex social and cultural contexts have forced a rethinking of the inclusion project, to take account of such factors as a predominance of mental heath problems associated with the conflicts, a hierarchy of disability which privileges the war wounded ahead of individuals with intellectual impairments, and a strong stigma associated with disability. Closs offers a reflexive account of her professional, personal and political selves and her engagement with children and families in these communities. Her experience leads her to conclude that the version of inclusion pushed by the NGOs is problematic and oversimplistic.

Part Three – pressing for change – contains accounts of Colloquium members who have engaged actively within policy and political spaces to press for strategic change. Mel Ainscow and Dave Tweddle's chapter, *Understanding and developing the role of the local education authorities in relation to inclusion and achievement*, examines the implications of the erosion of power Local Education Authorities (LEAs) in England and Wales for inclusive education practices. The authors report on their attempts to foster collaborative inquiry among students, parents, teachers and Local Authority staff as they attempt to explore ways of overcoming barriers to participation and learning in schools. They argue that this approach can create new partnerships, based on a critical appraisal, which could counter some of the closure fostered by national policies and which could encourage the kind of experimentation that will generate inclusive thinking and practice.

Daring to think otherwise? Educational policymaking in the new Scottish Parliament, contains an account of the process of educational policymaking in the first year of the new Scottish Parliament, reporting on the activities of the All Party Committee of Inquiry into special educational needs provision, to which I was adviser. In this role, I gained a unique insight into the tensions, uncertainties and contradictions of the policymaking process, which is rarely reflected in the subsequent documents produced. I argue that the establishment of a Scottish Parliament has created a 'new policymaking culture' (Hassan, 1999, p. 13) which is transforming 'conservatism and caution' into 'innovation and forward thinking' (ibid). During the Inquiry, the Members of the Scottish Parliament considered the first set of questions addressed in this book, concerning the goals and ambitions for inclusion, the forms of participation that are necessary to achieve these, and the changes in culture which are implied. This group of individuals appeared, to use Stephen Ball's (1998) phrase, to have succeeded in 'thinking otherwise' (p81) about inclusion.

Fernando Almeida Diniz provides an account of his attempts to address institutional racism and to operate within the 'racial spaces' in academic discourses and practices in educational policymaking, describing his 'creeping rage' and frustration. His critique makes use of Bell hooks' (1989) conceptualisation of rage as a catalyst to achieve critical consciousness and organised resistance. Almeida Diniz reframes inclusion in the context of social justice and attacks the race blind discourses of inclusion and the 'visibility of white supremacy' in research. He presents an ethical code for researching 'race,' racism and anti-racism, produced by SABRE, a network of black researchers within universities, local authorities and the black voluntary sector in Scotland and suggests strategies for the scrutiny of institutional racism by service providers.

In the final chapter of this section, *Teacher Education, Government and Inclusive Schooling: the Politics of the Faustian Waltz,* Roger Slee reflects on his engagement with politics and policy from inside the Queensland Government, where he has been seconded as Deputy Director General for two years. His unique insider/outsider perspective reveals the politicians' and officials' ideological and conceptual struggles as they seek to implement radical educational reform. Slee also offers a highly reflexive account of his own positioning in the political and policy process and of his attempts to encourage a particular kind of educational history making which is acceptable to students, families and communities.

The final chapter considers how the authors have addressed the four questions about goals, identity, ethics and consequences and discusses the themes which have emerged from their analysis. The book ends with a brief discussion about the kinds of consequences for young people and their families that might be acceptable, how these might be achieved, and, since accountability is still necessary, how we shall know if we have succeeded.

REFERENCES

Baldwin, S. & Cooper, P. (2000). How should ADHD be treated? Head to Head. *The Psychologist,* 13(12), 598–602.

Ball, S. (1998). Educational studies, policy entrepreneurship and social theory. In R. Slee, G. Weiner, & S. Tomlinson (Eds.), *School effectiveness for whom?* London: Falmer.

Ball, S. (2000). Performativities and fabrication in the education economy: Towards the performative society? *The Australian Educational Researcher,* 27(2), 1–23.

Ballard, K. (1999). *Inclusive education:International voices on disability and justice.* London: Falmer Press.

Barton, L. (1997) Inclusive education: Romantic, subversive or realistic? *International Journal of Inclusive Education,* 1(3), 231–242.

Biesta, G. (2001). Preparing for the incalculable. In G. Biesta & D. Egéa-Kuehne (Eds.), *Derrida & education.* London: Routledge.

Booth, T. and Ainscow, M. (1998). (Eds.), *From them to us:An international study of inclusion in education.* London: Routledge.

Clark, A, Dyson, A, and Millward, A. (1995) (Eds.), *Towards inclusive schools.* London: David Fulton.

Department for Education and Employment (1997) *Excellence for all children: Meeting special educational needs.* London: DfEE.

Derrida, J. (1990). Force of law: the mystical foundation of authority (M. Quaintance, Trans.). *Cardozo Law Review,* 11, 919–1070.

8 JULIE ALLAN

Derrida, J. (1992). *The other heading: reflections on today's Europe*, (P. Brault & M. Naas, Trans.). Bloomington and Indianapolis: Indiana University Press.
Derrida, J. (1997). The Villanova roundtable: a conversation with Jacques Derrida. In J. Caputo, (Ed.), *Deconstruction in a nutshell: a conversation with Jacques Derrida.* New York: Fordham University Press.
Derrida, J. (2001) A certain 'madness' must watch over thinking: Jacques Derrida's interview with François Ewald. In G. Biesta, & D. Egéa-Kuehne, (Eds.), *Derrida & education.* London: Routledge.
Hassan, G. (1999). The new Scottish politics: The establishment of a Scottish Parliament. In G. Hassan, (Ed.), *A guide to the Scottish Parliament.* Edinburgh: the Stationary Office.
hooks, B. (1989). *Talking back: Thinking feminist, thinking black.* Boston: South End Press.
James, P. (1994). Introduction: Rethinking politics. In P. James (Ed.), *Critical politics: from the personal to the global.* Melbourne: Arena Publications.
Kisanji, J. (1998). The march towards inclusive education in non-Western countries: Retracing the steps, *International Journal of Inclusive Education,* 2(1), 133–151.
McNeil, L. (2002). Private asset or public good: Education and democracy at the crossroads. *American Educational Research Journal,* 39(2), 243–248.
Nes, K., Stromstad, M. & Booth, T. (forthcoming) (Eds.), *Reforming teacher education: The challenge of inclusion.* London: Falmer Routlege.
Nunan, T., George, R. & McCausland, H. (2000). Inclusive education in universities: Why it is important and how it might be achieved. *International Journal of Inclusive Education,* 4(1), 63–88.
Salter, B. and Tapper, T. (2000). The politics of governance in higher education: the case of quality assurance. *Political Studies,* 48, 66–87.
Saul, J. (1997). *The Unconscious civilisation.* Harmondsworth: Penguin.
Scottish Executive (1999). *New Community Schools Prospectus.* Edinburgh: Scottish Office.
Slee, R. (1996). Disability, class and poverty: School structures and policing identities. In C. Christensen & F. Rizvi (Eds.), *Disability and the dilemmas of education and justice.* Buckingham: Open University Press.
Slee, R. (1997). Editorial. *International Journal of Inclusive Education,* 1(4), 307–308.
Strathearn, M. (2000). The tyranny of transparacy. *British Journal of Educational Research,* 26(3), 309–321.
Vidovitch, L. and Slee, R. (2001). Bringing universities to account? Exploring some global and local policy tensions. *Journal of Educational Policy,* 16(5), 431–453.
Ware, L. (Ed.), (forthcoming) *Ideology and the politics of inclusion.* New York: Teachers College Press.

PART ONE

BEYOND SCHOOLING

KEITH BALLARD

2 INCLUDING OURSELVES: TEACHING, TRUST, IDENTITY AND COMMUNITY

[The teacher's] questions were ones of identity (Connelly & Clandinin, 1999, p. 3)

A curious emotion stirred in Winston's heart. In front of him was an enemy who was trying to kill him: in front of him, also, was a human creature, in pain ... he... instinctively started forward to help her...as though he felt the pain in his own body. (George Orwell,1949, *Nineteen eighty-four*, p. 57)

... an emptying out of relationships (Ball, 1999, p. 10).

Michael Connelly and Jean Clandinin (1999) say that they use the phrase '*stories to live by* ... to refer to identity' (p. 4). This is an identity constructed and reported through narratives that link the person, knowledge, history and context of a teacher and their teaching. In this paper I use the idea of 'stories to live by' to examine how our own stories as researchers and teachers may interact with the stories of others in and beyond our communities and society. I am interested in the effects on us of ideological contexts and practices that I believe are in conflict with notions of trust and of community. If the dominant story in our various societies is one of individualism and of distrust, then a critical issue becomes what is it that we are to be included in? What are we to identify with, beyond our own values and preferences?

James (1994) says that in the fragmented, individualised and globalised world of New Right liberal economics, the 'sociality of identity' is being lost (p. 3). In part, this is because the concept of a society is challenged, and replaced with the idea that only the 'personal and familial' (p. 3) has meaning. In this context, rather than recognising and valuing our dependencies and interdependencies, which would seem to be central to the notion of an inclusive society, the term dependent is constructed as involving a 'lesser person,' one who cannot, or will not, fend for themselves (James, 1994, p. 3). This position supports only limited connections between and amongst people in communities and societies. It stands in contrast to John Dewey's (1916) view that democracy and the ongoing development of co-operative democratic institutions requires social participation, which includes a sharing of ideas and experiences based on an education 'which gives individuals a personal interest in social relationships' (p. 99). The disengaged individual has limited reason to identify with their wider society. The individual who identifies as connected with society has reason for engagement and participation.

11

J. Allan (ed.), Inclusion, Participation and Democracy: What is the Purpose?, 11-32.
© 2003 *Kluwer Academic Publishers. Printed in the Netherlands.*

Identity is a contested area that includes the idea that identity resides in the construction of differences, such as for gender or for gay or other minority groups (Zaretsky, 1994). Zaretsky notes Foucault as seeing identity as a construction of power discourses that exert control over us, assigning us to various groupings and making us who we are. This means that, for Foucault, identity is something for us to be liberated from. In this context, says Zaretsky (1994), the analysis of identity requires that we go beyond the subjective and interpersonal to consider identity in social, political and historical contexts. In that case it would seem important to examine notions of identity and difference in ways that foreground an uneven distribution of power and resources (Sleeter, 1993). This would acknowledge the complex interactions of the individual and their cultural, religious, social class, ideological and gendered senses of themselves (Kearney, 1998) that result in the 'multiple identities and identity choices that people make in practice' (Shakespeare, 1996, p. 109). Scheurich (1993), along with Fine and her colleagues (2000), reminds us of the enforced racialised identities that form and are sustained in racist societies, while in his analysis of 'whiteness' as a key issue of identity politics, Allen (2001) suggests that the predominant power of white identity expressed through an imposed global economic and military supremacy assigns an inferior identity to othered non-whites. This justifies the exploitation of their lands and labour in the 'structural dehumanisation of people of colour' (p. 482). For Grosze (1994), one response to such complexity is to work with both identity and difference in an ongoing discussion about the possibilities for new social relationships that may be negotiated from ethical and moral principles.

In addition to these various positions, there are those who see identity as a term describing who we think we are. In this context, Canadian reading researcher Frank Smith (1998) writes that 'the way we identify ourselves is at the core' of all learning because 'all learning pivots on who we think we are, and who we see ourselves as capable of becoming' (p. 11). Smith's claim might be understood when we make a decision that 'this has nothing to do with me.' We mean that the issue – economics, politics, gender, racism, disability – is of no interest to ourselves. It may be important to others, but we do not identify with it. If we have the power to exclude ourselves from participation in this issue, then we will not learn about it. The more that our social environment assigns us the power to disengage – for example, by an emphasis on the primacy of the individual – the less we need to contribute to and learn from dialogue with others. Smith (1998) refers to Vygotsky's socio-cultural theory of learning to suggest how much we would lose if we fail to learn with and from others, if we remove ourselves from what Vygotsky termed 'zone[s] of proximal development' within which 'we are helpless by ourselves but competent if we have assistance' (p. 85).

Skrtic (1995) writes of John Dewey's philosophy that it emphasises the ongoing construction and reconstruction of knowledge and social practices through 'dialogical discourse' (p. 46). This underlines the fundamental importance of education because it is through education that we 'are prepared to enter the conversation' (Skrtic, 1995, p. 46). Because we must learn to be democratic, says Skrtic, we need to create institutional settings and practices 'in which democratic identities, values and communities are cultivated' (p. 47). Skrtic suggests that 'identity must be central to social policy because its opposite, alienation, threatens community itself' (p. 47).

In this chapter I suggest that, for some of us, alienation is evident in our workplaces and in other aspects of our lives. This is an alienation imposed by the creation of environments that are designed to limit human relationships to controlled and contractual interactions focused on achieving specific predetermined goals. I contrast such disengaged experiences with alternative stories that are about identifying with others, a 'participatory consciousness' (Heshusius, 1994, p. 16), that reflects care and trust. I refer to evidence from research but also to writings by journalists and others commenting on people and their experiences. The intention is not to equate journalism and selected individual comments with research (although good journalists, like good researchers, are concerned with veracity, honesty, and critical evaluation of their interpretive stories). Rather, I use media and other sources to suggest that particular experiences, ideas and values are evident in the societies that I am referring to in this writing. While there will also be alternative experiences, values, views and interpretations, I have chosen to attend to some particular issues for this chapter to suggest that they form a context for teaching and teachers. I quote from research and from media sources to include voices other than my own commenting on issues that are of concern to me.

LOSING THE PLOT

This is of course my story, although, as with all accounts, there is much that will not be told and I acknowledge that like all stories this one is 'interpretive and partial' (James, 2002, p. 172). The story begins with a group of researchers sitting in the sun in Norway and Julie Allan introducing the idea of 'identity.' At the time, 'Who am I' seemed a self-indulgent thought, unworthy of public discussion. I am a university teacher and I live and work with school and university teachers who claim a commitment to equity, justice and inclusion in education and society. In this context (and at my age) my 'identity' as a teacher should not be especially difficult to articulate and subject to interrogation and analysis. Yet as I thought about it I realised that for myself, and for some others I talk with, our teacher identities, our 'stories to live by,' in Connelly and Clandinin's (1999) terminology, are at this time difficult to tell to ourselves or others, conflicting, for example in being both assertive and uncertain about who we are, and involving significant distress.

In my analysis, teaching and research in New Zealand is undertaken in a context of technicist models of curriculum and assessment, of 'accountability,' of 'performance management,' and the surveillance and control that all this entails. This is part of an alienating environment for teachers whose version of professionalism emphasises the complexity of their work and their personal responsibilities to children, young people, parents and society. Further stresses occur when we apply for research grants or other resources, or report on our work to educational and social agencies and institutions in New Zealand, because these work almost exclusively in a language of commercial transactions and corporatised management (Easton, 1997). Even if we can resist and subvert in our own writing for such purposes, to see government, ministries and universities retelling the story of our field in terms of mechanistic operations and competitive market exchanges creates tensions for and within our own narratives of who we are and why we teach. How do we find continuity? What is the plot in this tale?

Their plot is quite apparent – to redesign teaching along neoliberal New Right lines (House, 1998) and education as an international, commercial, tradeable commodity (Kelsey, 2000). This reflects the overwhelmingly commercialised environment of New Zealand. Each New Zealand state (publicly funded) school is a self-managing education 'provider,' competing with others in its community. Government scientific research has been organised into commercial Crown Research Institutes, competing for funds and charging for services. Public hospitals are commercial Crown Health Enterprises (CHEs) 'required to run as successful private sector businesses' (Kelsey, 1997, p. 4). Of the endless commercially driven reforms in the health sector, the retiring head of the Christchurch Hospital cardiology unit, Hamid Ikram, said:

> All this mucking about, and every day there's another state-run experiment which has fallen over. The reforms … have been hollow, derisory and expensive. They keep changing the logos and the mission statements. Everyone knows what our mission statement is. We're a hospital, we've been here before they had mission statements and we are not short of work – do they think all of us are idiots? (Knight, 2001, p. C4)

I think the answer is that they do think we are idiots. The New Right managerialists who comprise the New Zealand power elite believe that if only we would comply with the commercial market culture, its language and its values, we too could be included, and our organisations would become efficient and effective. Roger Douglas, architect of the Labour government's New Right agenda in 1987–1990, continues to say of health and education that the problems are not those of (clearly evident) chronic underfunding but 'about getting incentives right – they just don't understand human nature' (interviewed by Potter, 2000, p. A11). If we find the right balance of threats and rewards, individuals will perform and the system will work. This is a key assumption of the (present) Labour government's Tertiary Education Advisory Commission in its report on *Shaping the Funding Framework*. In its justification for introducing a 'performance-based research fund.' the Tertiary Education Advisory Commission (2001) writes that it assumes 'that there is a positive relationship between the use of explicit incentives for performance and the actual effort expended by academic researchers' (p. 88).

Concern about the Crown Health Enterprise (otherwise known as hospital) in the South Island city of Christchurch had, in 1998, led to some senior doctors writing a report under the title *Patients are dying*. In response, the Commissioner for Health and Disability, Robyn Stent, reviewed these claims. The Commissioner reported that she had found a 'dysfunctional and grief stricken health system' (Stent, 1998a, p. 1) in which hospital restructuring along commercial lines had limited the role of clinicians in planning and decision making. The Commissioner's report noted the role of the government's Crown Company Monitoring Advisory Unit (CCMAU), which had required 'a drive for efficiency [reducing costs by 10%] ... with minimal patient focus' (Stent, 1998b, p. 53). CCMAU had told the Minister that the financial targets were 'almost impossible' (Stent, 1998b, p. 52), but recommended that staff should not be told their budgets were unrealistic, as this 'will likely undermine their resolve to achieve the targets set' (Stent, 1998b, p. 53). One of the goals of the CCMAU was a 'drive to develop tension in the system' between clinicians (services) and management (funding) which would lead to cost savings (efficiencies) (Stent, 1998b, p. 53). What are the ethics implied by this view of human motivation and relationships in the workplace? What is the moral basis for relationships involving deception and the deliberate creation of distance and tension? Journalist Bruce Ansley (2001) said of the Commissioner's report that it described an environment 'bereft of trust' (p. 22).

Another example of commercialisation is in the area of research. Most funding for research in New Zealand is through a government organisation, The Foundation for Research Science and Technology (FORST). In a FORST newsletter, science providers (researchers) are told that, following restructuring, 'the Foundation is refocusing its investments ... from sector-based input funding to innovation-oriented investment ... [in order to] grow the innovation system' (Thompson, 2000, p. 2). The new structures involve 'four units – policy, portfolio management, investment operations and corporate development' (p. 2). A technicist language of corporate managerialism is also part of research grant application procedures for this agency. In recent communications, the Foundation for Research, Science and Technology (2002) invited funding applications for 'Advancements' (this means research) and said that the assessment criteria for applications are now known as 'Investment Signals' (previously called change messages).

In her comments on the government as the major funder of research in New Zealand, Maori researcher Linda Tuhiwai Smith (1999) notes that the processes and terminology involve research being identified as a 'product.' This is 'purchased,' copyrighted and owned by the state as part of the 'outputs' of the ministry or department concerned (Smith, 1999, p. 186). Smith sees this neoliberal market model as involving the commodification of knowledge which challenges 'Maori cultural values and practices' (p. 189). The research design requirements of FORST, says Smith, involves the 're-inscription of positivist approaches to scientific research,' which is implicated in the ongoing colonisation of Maori (p. 189).

It is the case that, at the time of writing, the present (1999–2002) Labour/ Alliance coalition government has said that it wishes to change the commercial and competitive emphasis in health and education. But some of those working as managers in present systems may find it difficult to comprehend the idea of public service, given the denigration of this concept over the last 15 years and its replacement by market principles. For example, Evan Begg, Director of Clinical

Pharmacology at Christchurch Hospital, interviewed by journalist Bruce Ansley (2001), said of present health managers that they continued to focus on commercial imperatives and that 'it's impossible for them to change their philosophies ... they were appointed because of them' (cited in Ansley, 2001, p. 24). Economist Brian Easton (2001) has said that New Right Labour and National (conservative) governments in New Zealand and a compliant media have closed off economic debate. This has meant that the majority of those in management positions know only the ideas of the rationalist market position. Easton claims that 'the level of economic analysis in New Zealand is stunted, and ideas that are a part of the normal overseas discourse are hardly ever discussed here, so policy is often misdirected' (p. 38). It is not just policy that may be misdirected in this context. It is the nature of our society and how we may participate in it that is being shaped by a singular focus on a commercial market ideology.

RELATIONSHIPS: INCLUDING OURSELVES AND OTHERS

Carol Witherell (1991) sees teaching as involving ethical issues centring around the 'nature of the self, the relation to self to other and to culture, and conceptions of knowing, meaning, and purpose' (p. 84). If we do not engage in an ongoing and critical way with such complex issues, suggests Witherell, then teaching will be taken over by a technology of assessment and instructional procedures that avoid the need to understand how our 'self develops and finds meaning in the context of relationship' (p. 90). In emphasising relationship as fundamental to human experience, Witherell draws on Nel Noddings' work on an ethic of caring relationships. These require an 'empathic understanding' of ourselves and others' actions, intentions and meanings (p. 90).

In her work, Witherell focusses on the 'centrality of human narratives in the attainment of moral identity' (p. 93). If we at some time hide or deny the identity we have constructed from our culture and history, we may lose the 'narrative unity' of our self, and until such a conflict is resolved we may live as a false self, creating uncertainty about how we should be among others. Witherell is not referring to a selfish, singular or static identity. Her emphasis is on relationships and on an ongoing interrogation and reconstruction of ourselves in relationship to others. Witherell (1991) makes evident the transactional nature of identity. She refers to work on infants that emphasises that they become a person through social interchanges with consistent others. Human development is thus seen as grounded in relationships and in the moral quality of those relationships.

Witherell and Noddings (1991) emphasise the self as formed through experiences which involve caring and being cared for, and which are based on trust. They refer to Martin Buber's (1965) notion of inclusion in which a teacher, for example, 'includes' themselves and 'lives through' (citing Buber, 1965, p. 97) a child's experience, sensing and anticipating the child's physical, social and emotional state as they respond to or engage with an event or activity. The idea of including oneself 'with' another is suggested by Canadian researcher Lous Heshusius in her analysis of modes of consciousness. Heshusius (1994) notes that western (positivist) thought emphasises the self as an independent identity that believes it knows best when it is distant, removed and unconnected to that which the person would know. This 'alienated mode of consciousness' (p. 17) separates what is believed as real from notions of values and ethics.

In contrast, suggests, Heshusius, 'participatory consciousness...involves [our] identification' with who and what we wish to know (p. 16). She refers to the work of Nobel prize geneticist Barbara McClintock and other scientists who speak of their work in terms of a 'deep passion' for and 'identification' with the things they wish to understand (p. 17). We might think of such people as those who 'love' their work, and Heshusius says that participatory consciousness may resemble being 'in love,' involving a knowing that we find difficult to articulate, a state of 'complete attention' in which the self is not separate or in charge, not objective (object like), 'alienated (and alienating)' but engaged in a 'participatory quality of attention' (p. 18). Such a consciousness does not separate fact and value, so that knowing and being, 'ethics and epistemology, are acknowledged as inseparable' (Heshusius, 1994, p. 20). In this way we acknowledge connectedness, kinship and a self-other unity. Our 'identification' with another is our way of knowing them, a striving for a consciousness of participation with another.

Dominant western cultural thought, and dominant positivist paradigm science, denies such connection and supports, instead, distancing and therefore alienating, relationships. This is evident in political and social ideologies that emphasise the individual and that have created community and working contexts in which people are separated beings.

Don't trust me, I know what I am doing

In his writing about New Right economic rationalism, John Codd (1999) reminds us that the changes made to all aspects of education, social policy and economic practice in New Zealand since 1984 (when New Right reforms began) were grounded in a theory of humanity as fundamentally individual, self-interested, 'rational utility maximisers' (p. 46). Each of us is deemed to seek maximum gain for ourselves in whatever we do. Our communities and institutions are thought of in terms of individuals and their behaviour. This means that moral preferences are merely the subjective choices of individuals and there is no such thing as 'the public good' because there is no such entity as a 'society' which is not reducible to individual experiences (Codd, 1999, p. 46).

From the premise and ideological belief that we are all motivated by self-interest, arises the position that we are not to be trusted. We need incentives to make us work; our schools and other institutions must operate in an environment of marketplace contestability so that we must constantly be threatened to perform or perish, and we must be watched and endlessly reviewed, assessed and audited to ensure that the purchaser (eg employer, student, parent) gets maximum (efficient) and quality benefit from the provider (eg teacher, lecturer, principal).

Codd says that 'trust' involves an 'attitude or disposition' reflecting ideas of 'fairness and respect ... and virtues such as honesty ... friendliness and care' (p. 49). The idea of trust is central to social capital theory because, Codd explains (after Putnam, 1993), it is the 'social cement by which norms and networks are connected.' Trust is in fact, cumulative because 'trust breeds more trust and conversely distrust breeds more distrust' (p. 50). The relentless assessment, auditing and surveillance systems that operate in New Zealand state schools and in the university system are the mechanisms of low-trust institutions in a low-trust environment. In terms of the effects of this environment on its citizens, Law professor Jane Kelsey (1997) has said that in New Zealand, our predominantly (both Labour and conservative) New Right politicians and Treasury have ignored 'the impact of an individualised, privatised and internationalised society on human development, cultural identity and the sense of belonging to a community that cares' (p. 11).

A low-care environment is one in which we will not reach out to others. We cannot trust them, so our relations are contractual. Writing down what is to be done is the only way we can 'trust' it will be done. Our engagement with others thus becomes a technical matter, indeed one that is described in increasingly fine detail, requiring a particular technicist language of charters, governance, goals, objectives, strategies, profiles and portfolios. For some of us this mechanistically prescribed world is alienating and excluding. English researcher on educational policy Stephen Ball (1999) describes us as living in a 'world of judgments ... a performative society' (p. 1) in which we are constantly watched, recorded and evaluated, and in which our personal worth is the judged quality of our performance. Power resides with those who determine what is to comprise 'quality.' All this involves redefining what is means to be a teacher or lecturer, and new identities are constructed within a discourse of objectivity, outcomes and accountability.

In such a context, says Ball, there is an 'emptying out of relationships' and 'authentic social relations are replaced by judgemental relations' (p. 10). 'Impression and performance' (ibid) replace a teacher's sense of authentic professional work, and constant auditing and evaluation create both a 'spectacle' (p. 11) and a press toward fabrication. As teachers and lecturers become embedded in these concepts and practices, they become self-regulating – surely the ultimate controlling achievement of the elaborate machinery of the gaze. Then, says Ball, 'the heart of the educational project is gouged out and left empty. Authenticity is replaced by plasticity' (p. 16).

Ball refers to Lyotard's view that the 'commodification of knowledge,' the corporatisation of schools and universities with the purpose of selling learning as a product in an international marketplace, 'changes what academic work is' (p. 25). By making knowledge an external product (in New Zealand, schools and universities are all referred to as 'providers' by the Ministry of Education), relationships in learning are 'de-socialised' (p. 26). Some, says Ball, will readily commodify themselves and take on the identities of a 'new commercialised professionalism' (p. 26, citing Hanlon, 1998, p. 52). For others, the performative institution is alienating and dehumanising and they no longer feel included.

'The corrosion of character' (Sennett, 1998)

In his book, *The Corrosion of Character*, sociologist Richard Sennett examines the effects on people of workplaces designed to maximise performance and profit. He begins by describing the experiences of Enrico, an American blue-collar worker of 25 years ago. With employment, union protection and a government pension plan, Enrico had 'carved out a clear story for himself ... a narrative ... of self respect' (p. 16). His son, in contrast, works within the contemporary context of fast capital, which demands rapid response to ensure ongoing maximisation of profit. Contracting out by large firms results in individual employment and short-term contracts. Within the corporate workplace there is a similar emphasis on fragmentation with jobs being flexible and therefore contingent on the need for particular tasks to be done. The slogan 'No long term' (p. 22) reflects the need for both rapid skill changes and the corporate wish for flexibility achieved through the replacement of long-term jobs by short-term projects.

Sennett argues that 'No long term' corrodes trust, loyalty and mutual commitment' and 'detachment and superficial co-operativeness' are likely responses to such an environment (p. 24). In the workplace there is an emphasis on 'weak ties,' so that teams may disband and different teams reform where needed. The idea of the team is emphasised, but it is a fiction used to imply that individuals are not in fact competing with one another and that there is a 'leader – a most cunning word' in modern management designed to persuade that the person is on your side (p. 111). Teamwork involves peer control of the work group and its output, requiring of the workers 'masks of co-operativeness,' a form of 'deep acting' (p. 112, after Kunda, 1992, p. 56) and a 'fiction of a community at work' (p. 113). In such environments, says Sennett, the system 'radiates indifference.' For the person of the worker, the 'absence of trust' means that 'there is no reason to be needed' (p. 146).

Sennett describes our character as 'the ethical value we place on our own desires and on our relations to others ... the personal traits which we value in our selves and for which we seek to be valued by others' (p. 10). Character, says Sennett, emphasises our 'emotional experience' and is expressed through long-term commitment, loyalty and goals (p. 10). Our character involves our beliefs and behaviours that establish and sustain our relationships with others. Through such relationships we achieve an identity – we know who we are. The elderly and retired Enrico knew who he was in such ways. From the experiences of his son Rico, forced through downsizing and restructuring to move from job to job and place to place, eventually working alone as an independent consultant, Sennett asks, 'How can a human being develop a narrative of identity and life history in a society composed of episodes and fragments?' (p. 26). Of such a reductionist society I ask what it is that people are to be included in?

Participation and community: Who cares?

From his accounts of worker experiences in various companies, Sennett presents evidence that the alienation and stress engendered in the performative, low-trust workplace may carry over into a worker's family and community. There are reports of anger in people's lives and of domestic violence related to workplace events. Enrico talked of his concern about what values his children may learn from their part in his experiences.

The corrosion of character can occur in other ways with similar disruptive effects to how we sustain an identity and participate in community. In an article on children of the 'Rogernomics revolution' (named after the Minister of Finance, Roger Douglas, in the 1984–1990 Labour government), journalist Philip Mathews reported Law professor Jane Kelsey saying that the majority of her students had known nothing other than the market driven policies and agendas of 1984 (Mathews, 1999). Lester Oakes, chief executive of the government's Career Services, said that today's young people are focused on 'putting a price on their own skills ... no one subscribes to notions of long term loyalty' (Mathews, 1999, p. 20). This is consistent with Kelsey's view that students have learnt the intended message that tertiary education is a private good that they must pay for. Students therefore focus on what they personally will gain from their efforts. Not only is a notion of public good as a citizen 'downplayed, but also the importance of having a broad, knowledgeable, thinking population is downplayed' (Mathews, 1999, p. 20).

In talking with some young graduates, Mathews quotes one as telling him that 'our generation could be considered selfish, but I think it is part of having to be. It's look after number one ... that pervades all your thinking ... it goes into your relationships with people. We are all islands ... It does mean no loyalty ... That's the real cost' (Mathews, 1999, p. 20). Another student said 'student loans and fees ... encourages self-interest' (p. 22) and another, 'we have known nothing but that selfishness is a virtue' (p. 22). Two years after these comments were recorded, Richard Pole, President of the New Zealand Medical Students' Association, wrote that the emphasis on 'market ideology' meant that students were 'being forced, through the cost of one's education, to concentrate on the economic value of education rather than its value as a public good' (Pole, 2001, pp. 15–16). Pole claimed that one effect of high medical student debt is that most students plan to leave New Zealand for higher paid work elsewhere, while others 'will pursue the higher paid procedural-based specialities,' meaning 'fewer GPs ... fewer mental health workers and fewer public health physicians' (p. 16).

In a similar comment, a New Zealand medical student, Julie Fitzjohn, wrote as a trainee intern at Harvard Medical School. She said that student fees in New Zealand are replicating the high fees and 'massive loans' evident in America. The results at Harvard, she claimed, are that the students' 'focus is entirely on the economic value of their study, with little social good will left ... and only the market value of their degree in mind' (Fitzjohn, 2001, p. 6). She suggested that similar repercussions are likely to be seen in New Zealand.

Research may show such proposed consequences to eventuate or not. People's stated values of selfishness may not be enacted in self-serving ways or may change. Nevertheless, these statements in the public arena signal a willingness to articulate an unease about social values, relationships and the 'public good'. At least these various statements suggest people feel alienated from a notion of a collaborative society that they think should be valued.

For some, the commercialised and managerialist workplace is where they experience significant pressure to focus on corporate goals rather than on broader notions of public good and community well-being. Public agencies, operating as if they were a profit-making business, erode collaborative forms of professional identity and create ethical tensions that impair trust and question loyalty.

Educational researcher Alan Hall (1999) sees the move toward a more individualised, and therefore fragmented, society as having significant implications for teachers. The New Zealand competitive market model of education has each school as self-managing and resourced according to the number of students it enrols. State-funded schools engage in advertising (including television advertisements for some) and 'image management' (Hall, 1999, p. 3). Families seek a 'positional advantage' in employment and social standing for their children, which they think will occur from attending a more successful school (Hall, 1999, p. 2). The evidence, says Hall, is that those recruited to successful schools are higher-achieving students from more stable families. This leaves other schools with a student profile and unstable roll that makes education in that setting more difficult.

Hall raises the question of teacher ethics in this context. Do teachers have a responsibility only to the students in their school, or is their professional duty wider than that, encompassing a concern with the education and well-being of all children in their society? Educational success influences future life chances. The actions of a school that may harm the educational achievements of another school may be seen as an issue of social justice.

Hall records that prior to the New Right school reforms of 1989, New Zealand parents saw the government as responsible for education. Subsequently the contract became one between parents and each school board of trustees as a stand-alone provider of education. The idea that education is just another commodity to be traded in a marketplace has meant that relationships between families and schools, and students and lecturers, are increasingly defined and written in terms similar to that of a commercial contract. As Hall (1999, after May, 1988) notes, 'in a commercial relationship each agent attends only to the interests of those he or she represents' (p. 10). This is a relatively low-trust environment requiring a written agreement because the individuals involved are assumed to be essentially self-interested.

Hall contrasts this with a context of professional ethics in which there is an emphasis on personal integrity and a commitment to the client that goes beyond self-interest. He refers to May's (1988) position that contracts are 'external,' while 'covenants' are 'internal' and support the development of trusting, collaborative relationships (p. 9). Competition between schools requires teachers to focus on what is good for their school and students. They contract with parents and students to do that. In so doing they risk harming other students and other teachers. Their professionalism may become focused on and even limited to meeting their obligations to a particular contract. It becomes more difficult for them to show concern for educational and social issues beyond that limited relationship. One way in which many teachers reach beyond the particular to wider social responsibilities is through their professional unions. It is because of this that the New Right has such a strong emphasis on discrediting these professional bodies. As O'Neill and Jolley (1996/97) note, institutions such as unions have 'historically tempered market relations' and are attacked by the neoliberal New Right because they stand in the way of 'remodel[ing] all cultural forms, processes and institutions along the lines of commercial enterprise' (p. 232).

A similar concern is recorded by journalist Bruce Ansley (2001) in his interviews with some New Zealand health professionals. Of the commercialised health system, a former Director-General of Health, George Salmond, said that 'so much trust has been eroded' (p. 24). Salmond, who quit after 20 years in health management, says that health involves collaboration and 'goodwill' among and between medical practitioners and the community. 'To get excellence,' says Salmond, 'you need external regulation, but much more – you need people who are proud of what they do' (p. 24). A rheumatologist, Peter Moller, told Ansley that he believed medical doctors had been moved from 'a world of professionalism ... to a police system where you fill in forms' (p. 24).

If we cannot be proud of what we do, what might be our motivation for doing it? It could be that we continue in such work mainly out of financial necessity or for economic gain. That would seem a limited and selfish position to be forced into. In Sennett's terms, it would seem the corrosion of character. A similar concern has been expressed by Miles Little, Professor of Surgery at the University of Sydney. Little (1995) sees the new business focus in health and education as distracting professionals from the essentially moral aims of their work. He suggests that an environment of 'missions' and 'visions' in which 'everyone must be 'accountable' to someone else' (p. 89) erodes morale because commercial imperatives are seen to replace professional values.

'It takes away your soul' (Locke, 2000)

In exploring the nature of professionalism, researcher and teacher educator Terry Locke (2000) identified criteria that include specialist knowledge and expertise, autonomy and self-regulation, and responsibility and altruism as the basis for professional work. In tension with a professionally controlled autonomy, Locke contends that in New Zealand, Australia and England, the neo-liberal New Right state has imposed a highly structured curriculum and prescribed assessment strategies that shape teachers' work toward provision of externally determined 'outcomes.'

Along with others (Robertson, 1996; Smyth, 1993), Locke sees teachers losing the ideological struggle to influence both the curriculum and teaching strategies in classrooms. A 'new professionalism' emerges in which the teacher becomes an expert in compliance. The volume of work required by a highly technicist and reductionist curriculum, and the demands of administrative surveillance and reporting, force the teacher toward achieving measured 'learning outcomes' and away from the complexities and uncertainties of educating children in a critically thoughtful way.

In his study of New Zealand high school teachers of English, Locke found that most (61.7%) preferred a definition of professionalism that involved a 'commitment to the well-being' of students and responsibility 'to speak out' on 'matters of educational policy and justice.' The alternative 'new professional' definition involved a teacher who 'manages their students' well, and achieves the 'outcomes' and 'professional standards ... established by the Ministry of Education' (Locke, 2000, pp. 14–15). Locke reports a comment from a teacher identifying with the first definition, but who described the effects of losing their autonomy as 'playing someone else's silly game ... [being] reduced to a cog in a machine ... I'm not interested in teaching English as this sort of person. It takes away your soul' (Locke, 2000, p. 22).

Locke concluded from his study that, while there existed a group who endorsed the ideologically driven emphasis on discrete, measurable outcomes for teaching and teachers, there was evidence for the majority of a sense of erosion of professional autonomy and integrity. The erosion of teacher character is not simply a result of the New Right's overwhelming success in reforming New Zealand education along managerialist technicist lines. Robertson (1996) argues that globalised post-Fordist capitalism demands a manipulable, flexible labour force, technical skills (including team work) and a commitment to individualism and privatisation. This requires the redirection of education achieved, as Robertson suggests, through 'successively more vicious attacks on teachers' competence ... [and] their alleged failure to be more scientific, and therefore professional' (p. 37).

A scientistic emphasis, an identity with neo-liberal thought, and statements attacking teachers have been evident in the widely publicised views of Judith Aitken, Chief Review Officer of the Education Review Office, the government agency that replaced the former inspectorate and now 'audits' New Zealand schools. Aitken (2000a) has claimed that there is 'international approval' of New Public Management and refers to the 'dog in the manger' grievances of those who lament a loss of 'relationships of trust' (p. 1). Aitken's criticism of teachers' concern for trust is particularly interesting. This is especially so in a context where, for example, a Ministry of Social Policy report on the government's relationships with community groups concludes that 'a decade of ... state sector reform has left many in iwi [Maori] and community organisations mistrustful of government' (Wilson, 2001, p. 10). As one respondent to this study said, 'We have learnt not to trust' (p. 16). Clearly it is not only teachers who are expressing disquiet over the effects of New Public Management. Nevertheless, stating her priorities for education, Aitken (2000b) said that: 'on a scale of one to ten I would put assessment and the knowledge economy right up there at 9.5!' Yet, she said, teachers lack 'valid and reliable information' about student learning (p. 1) and 'problems of poor teaching and low quality professional leadership are ... entrenched' (2000a, p. 3).

What I find particularly interesting about the New Right assertion that it has a scientific basis for its practices (and that teachers do not) is that empirical research on the market school system in New Zealand shows it to be in serious trouble. Schools have become increasingly divided along socio-economic and ethnic lines, there is increasing inequality of resources, and there is a related decline in student performance in those schools that are the market losers in this competitive system (Harker, 1999; Lauder et al, 1999; Riske & Ladd, 2000). Although such evidence is there, Aitken (2000a) referred to those opposing the New Right marketisation of education as 'inhabitants of old and outmoded intellectual ditches' whose 'essentially industrial agencies' (teacher unions) 'speak for and on behalf of a well-cloned body of teachers and school principals' (p. 4). Aitken (2000a) asserted that 'many of our schools are centres of complacency. Many of their professional employees are easily satisfied with the quality of their own work' (p. 4) and claimed that the 'firm or company has been far more powerful as an instrument of public education than the school in the past 50 years in New Zealand' (p. 5).

It is not difficult to see how such a discourse is part of a drive to create the teacher as a 'manager of resources' directed to achieving 'pre-specified learning outcomes and targeted performances,' which produce students oriented to the 'new ideology' of 'market flexibility' (Robertson, 1996, p. 47). Robertson (1996) sees teachers as increasingly constrained by externally controlled requirements directed toward a right-wing government's 'need to establish ... new conditions for accumulation' (p. 51). Teachers therefore serve the ideology and structures of globalised capital, their professionalism as autonomous agents who care for children replaced by the 'depersonalised authority' (Robertson, 1996, p. 51) of the manager of learning outcomes.

TEACHING AND COMMUNITY: WHERE DO I BELONG?

Writing of the New Right reforms in New Zealand initiated by the 1984–1990 Labour government and continuing unabated since then, Peters (1995) says that the 'reform process itself was profoundly anti-democratic' (p. 35). He refers to writing by the architect of the reforms, Labour Minister of Finance Roger Douglas, which emphasised that 'speed is essential' for achieving radical change toward the market society, and in which generally, says Peters, there is a reliance on 'almost limitless executive power ... [and] a deep suspicion of the processes of democracy' (p. 35). Opposition is dismissed as 'provider capture' or as the failure to successfully use PR to market and sell a policy. The voter has been constructed as consumer in a society that is now subordinated to the market.

Further evidence for the undemocratic nature of the reforms is suggested by Greg & Howard Lee (1999). They cite a Ministry of Education commissioned account of the educational reforms (Butterworth & Butterworth, 1998) as recording that 'the education sector was ripe for change' (p. 14, cited in Lee & Lee, p. 256) and that policy makers knew 'what needed to be done' (p. 11 cited in Lee & Lee, p. 256). As the Lees suggest, this seems to imply that the public consultations and forums of the time were a public relations exercise, rather than a genuine concern to consider public views on education. Such an analysis is supported by Ken Rae

(1999), who writes of his experiences as a senior policy analyst during the initial reform years. He emphasises the key role played by an ideologically driven Treasury and other advisers, 'driven by their NPM [New Public Management] vision ... of a world ordered ... by ... market relationships ... where managers manage and the operatives obey instructions' (p. 2). In this context consumers are to be persuaded of the rightness of the reforms. They must be sold a new way of thinking and speaking about education.

The language, and therefore the thought, of education is clearly to be that of the market. Alan Barker (1995), the 'strategic manager' for the New Zealand Qualifications Authority, writes that qualifications 'act as a form of currency in society' (p. 15) and that we must create new forms of assessment and qualifications to remove 'barriers to the attainment of the currency' (p. 16). The 'purchaser demands' of students will require that assessment be in 'precise terms' and not 'open to subjectivity' (p. 21). Barker asserts that to achieve these goals a new language of education is required and that this 'language will be intensely resisted because it attacks a mind set and traditional power base' (pp. 19–20). Resistance has had little success. Many, perhaps most, teachers and student teachers now talk in terms of 'learners' (rather than children) who are to achieve 'outcomes.' This is the language of the curriculum documents. It seems to me to represent a technicist, non-human discourse.

In one of the quotes that opens this paper, George Orwell's Winston reached out to help someone 'instinctively,' identifying with her pain. Recently I have found myself reaching out in some form of identity with an aboriginal child hurt by discrimination and described in a thoughtful paper by Australian researcher Merridy Malin (1999). I read this some time ago but she continues to live with me for the moment. I cannot think of her as a 'learner.' She has a name, Naomi, and in my imagination I see her in the classroom, assertive, but harmed nevertheless.

I think of the terminology of 'learner' in the context of Stephen Ball's (1999) description of an 'emptying out of relationships' (p. 10). Surely naming children in this way is meant to distance us from them, to ensure that we focus on achieving the 'learning outcomes' specified for each prescribed 'standard' without the distraction of a close involvement with the person of the child? What will children think? Malin points out that, as a non-aboriginal academic, she cannot really know what went on in the mind of a five-year-old aboriginal child. Yet, in her work, Malin identifies with both the child and her teacher, who she fears may be harmed when marginalisation of the child is made public through the research report. Malin proposes that if teachers allow us into their classrooms so that we may undertake research focused on equity, then we should write in ways that are protective of the teacher's well-being. That would seem to be an ethical and an inclusive position to take. Yet, it is incidents such as that between this teacher and the child Naomi that are the daily, lived, and surely cumulative, experience of racism for many children in many societies, and it is clearly important that they should be known.

In this regard another Australian academic, Lynne Alice (1993), refers to her experiences of attending conferences on post-colonialism that often fail to include indigenous people and that therefore sustain a dominant and excluding European view. In striking contrast, Alice reports aboriginal scholar and activist Roberta Sykes at a *Postcolonial Fictions* conference (in December, 1992) saying:

> Postcolonial...? What!
> Did I miss something?
> Have they gone? (Alice, 1993, p. 41)

And so who is missing from our inclusion project? Is the recognition that there are missing persons significant enough for us to say that we are at least wanting to be inclusive? Is American writer Alice Walker's (1997) intention to 'not harm anyone or anything in this moment' (p. 207) enough to strive for? Her own activism – against racism, violence, tyranny and the genital mutilation of women; against the use of western corporate power to harm less powerful people; and for literacy, nutrition, freedom, democracy and ecological sustainability – suggests we should think of acting in more transformative ways.

At least we might strive to reduce exclusion and harm – as we see it – in classrooms, schools and other settings in which we have involvement. How we 'see it' needs to acknowledge the importance of an ongoing critical interrogation of our 'seeing'. That cannot be done alone. It needs to be responsive to others. It requires that we make ourselves vulnerable so that these selves may be re-formed by new understandings. Thus, who we are – our identity – will change as we change our understanding of ourselves. It seems to me that a participatory democracy requires participatory identity. That is, for participation to occur, we must want to be with, and therefore know of, others. In terms of knowing others, those of us in the dominant white group may not claim to know, for example, about racist and other deeply harmful experiences that do not directly affect our lives (Cochran-Smith, 2000). We must shift from 'naïve notions of pluralism to understanding [how] ... unacknowledged white supremacy inhibits any authentic project for diversity' (Hytten & Adkins, 2001, p. 437; Lawrence & Tatum, 1997). Nevertheless, if we do not strive to know others in some way, we ignore and exclude them, and therefore diminish the possibility of a democratic society (Fine et al, 2001). The child 'Naomi' is an instance of this. The failure to recognise our own racism and other forms of possibly unintended violence against the identity and well-being of others is another instance of a failure to create an inclusive community.

Naming and treating people as 'providers,' as 'human resources,' as 'learners' producing educational 'outcomes,' and as sites for 'performance management,' also, I believe, acts against inclusion. This language constructs depersonalised, unitised 'others' who we can know primarily, perhaps only, in terms of criteria created and sustained within the discourse of an individualistic and mechanistic ideology. Such a separatist discourse, I believe, requires resistance, and should be challenged with alternative positions that assert the value of uncertainty in human relationships, of trust, of difference, of care and of love.

Connelly & Clandinin (1999) say that the question of identity arises when we ask 'who am I?' in my classroom, place of work, or our other stories of other situations (p. 3). For the moment I am, in this text, as ideologically driven as those whose ideas and actions I have contested here. I am not sure if this story will have a happy ending.

PARTICIPATION AND DEMOCRACY

Along with those I have chosen to present in this paper, I suggest that there exists at this time in New Zealand and in a number of other societies a dominating ideology of individualism. This serves to justify selfishness and the view that the wellbeing of those who have fewer resources and are less powerful is their concern, not ours (Galbraith, 1992; Saul, 1997). In this paper I have presented this ideology as a culture of separateness which replaces trust and loyalty with a technology of contractual arrangements that define, monitor and evaluate what we do through increasingly elaborate systems of surveillance. Our reason for doing our work, for example, is deemed to be an external reward rather than an internal sense of satisfaction for the rightness of a job well done. In this context, for some of us at least, it becomes difficult to reconcile who we are, our narratives of identity, with responses to us that are concerned primarily with what we 'provide' and how well the quality of our product meets criteria and standards that have been determined elsewhere. In this mechanistically ordered world, the purpose is self-betterment through competition in commercially arranged markets. There is less concern with inclusion in wider societal networks that we might contribute to and benefit from.

I have suggested that identity is formed in relationships. Competitive relationships must involve success and acceptance for some and, by implication, failure and rejection for others. While success and failure are part of human lives, what I refer to here is the dominance that these experiences are assigned in New Right commercialised societies. American researcher and child advocate James Garbarino (2000) refers to evidence that across-cultures rejection has negative consequences for child development, eroding a sense of integrity, self-worth and identity. I suggest that, as adults, our development is impaired when we experience alienation from not just our workplace but from a notion of education and of society that is part of who we are. It is difficult to participate in that with which we do not identify.

Am I concerned about exclusion because my side in the ongoing struggle over values and ideology in society has, for the moment, lost? The answer has to be yes, and recognises that the neoliberal New Right may eventually feel alienated and excluded if a new order emerges to replace their world view. But a democracy is about living with diverse ideas and so, as John Ralston Saul (1997) has said, it is not about certainty and a comfortable stability. A democracy is also about participation. Societies such as New Zealand, America and Britain have in recent times deliberately created poverty and significant inequalities in income and education. In so doing they have reduced participation in political and social processes and therefore have impaired social cohesion and the achievement of democracy (Galbraith, 1992; Garbarino, 2000; House, 1998; Kelsey, 1993; Waldegrave et al, 1999).

For these societies the dominant view is that the individual 'self' is sufficient. Yet they have created physical and social environments that make it increasingly difficult for the self to survive without fear of at least physical harm from others. Cultural historian Morris Berman (1989) writes of the 'self' that it is a complex notion that in the middle ages referred to the soul. Perhaps it is from our soul that as individuals we feel impelled to reach out to others? At least it seems a deeply felt need and wish. For example, Australian historian Henry Reynolds (1998) has written an account of Europeans who, since the arrival of the colonisers in the mid 1700s, have stood against the racist and murderous harm done by other settlers to Australian aborigines. They show, I think, an identity with those being harmed. For example, James Douglas, President of the Royal Society, advised Captain Cook and those with him on the ship Endeavour in 1768, that the 'natives' they may meet on their journeys should be treated with the 'utmost patience and forbearance' as they 'are human creatures ... equally under [God's] care' as ourselves (in Reynolds, 1998, p. xii).

Reynolds records that in 1842 a Sydney barrister, Richard Windeyer, gave a lecture in which he criticised aboriginal society and argued, as he had before, that aborigines had no right to the land. In his written lecture, Windeyer asserted the soundness of his case. Nevertheless, he also indicated a felt unease. As Reynolds records, Windeyer wrote in his text a rhetorical question indicating his uncertainty and then asked, 'What means this whispering in the bottom of our hearts?' (in Reynolds, 1998, p. 21).

Participation is, I suggest, about a sense, a feeling, in our hearts perhaps, of being part of something such as an idea; a belief system; humanity; the wider life world. It is a consciousness (Berman, 1989; Heshusius, 1994, 1995) not self-absorbed but a 'self reflective ... critical consciousness' (Fine et al, 2000, p. 108) through which we strive not to be alone and to identify our self in another. Inclusion, therefore, is about ourselves.

Reynolds (1998) presents the words of an anonymous European settler published in the weekly Queenslander in 1880. This bushman had previously said that he had taken part in the murder of aborigines and that he opposed those who showed support for these people. He then wrote, 'Is there room for both of us here? No. Then the sooner the weaker is wiped out the better' (in Reynolds, 1998, p. 115). Perhaps all of exclusion is of this kind.

Where do we stand in comparison with this Australian bushman of more than a century ago? Economist and photographer Sebastião Salgado (2001) has photographed people around the world who are left without work, homes, land or resources. His exhibition was at the Edinburgh City Art Centre at the time of a research meeting in nearby Stirling where the project of which this chapter is a part was being discussed. Salgado wrote, 'I sometimes saw 10,000 people die in a day' (p. 19). He identified the death of these children and adults 'with this new economic system' and said that 'there is an economic problem at the start of all these stories' (p. 19). John Berger (2001, p. 19), in his review of Salgado's work, says that four people out of five in the world are harmed by the economic policies and practices we call globalisation. Have we – the we of whiteness and power in my case – decided that the sooner they are wiped out, the better?

Allen (2001) describes globalisation as a 'form of white identity politics' creating and sustaining 'power and privilege that benefits even poor whites over non-whites because 'access to equity [is] distributed along racial group lines' (p. 478). Such institutionalised unfairness, such wilful oppression, brings into question the ethical and moral character of presently dominant systems of thought that are replicated through our schools and other institutions. An alternative story might be written and new identities formed if we were to strive to understand and be part of an inclusive agenda that would share power, value interdependencies, and create environments that foster and sustain democratic participation and social justice.

REFERENCES

Aitken, J. (2000a). *Where are the heroes? Educational leadership in recent times.* Address to the New Zealand Education Administration Society Biennial Conference, 19 January, Waitangi (NZ).

Aitken, J. (2000b). *Probability or proof – inference or information.* Address to a Teachers' Refresher Course Committee (TRCC) Seminar, St Hilda's Collegiate, 12 April, Dunedin (NZ).

Alice, L. (1993). 'Unlearning our privilege as our loss': Postcolonial writing and textual production. *Women's Studies Journal,* 9(1), 26–46.

Allen, R. L. (2001). The globalization of white supremacy: Toward a critical discourse on the racialization of the world. *Educational Theory,* 51(4), 467–485.

Ansley, B. (2001). Recurring condition. *New Zealand Listener,* 178, 26 May-1 June, 22-24.

Ball, S. J. (1999). *Performativities and fabrications in the education economy: Towards the performative society.* Paper presented as the Frank Tate Memorial Lecture and keynote address to the Australian Association for Research in Education Annual Conference, Melbourne.

Barker, A. (1995). Standards-based assessment: The vision and broader factors. In R. Peddie & B. Tuck (Eds.), *Setting the standards: The assessment of competence in national qualifications.* Palmerston North (NZ): Dunmore Press.

Berger, J. (2001). Tragedy on a global scale. *Guardian Weekly,* June 7–13, p. 19.

Berman, M. (1989). *Coming to our senses: Body and spirit in the hidden history of the west.* New York: Bantam Books.

Buber, M. (1965). *Between man and man* (Ronald G. Smith & Maurice Friedman, Trans). New York: McMillan.

Butterworth, G. & Butterworth, S. (1998). *Reforming education: The New Zealand experience, 1984–1996.* Palmerston North (NZ): Dunmore Press.

Cochran-Smith, M. (2000). Blind vision: Unlearning racism in teacher education. *Harvard Educational Review,* 70(2), 157–190.

Codd, J. (1999). Educational reform, accountability and the culture of distrust. New Zealand *Journal of Educational Studies,* 34(1), 45–53.

Connelly, F. M. & Clandinin, D. J. (1999). Knowledge, context and identity. In F. M. Connelly & D. J. Clandinin (Eds.), *Shaping a professional identity: Stories of educational practice.* New York: Teachers College Press.

Dewey, J. (1916). *Democracy and education: An introduction to the philosophy of education.* New York: The Free Press.

Easton, B. (1997). *The commercialisation of New Zealand.* Auckland: Auckland University Press.

Easton, B. (2001). Locked out: Of free press and free economics. *New Zealand Listener,* 178, 26 May-1 June, p. 38.

Fine, M., Weis, L., Weseen, S. & Wong, L. (2000). For whom? Qualitative research, representations, and social responsibilities. In N. K. Denzin & Y. S. Lincoln (Eds.), *Handbook of qualitative research* (2nd edition, pp. 107–131). Thousand Oaks: Sage.

Fitzjohn, J. (2001). Student loans: Letter to the editor. *The Press* (Christchurch, NZ), Monday 15 January, page 6.

Foundation for Research, Science and Technology (2002). Formulation for Research Science and Technology, Draft investment signals for 2002. Retrieved June 8, 2002, from http://www.frst.govt.nz.

Galbraith, J. K. (1992). *The culture of contentment.* London: Penguin Books.

Garbarino, J. (2000). Children's rights in the ecology of human development. In A. B. Smith, M. Gollop, K. Marshall & K. Nairn (Eds.), *Advocating for children: International perspectives on children's rights.* Dunedin, NZ: University of Otago Press.

Grosz, E. (1994). Identity and difference: A response. In P. James (Ed.) *Critical politics: From the personal to the global.* Melbourne: Arena Publications.

Hall, A. (1999). *Some ethical questions for teachers arising from inter-school competition.* Paper presented at the Conference of the Australian Association for Research in Education and the New Zealand Association for Research in Education, Melbourne, 29 November-2 December.

Harker, R. (1999). *Innovations for effective schooling.* Panel discussion, 28 August. Unpublished paper, College of Education, Massey University.

Hanlon, G. (1998). Professionalism as enterprise. *Sociology,* 32(1), 43–63.

Heshusius, L. (1994). Freeing ourselves from objectivity: Managing subjectivity or turning toward a participatory mode of consciousness. *Educational Researcher,* 23(3), 15–22.

Heshusius, L. (1995). Listening to children: 'What could we possibly have in common?' From concerns with self to participatory consciousness. *Theory into Practice,* 34(2), 117–123.

House, E. R. (1998). *Schools for sale: Why free market policies won't improve America's schools, and what will.* New York: Teachers College Press.

Hytten, K. & Adkins, A. (2001). Thinking through a pedagogy of whiteness. *Educational Theory,* 51(4), 433–450.

James, C. E. (2002). Achieving desire: Narrative of a black male teacher. *Qualitative Studies in Education,* 15(2), 171–186.

James, P. (1994). Introduction: Rethinking politics. In P. James (Ed.), *Critical politics: From the personal to the global* (pp. 1–6). Melbourne: Arena Publications.

Kearney, C. (1998). Deep excavations: An examination of the tangled roots of identity in modern cosmopolitan societies. *International Journal of Inclusive Education,* 2(4), 309–326.

Kelsey, J. (1993). *Rolling back the state: Privatisation of power in Aotearoa/New Zealand.* Wellington, NZ: Bridget Williams Books.

Kelsey, J. (1997). *The New Zealand experiment: A world model for structural adjustment?* Auckland: Auckland University Press & Bridget Williams Books.

Kelsey, J. (2000). GATS – what does it mean? *AUS Bulletin,* 46, July, 6–7.

Knight, K. (2001). Doctor loses heart over health reforms. *Sunday Star Times,* 22 April, C4.

Kunda, G. (1992). *Engineering culture: Control and commitment in a high-tech corporation.* Philadelphia: Temple University Press.

Lauder, H., Hughes, D., & Watson, S. (1999). The introduction of educational markets in New Zealand: Questions and consequences. *New Zealand Journal of Educational Studies,* 34(1), 86–98.

Lawrence, S. M. & Tatum, B. D. (1997). White educators as allies: Moving from awareness to action. In M. Fine, L. Weis, L. C. Powell & L. M. Wong (Eds.) *Offwhite: Readings on race, power and society.* New York: Routledge.

Lee, G. & Lee, H. (1999). Essay review: Reforming education, rewriting history. New *Zealand Journal of Educational Studies,* 34(1), 255–259.

Little, M. (1995). *Health, education and the virtues of efficiency:* The Everett Magnus Oration presented at the Sixteenth Biennial Conference of the Australian and New Zealand Association of Maxillofacial Surgeons. New Zealand Dental Journal, 91, 89–93.

Locke, T. (2000). *Curriculum, assessment and the erosion of professionalism.* Paper presented to the 18th World Congress of Reading, July, Auckland (NZ).

Malin, M. (1999). *An undebated conundrum in the ethics of classroom research: The conflicting rights of researcher, teacher and student within an agenda of reform.* Paper presented to the Conference of the Australian Association for Research in Education and New Zealand Association for Research in Education, 29 November-2 December, Melbourne.

Mathews, P. (1999). Right on: The generation who have inherited the Rogernomics revolution come of age. *Listener,* 9 October, pp. 19–22.

May, W. F. (1988). Contract or covenant? In J. C. Callaghan (Ed.), *Ethical issues in professional life.* New York: Oxford University Press.

O'Neill, A. M. & Jolley, S. (1996/97). Privatising curriculum. Constructing consumer society. The technology curriculum: The politics of food – women's work? To high tech or oblivion. *Delta,* 48(2), 49(1), 221–248.

Orwell, G. (1949). *Nineteen eighty-four.* Harmondsworth, Middlesex: Penguin Books (1954 edition).

Peters, M. (1995). The marketisation of education and democracy: A response to Professor Michael Apple. In M. Olssen & K. Morris Matthews (Eds.), *Education, democracy and reform.* Auckland: New Zealand Association for Research in Education and Research Unit for Maori Education.

Pole, R. (2001). Letter to the editor. *North and South,* March, pp. 15–16.

Potter, T. (2000). Roger, but not over and out. *Sunday Star Times,* 19 March, page A.11.

Putnam, R. D. (1993). *Making democracy work: Civic traditions in modern Italy.* Princeton, NJ: Princeton University Press.

Rae, K. (1999). *Reforming education – was this indeed the New Zealand experience?* 31 August, unpublished paper, Porirua, Wellington, NZ.

Reynolds, H. (1998). *This whispering in our hearts.* St Leonards, Australia: Allen & Unwin.

Riske, E. & Ladd, H. (2000). *When schools compete: A cautionary tale.* New York: Brookings Institution Press.

Robertson, S. L. (1996). Teachers' work, restructuring and postfordism: Constructing the new 'professionalism'. In I. Goodson & A. Hargreaves (Eds.), *Teachers' professional lives.* London: Falmer Press.

Salgado, S. (2001). Displaced children. *Guardian Weekly,* June 7–13, p. 19.

Saul, J. R. (1997). *The unconscious civilization.* Ringwood, Victoria: Penguin Books.

Scheurich, J. J. (1993). Toward a white discourse on white racism. *Educational Researcher,* 22(8), 5–10.

Sennett, R. (1998). *The corrosion of character: The personal consequences of work in the new capitalism*. New York: W. H. Norton.

Shakespeare, T. (1996). Disability, identity and difference. In C. Barnes & G. Mercer (Eds), *Exploring the divide: Illness and disability*. Leeds: Disability Press.

Skrtic, T. (1995). Power, knowledge and pragmatism: A postmodern view of the professions. In T. Skrtic (Ed.) *Disability and democracy: Reconstructing (special) education*. New York: Teachers College Press.

Sleeter, C. E. (1993). Advancing a white discourse: A response to Scheurich. *Educational Researcher*, 22(8), 13–15.

Smith, F. (1998). *The book of learning and forgetting*. New York: Teachers College Press.

Smith, L. T. (1999). *Decolonising methodologies: Research and indigenous peoples*. London: Zed Books.

Smyth, J. (1993). Introduction. In J. Smyth (Ed.), *A socially critical view of the self-managing school*. London: The Falmer Press.

Stent, R. (1998a). Health and Disability Commissioner's investigation into Canterbury Health Ltd. Retrieved on February 7, 2002, from http://www.hdc.org.nz.

Stent, R. (1998b). *Canterbury Health Ltd: A report by the Health and Disability Commissioner*. Wellington: Health and Disability Commissioner.

Tertiary Education Advisory Commission (2001). *Shaping the funding framework: Fourth report of the Tertiary Education Advisory Commission*. Wellington: Tertiary Education Advisory Commission.

Thompson, S. (2000). Moving into higher gear. *Foundation*, 39, March, p. 2.

Waldegrave, C., King, P. & Stuart, S. (1999). *The monetary and consumer behaviour in New Zealand of low income households*. Wellington: The Family Centre Social Policy Research Unit.

Walker, A. (1997). *Anything we love can be saved: A writer's activism*. London: The Women's Press.

Wilson, D. (Chair) (2001). *Communities and government – Potential for partnership: Whakatōpü whakaaro*. Wellington: Ministry of Social Policy.

Witherell, C. (1991). The self in narrative: A journey into paradox. In C. Witherell & N. Noddings (Eds.), *Stories lives tell: Narrative and dialogue in education*. New York: Teachers College Press.

Witherell, C. & Noddings, N. (1991). Prologue: An invitation to our readers. In C. Witherell & N. Noddings (Eds), *Stories lives tell: Narrative and dialogue in education*. New York: Teachers College Press.

Zaretsky, E. (1994). Identity theory, identity politics: The separation between the public and the private. In P. James (Ed.), *Critical politics: From the personal to the global*. Melbourne: Arena Publications.

MARIT STRØMSTAD

3 'THEY BELIEVE THAT THEY PARTICIPATE ... BUT': DEMOCRACY AND INCLUSION IN NORWEGIAN SCHOOLS

INTRODUCTION

Is it possible to imagine a truly inclusive school that is not also a democratic school? Can a truly democratic school close its doors to any student? Democracy, in this chapter, does not refer to a political system or form of government, but to a social phenomenon. In a democracy, people are participating and are empowered to make decisions and politics concerning themselves and society. Such decisions are, however, constrained by the principles of nonrepression and non-discrimination (Levin, undated). For the last 2–3 years a colleague, Kari Nes, and I have been engaged in a project aimed at evaluating the inclusiveness of schools in Norway. We both came from special education and like many others with that background, we thought about inclusion as primarily related to students who had not formerly been a part of the mainstream school system, namely students with special needs. The aim was to include them and still give them the benefit of special education, but along with others (eg. Skritc, 1995, Haug, 1998, Thomas & Loxley, 2001) we began to question the knowledge base of special education. This chapter explores the relationship between inclusion and democracy. It first outlines the legal demands for inclusion and democracy in Norwegian schools. This serves as a background for the presentation of some findings from the project and parallel findings. Finally, it asks whether school democracy can enhance inclusion in both school and society and considers to what extent democratic ideas are used as a scaffold for the development of inclusion.

INTEGRATION AND INCLUSION IN NORWAY

Norway has a unitary compulsory school system and there are few private schools. Statistics indicate that more than 98% of students go to their local school (Tjernshaugen, 2002), which is free and open to every child irrespective of cultural background, ethnicity, ability or gender. One school for all has been the principle, though there have been contrasting views as to how this ideal should be interpreted and put into practice.

Norway had state special schools until 1991, when the system was dismantled. Institutions and schools for mentally retarded were closed down in 1990 and from

33

J. Allan (ed.), Inclusion, Participation and Democracy: What is the Purpose?, 33-47.
© 2003 *Kluwer Academic Publishers. Printed in the Netherlands.*

1991, the local authorities were given total responsibility for the education of all children living in their area. Though state special schools existed for more than a hundred years, relatively few students attended them. The number was at its highest in the 1970s, but even then there were only around 3,500 students (less than 0.1%) enrolled. Most children went to school in their local municipality, but that did not necessarily mean that they were included. According to Haug (1998), 3,000 students in the elementary school received offers of segregated placement in 1996 – five years after the special school system was abandoned.

Inclusion is a relatively new concept in Norwegian education policy. Integration has been on the agenda since the middle of the 1960s, however, the concept of integration proved to be ambiguous, and the understanding and practice of integration in Norway – as in other countries – has varied greatly. According to Haug (1998), there were at least two different integration discourses. One of these was characterised by the concern for individual needs, what Stangvik (1997) terms an individual-oriented paradigm. This led to a more or less segregating practice where the ideas of the special school system were implemented in the ordinary schools. Thus students in some ways were assimilated while the schools remained largely unchanged and did not accommodate to the diversity of students. The more inclusive integration discourse focused on every student's right to be part of a social community. Although this was the official policy, the implementation was left to the local school authorities or individual schools and many students were still given a largely segregated education in the local school.

In 1997, the new Curriculum for the 10-year compulsory school in Norway (L97) laid down that schools should be inclusive and accommodate all students: 'The compulsory school is based on the principle of one school for all' (L97, p. 62). The danger is, however, that inclusion, as integration was in the past, is concerned only with special education. Teachers express their worries about 'including' individual children, being less concerned with making the school or class inclusive to meet the demands of diversity. This points to a dangerous narrowing of inclusion and a repetition of the debate on integration. Inclusion seems to be understood as merely a reform of special education with the same basic assumptions.

Inclusion and democracy

Inclusion is not about bringing somebody who has been formerly excluded into an environment that has not adapted to normal diversity. Inclusion is about diversity living and working together. Is not this the core of democracy as well? Democracy – like inclusion – can be variously interpreted, but interaction between people is central to any definition. Dewey's (1961) view of democracy is of great relevance for the inclusive school and specifies the salient goals:

> A democracy is more than a form of government; it is primarily a mode
> of associated living, of conjoint communicated experience. The extension
> in space of the number of individuals who participate in an interest so that
> each has to refer his own action of that of others, and to consider the action

of others to give point and direction to his own, is equivalent to the breaking
down of those barriers of class, race, and national territory which kept men
from perceiving the full import of their activity (p. 87).

Education for democracy has been an ideal in Norway for many years, dating
back to the Enlightenment of the people-programme of the Left party in the
1880s. Enlightenment had a double function, as both the basis and the aims of
democracy. It was realised that a democracy that was not based on general education could threaten its own existence. Education, therefore, was needed to sustain
democracy.

According to Slagstad (1998), 'an enlightened people is a powerful people who
wants to decide its own destiny' (p. 107). Education has been seen by the Norwegian
Labour Government as a means to reduce class distinctions and social barriers
between people and the Norwegian unitary compulsory school was developed as a
means of achieving this. It was, however, 'built up with the normal pupil in mind'
(Haug, 1998, p. 25). Though the aim of education was democratisation of society,
school practices were far from democratic. They resembled what Senge (2000)
describes as a school modelled on an assembly:

> While the assembly-line school system dramatically increased educational
> output, it also created many of the most intractable problems with which
> students, teachers and parents struggle to this day. It operationally defined
> smart kids and dumb kids ... It established uniformity of product and process
> as norms, thereby naively assuming that all children learn in the same way
> (pp. 31–32).

This was a teacher-centered, rather than learner-centered, school. Special schools
and special education as a profession emerged in response to a need to accommodate those children who did not fit the unitary school. As early as 1881, a
first law considering the abnormal child's right to be educated was established in
Norway. This at least offered some education to people who had hitherto had no
opportunities. The 'school for all' did not, literally, mean 'all.' The undemocratic
practice in schools excluded those who 'fell off the assembly-line.' School is also
a preparation for societal life. How could those who were rejected even by their
local school ever be equal participants in their local society?

When 'Blom-komiteen,' a public committee, discussed integration in the 1960s
(Kirke-og undervisningdepartementet, 1970), on the one hand, they realised the
importance of diversity in classes as a preparation for life in a diverse society; on
the other hand, they were concerned about individual needs and the consideration
for the other students. The White Paper preceeding the dismantling of the special
schools (Utdannings- og forskningsdepartementet, 1989–90) emphasises the right
to equality and adapted education. Individual needs are central and the paper states
that nobody shall be integrated just for the the sake of it. Both documents clearly
indicate an 'us' and a 'them.' Nothing is said about diversity being valued.

Did any democratic ideals shape these considerations? One might say that the
right to belong and participate is a democratic right, but all the same it seems that

the focus was on individuals rather than on the expansion of democracy. Norway was a welfare state, and those who had not yet had their share of prosperity were now invited in. The emphases on individual rights are revealing. The supporters of integration – now inclusion – still hold out that children with special needs have the right to be present at the local school. What about the rights of other students to experience the normal and natural diversity of human life? Diversity is an essential condition for democracy. Only societies where the normal diversity of mankind lives together and refer their actions to those of others can be truly inclusive and have room for everyone. In such a society, every participant has individual needs but nobody has special needs. Real understanding can be fostered through learning about each other's differences.

Perhaps it is time to stop discussing individual needs and rights and to look instead at how democracy is practised in schools. Being together is not necessarily sufficient for understanding and care to develop between people. Students, as well as staff and carers, must realise that their words and actions are important to others because they have impact on others' lives, feelings, and self-image. That can be obtained by deliberate democratic practice in schools and classrooms. The major goal is to create 'within the school a climate of tolerance and respect encouraging the development of democratic culture' (UNESCO 2001, p. 20). Such a climate is essential in an inclusive school.

Laws and prescriptions concerning student democracy in Norwegian schools

School laws and The National Curriculum for the 10-year compulsory school in Norway (L97) requires students, parents and staff to participate in democratic leadership of the school on different levels and in various ways. The National Curriculum for the 10-year compulsory school in Norway prescribes democratic ways of working and decision-making in the classroom as a preparation for social life. It states that education must promote democracy, national identity and international awareness. But it is not sufficient merely to learn the theory of democracy. It has to be done in practice as well: 'School is a society in miniature that should be used actively for learning such skills. The learners must be spurred to engage in decisions, for their ability to participate is strengthened by use' (L97, p. 48). Today's education must encompass:

> Experience in making decisions with direct and clear consequences for oth-
> ers. This implies training in making and following rules, practice in making
> decisions in tangled situations, exercising *crisis skills*, i.e. the ability to act
> when faced with unexpected troubles or unfamiliar tasks, etc. Taken together
> these represent coaching in social responsibility (ibid).

The democratic practice in the classroom is not democracy through representation, but a place where every student has the right to voice his or her opinion and be listened to before a decision is taken. This is of particular importance when it comes to the students' choice of learning material and working methods: 'As they share in planning and influencing their own school work, they gain experience in democracy in practice' (ibid, p. 70).

Each class in the primary and lower secondary school must have a class council, whose responsibility is to promote the interests of all the students in the class and, in co-operation with the teachers and the parents, to work to create a satisfactory environment in the class. The class council is also expected to represent their views at school level. Each primary and lower secondary school has one council for class levels 5–7 and one for class levels 8–10 consisting of one representative from each class. In co-operation with teachers and parents, the council's primary responsibility is to promote the joint interests of every student and to work to create a satisfactory school environment. The council organises its own activities. Teachers, headmasters, parents and class councils can submit matters to the council, which decides independently what matters to engage in. The overall aim is that children should learn to take responsibility for their own learning and well-being and for that of their peers.

The prescriptions cited above have certain consequences for classroom activities. It represents a substantial change from the traditional teacher who primarily was an intermediary of knowledge. L97 characterises the class as a working team and the teachers as leaders of the pupils' community of work. One of the practical consequences is that teachers must decide less than they have formerly done, with more decisions being taken by the students. This shift in the locus of decision-making has been occurring gradually over time, but is more explicitly expressed in L97 than it was in former curricula.

Students are supposed to be actively engaged in setting their own goals and evaluate their own learning, but their responsibility is not restricted to their own learning. They must recognise what influence they have on other students' success or failure in academic work as well as socially. Students should participate in the making of rules for schools and classroom and other things essential to their motivation and well-being. Staff are expected to engage students in conversations that enhance critical thinking and promote values education, and diversity must be on the class-room agenda.

In practice, this means that after a few days together, even the first-graders have mapped each other's strengths and weaknesses. If this is not managed carefully through open conversations about the normality of difference and the importance of mutual respect and understanding, pupils may find themselves harshly judged by their peers. Such openness is not easy and perhaps demanding on staff, but is necessary in order to cultivate an understanding of diversity as natural and normal. This kind of student democracy does not entail that staff give up their position of authority. Even in a democracy there are things that are not negotiable and recognising this is part of democratic education. Students need the support of adults in order to develop their democratic skills. The challenge is finding the optimal balance and level of support. Openness about differences is also important for orchestrating adapted education. In academic work, student achievements will vary and 'Every element in the learning process – syllabus, working methods, organisation and learning materials – must therefore be implemented with the abilities of different pupils in mind' (L97, p. 64). The teacher cannot keep these differences a secret. The students must learn through openness to accept and respect the achievements of all.

EVALUATING INCLUSION: LOOKING FOR DEMOCRACY?

The Curriculum for the 10-year compulsory school in Norway (L97) lays down a requirement for inclusion. But how is inclusion to be carried out? What is it to be an inclusive school? When we started our evaluation of inclusion in Norwegian schools, we had to operationalise the concept and decide what to look for. A natural starting point was to explore the application of the concept in L97. At one point in the document, inclusion clearly relates to students with special needs: 'As a community, the compulsory school must be inclusive. Pupils with special needs must be given the opportunity to play an equally important part in the social, academic and cultural community' (L97, p. 64). Elsewhere, however, it seems to be more widely employed: 'In order to meet pupils' different background and abilities, the school for all must be an inclusive community with room for everyone. The diversity of backgrounds, interests and abilities must be met with a diversity of challenges' (op.cit., p. 63). The document also states that: 'While compulsory school education is based on a clear set of values, it must also be inclusive and respect different views of cultures, faith and values' (op.cit., p. 63). The term inclusive is only used explicitly in these three contexts; elsewhere, it makes more indirect references, for example in relation to co-operation between students, staff, staff and carers. Though L97 may be differently interpreted, at least the general part of it describes the inclusive school. It emphasises very clearly the importance of interaction between students:

> The school is a workplace and a meeting place for everyone. It is a place where pupils come together, learn from and live with differences, regardless of where they live, their social backgrounds, their genders, their religions, their ethnic origins, their mental and physical ability (op.cit., pp. 62–63).

The Index for Inclusion (Booth et al, 2000) has helped to operalise inclusion. The indicators and questions in the Index enhance awareness about how inclusion can be put into practice. Inclusion in the Index seems to be consistent with L97. With few alterations, the English material can easily be applied in Norwegian schools. Participation in a social, academic and cultural community, not only for students, but for staff and carers as well, seems to be central in L97. From the Index for Inclusion, and from literature on inclusion (eg. Ballard, 1995; Allan, 1999; Ainscow, 1999), we have identified the following list of characteristics:

1. How does the school cater for students' right to learn in an academic community?
• An inclusive school must give adapted education so that all students can be exposed to challenges in keeping with their abilities and interests.

- Giving adapted education to a diversity of students demands a variety of methods in classrooms. Students must be taught to take a certain responsibility for their own learning. They must be able to do parts of their work at school independent of help.

2. *How does the school cater for students' right to be part of a social and cultural community?*
- The school and class environment is the working place of students where they must feel safe and well to do their best. The school must look out for exclusionary attitudes among students as well as in teachers.
- The right of students with special needs to belong must be upheld. Though categorisation of students, in my opinion, is inconsistent with inclusion because it presupposes pathology, it is widely practised partly because a diagnosis may release extra resources. Categorised students are a vulnerable group, and schools have to be committed to their right to belong.
- The right of students from minority groups to belong must also be upheld. This group is vulnerable to exclusionary pressures. Thus it is urgent that schools take special precautions to secure their social and cultural inclusion free from pressure towards assimilation.
- Gender equality. An inclusive school offers the same opportunities to boys and girls.

3. *How is school democracy practised?*
- School is a preparation for life in a society where people are expected to live and develop together. This calls for practical knowledge in democratic principles for how decisions are taken, respected and lived up to. Schools and classrooms must be arenas where democracy is practised.
- Parents and carers should be part of school life because they have the main responsibility for their children and thus should influence their learning situation. They also represent the local culture which is an important basis for schools.
- Co-operation between staff is essential to the development of the school as a learning environment and workplace.

Looking at the characteristics of the inclusive schools listed above, it seems that democracy may be the most important characteristic because it both includes and is a premise for the others. Would a truly democratic school, just by being democratic, aim at all the other points mentioned?

It seems easier to provide adapted education and to employ different teaching methods in democratic co-operation with the students than to expect everyone to do the same thing at the same time and in the same place. It also seems plausible that students who share the responsibility for the school and classroom rules would feel more committed to live up to their own rules than students who are not consulted. Repression and discrimination will be removed when people explore their diversity through open conversations and experience.

How is democracy practised in the schools? Are students actually given any possibilities for real participation? Once student councils and similar structures are positioned, what kind of information do they get? What kind of decisions are they invited to take? Are they regarded as important and do their opinions have any impact on the development of school practice? And what about democracy in the classroom?

In our research project on inclusion, we distributed questionnaires to all the staff in the 33 schools, all the students of 4th, 6th and 9th grade and their parents, a total number of more than 3,000 informants. In our questionnaire, we asked both students and staff about democratic practice. Do students take part in rule-making in the classroom? Do they have any influence on teaching methods and learning material? Do they work together? Do they contribute to setting goals and evaluation? The questionnaire contained a number of statements to which one should declare a level of agreement on a five-point scale. In the following account categories were merged and reduced to 'agree' and 'disagree.'

With data from the questionnaires as a background, we undertook case studies (Yin, 1994) in five of the 33 schools. In these schools, we observed lessons and breaks and interviewed students, staff, and parents. We focused on democratic practice, students' participation and their attitude to diversity.

EXPERIENCES OF STUDENT DEMOCRACY

The findings from our research are used to illustrate certain points regarding student participation. One of the statements in the questionnaires to staff as well as teachers was that students had been participating in the making of classroom rules. Discrepancy between student and staff perception – not to say construction – of reality was evident in the answers to this question as to several others. In four schools out of 33 (some of them very small), all students agreed to the statement while staff agreed in 15 schools. In 13 schools, less than 80% of the students agreed, compared with only four schools in which the same proportion of staff agreed. In group interviews, the students were somewhat vague about the use of rules in the classroom. Some were not aware that class rules existed at all, while others said: 'They are there on the wall, but nobody ever looks at them.' Had they been active in the making of rules? 'In a way,' some answered. 'But it actually is the teacher's doing. We wrote a lot of proposals on the blackboard. Then the teacher made his choice. It is always like that. They say that we are to decide, but they do it.' Another group said: 'the teacher proposed some rules and we agreed.' Few students saw the rules as having any influence on classroom behaviour: 'Those who don't mind don't mind rules either.'

One group of teachers described students' participation in decision-making more generally, indicating that they made plans in co-operation with the students: 'But the students very often feel ... they know ... they believe that they participate ... they know that they are managed by us even though they are allowed to express their meanings. But we try.' Another statement was: 'Students are engaged in evaluating their own behaviour.' A majority of teachers agreed while students were less sure.

In the interviews, we tried to explore students and staff attitude to diversity and inclusion. Students were well aware of differences and expressed tolerance, but sometimes their choice of words demonstrated that there existed an 'us' and 'them.' For example, one student said: 'I think it is better for them to be in a group outside the classroom. It must be embarrassing for them when the teachers give them material to work with that is quite different from what we do.' Another student commented that 'they could just as well sit in the class-room with their teacher. Outside the class-room they do nothing, and the teacher expects nothing from them.' 'There is nothing wrong with her,' said yet another group, referring to a school-mate who spent much time outside the class: 'she just is in the cafeteria. She belongs to the class, only that she is in a way several years younger than us.' Several students complained about the level of noise in classrooms. They wanted the teachers to be firmer and to calm the boisterous classmates down or eventually even throw them out. 'But it looks like teachers do not know what to do.'

Teachers were in two minds about diversity in their classrooms. On the one hand they voiced the politically correct opinions; on the other hand, they found it difficult to respond to diversity. One teacher said firmly: 'It is important for every-body that they stay together! In class they can support each other.' Other teachers, however, were more doubtful about this: 'In our school some students prefer the segregated setting. And look at them during breaks. They keep to themselves even then. I think we do wrong.' One teacher described students who left their special classes five minutes before break, indicating that it was important to them to go to the playground with their friends from the classroom and not from the separate setting. Many teachers were of the impression that students were accepted members of class community in spite of their separate lessons.

Were differences ever talked openly about? The students said that teachers sometimes talked about students with certain problems when they were not present: 'The teacher should not do that. Some of our classmates cannot be trusted with such information. They bully him.' The students did not know whether or not the infor-mation had been given with the permission of the individual students concerned. Teachers expressed the view that openness was necessary because students knew about individual differences in any case. Interestingly, diversity and differences were never discussed during our observation of lessons.

One of the statements to the students was: 'We have a voice as to what to learn in school.' In 26 (out of 33) schools, less than 50% of the children expressed some level of agreement. We looked at the teachers' agreement to the statement: 'My students participate in setting their goals in subject matters.' Less than 50% of the teachers agreed in 13 schools. It was also of some interest to find out whether the students participate in assessing their learning. Only in one school did all the teachers agree that this was the case. In 13 schools less than 50% of the teachers asked the students to evaluate their own learning outcome. These responses suggest that students in the 33 schools of this municipality are not significantly involved in setting goals and evaluating learning outcomes.

The findings reveal a discrepancy between students' and teachers' conception of realities in schools. This is further demonstrated by the response to the statement: ' In some lessons the students are allowed to choose their own tasks.' In 18 schools, 100% of the teachers agreed. But when students were posed the same statement, only in one school did 100% of the students agree. In 20 schools, less than 80% agreed that they could choose tasks in some lessons. It is surprising to find that so many students, and even a certain amount of teachers, were of the opinion that students were not given the opportunity to choose their own tasks. We know from our observation that some schools gave the students some opportunities to chose. Subjects were organised into three 'paths' of different challenge. Students were free to change levels for each period. Differentiation was, however, mainly restricted to the number of pages to read or the degree of difficulty in questions to answer. The students liked the system: 'It gives everybody a choice. I can chose an easy path in English if I have much Norwegian to do in the same period.' But they also stated that some students chose the easiest way: 'They are too lazy to do their best.'

We interviewed student councils in five different schools about their work. What did the councils do? What matters did they look into? None of the councils had any influence on school development plans, action plans or activities in the classroom: 'That is not our business.' Matters submitted were mostly practical questions: What to sell in the cafeteria? How to spend the money from the cafeteria sales? What ought to be repaired in the playground? One of the councils had independently made their own investigation into bullying and school environment. They reported that numerous students felt uncomfortable during breaks. They were afraid of a gang of boys who had occupied parts of the playground and terrorised younger students. No action, however, was taken on their behalf: 'We gave out material to the school, but nothing has happened.'

Teachers reported more co-operation between students than did students. Teachers also said that co-operative groups were changed to give students the opportunity of different partners. The students generally said that they co-operated with friends and seldom changed partners. In some classes, co-operation was not allowed and teachers indicated that this was because of the high level of noise generated.

Parallel findings

Our research was restricted to one municipality and cannot be generalised across Norway. There are, however, some interesting parallels with findings from other studies.

Skaalvik and Skaalvik (1996) compared teaching methods within two research projects set ten years apart – in 1983 and 1993 – and concluded that pedagogical practice in classrooms seems to have changed very little. The blackboard and teacher directed practice remained dominant. Students did some individual work in both cases, but mostly used the same material. This kind of teaching leaves all the control to the teacher and the students have very little responsibility for their learning. They just do as they are told. Nordahl (1998) found that teachers seem to prefer students who yield to their authority and reproduce the required behaviour and knowledge. Students who oppose are judged to have insufficient social competence and are regarded as problematic.

In 2001, The International Association of Educational Achievement published their findings from the *Civic Educational Study*, where 90,000 14 year old students from 28 countries had been asked about their understanding of, and attitude towards, different democratic principles and practices. Data show that Norwegian students have more than average theoretical knowledge about democracy compared with their peers in 28 different countries. They have the politically correct opinions and attitudes regarding what is important for the maintenance and further development of a democratic country. Yet only 30% of the 9th graders take any interest in politics and a mere 14% want to join political parties (KUFAktuelt, 2001).

Data from the research demonstrate that reality and vision are incongruent. Teachers tend to have a vision that emphasises critical thinking or values education, but when it comes to teaching methods, teachers overwhelmingly report that in the teaching of civic education, most emphasis is placed on knowledge transmission (Torney-Purta, et al, 2001). National findings correspond with these data. In 2001, The Department of Education in Norway (KUF, 2001) reported that one out of two parents are of the opinion that students should have more influence in schools. In 1999, Thuen found that 53% of the 9th graders do not participate in decisions as to the choice of teaching and learning methods (Arneberg and Overland, 2001). The Children's Ombudsman in Norway reports that many of the complaints received come from students who are not listened to by their teachers (Barneombudet, 2001). He argues that the assumption made that democracy can be learned through reading about it in textbooks is false and on the contrary makes children passive.

Two young Norwegians were interviewed before they left for a UN conference concerning *A World fit for Children*. They were of the opinion that Norwegian children were seldom heard and that participation was often symbolic rather than real (Speed, 1992).The picture is, however, not entirely bleak. According to the IEA investigation, Norwegian students report especially open climates for classroom discussions. Furthermore, female students perceive their classrooms as more open than do males.

A FAKE DEMOCRACY?

The students we have spoken to appear to have a limited influence on planning, setting goals and evaluating outcomes in subjects and in their behaviour. It is possible that students underrate their participation, but this would have to be substantial to explain the discrepancies between student and teacher rating. A plausible explanation is that teachers overrate student participation, either because they truly believe that students participate more than they do or because there is a certain amount of lip service on their part. It is, however, not unexpected to find that teachers and students conceptualise school practice rather differently. Nordahl (1998) found the same when he looked into teachers' and students' perception of the variety of teaching methods and choice of material in schools in Oslo. It also appears that the dichotomy between 'us' and 'them' is not sufficiently challenged. Diversity is undoubtedly present in Norwegian schools, but it is questionable whether students learn to live together and foster mutual responsibility and respect, or whether they just co-exist.

The conversations with students and teachers and experiences within a variety of classrooms provoke the question: Do Norwegian students fall prey to a fake democracy? Practices vary, and of course some schools try hard to be more open to student voices, but the overall impression is that much is actually a play for the gallery, a pseudo-democracy where children are encouraged to have a voice, while little importance is attached to what they say. Both students and teachers state this very clearly. The phrase 'give them the feeling or impression of participation' is often used. What if students realise that when in reality they have very little influence? Does that foster democracy? Does that enhance responsibility, tolerance, understanding and all those pretty formulations in educational rhetoric? School is a preparation for life, but is also much more than that. To the students, school is life. Their opinions and views are of importance today. If democracy is not practised actively in schools, how can people be expected to suddenly realise its importance at the age of 20? Students learn about democracy through the ways that decisions are made in their schools.

Senge (2000) argues that we are still in the grip of the industrial heritage of schools, with its assumptions about students and learning. Ironically, the solution he suggests is to listen to students voices:

> Industrial-age schools have a structural blind spot unlike almost any contemporary institution. This blind spot arises because the only person who could in fact reflect on how the system as a whole is functioning is the one person who has no voice in the system, no power to provide meaningful feed-back that could produce change. That person is the student (p. 58).

Vestby (2002) points to the fact that the idea of children's participation and influence is rather new. The existence of a democratic childhood is less than 20 years old and we still have not realised the real implications of this. Children traditionally needed care and protection and it has taken some time to recognise their need for a voice in matters concerning their life and environment. Children's opinions may prove useful, rather than troublesome.

Teacher education in Norway is not adapted to the ideals of comprehensive schools, in which the newly educated teachers are going to work. Even though the students have regular practice in schools for several weeks during education, they do not acquire the necessary skills to operate democratically in the classroom. There are at least three reasons for that. First, they have gone through a very traditional school themselves, and they have presumably adapted to the system. Thus the ideals of the teacher-centred classroom are ingrained. Secondly, teacher education does too little to change those attitudes in students. On the contrary, they are more or less confirmed and strengthened through a teacher training which is following the same principles. Subjects are taught separately, and students are expected to sit relatively passively and receive information from teachers who know their subjects well, but who may never have worked with children. They are taught theoretically about teamwork and the thematic organisation of subjects, but that theory is seldom put into practice during their education. Thirdly during practice in school they often meet with teachers who still teach using traditional methods. Some even tell the students that what they learn at college is 'mere theory and impossible to put into practice because children are unable to concentrate and cannot work independently.' The outcome is that students leave their training with only a half-hearted conviction that change is required and possible. When they start working they will submit to the prevailing attitudes of the staffroom. Thus the system reproduces itself.

Teacher training still makes a definite distinction between education and special education. These form separate strands of the curriculum and the textbooks they read highlight individuals' special educational needs. Individual deficits are emphasised in the textbooks written by professionals. Students inevitably leave college with little understanding of diversity as a premise for democracy.

WOULD DEMOCRATIC PRACTICE MAKE A DIFFERENCE?

Trying to change society through school is nothing new. Some say it has never had any success. The mutual process of exchange and influence between school and society is, however, difficult to map. And what options are there? School is the only place where the experience of diversity can be imposed on people. It is the only arena where people cannot evade contact with people who are different from themselves and thus get the chance to adapt their attitudes and be freed from their fear of what may seen strange and threatening. There has always been diversity in schools. In many ways, it has been more or less purposefully unrecognised and ignored. As a consequence of changes outside schools, for example social reforms and immigration, diversity inside schools has expanded and cannot remain unrecognised either by students, staff or parents. History has proved that accepting differences and living in peaceful co-existence with those who seem strange does not come easy to mankind. It is a competence we must aquire through practice and experience. An inclusive and democratic school is the arena best suited for this learning.

Beem (1999) holds that the building of community and trust requires face-to-face encounters and interaction between people. Without interaction trust decays and this may lead to serious problems in society and a decline in social capital within it. Social capital consists of active connections among people: 'the trust, mutual understanding, and shared values and behaviours that bind the members of human networks and communities and make co-operative actions possible' (Cohen & Prusak, 2000, p. 4). A truly inclusive and democratic school would see a growth in social capital as one of its outcomes.

Is this Utopia? Definitely! According to Mannheim (1972), utopia is 'that kind of orientation which transcends reality and which at the same time breaks the bonds of the existing order ... Only in utopia and revolutions is there true life' (pp. 173–178). Isn't that what we want to through inclusion and democracy in school and society? If we lose sight of utopia, we lose our energy as well. 'The disappearance of utopia brings out a static state of affairs in which man himself becomes no more than a thing' (pp. 263–64).

REFERENCES

Ainscow, M. (1999). *Understanding the development of inclusive schools.* London: Falmer.

Allan, J. (1999). *Actively seeking inclusion: pupils with special needs in mainstream schools.* London: Falmer.

Arneberg, P. and Overland, B. (2001). *Fra tilskuer til deltaker.* Oslo: nks-forlaget

Ballard, K. (1995). Inclusion, Paradigms, Power and Participation. In C. Clark, A. Dyson & A. Millward (Eds.), *Towards Inclusive Schools.* London: David Fulton Publishers.

Barneombudet (2001). *Forskrift til opplæringslova – høringsuttalelse.*

Beem, C. (1999). *The Necessity of politic. Reclaiming American public life.* Chicago: University of Chicago Press.

Booth, T., Ainscow, M., Black-Hawkins, K., Vaughan, M., & Shaw. L. (2000). *Index for Inclusion.* Bristol: Centre for Studies on Inclusive Education.

Cohen, D. & Prusak, L. (2001). *In Good Company. How social Capital makes organisations work.* Boston: Harward Business School Press.

Dewey, J. (1961). *Democracy and Education.* New York: The Macmillian Company.

Haug, P. (1998). Norwegian Special Education. In P. Haug, & J. Tøssebro (Eds.), Theoretical perspectives on Special Education. HøyskoleForlaget, Norwegian Academic Press.

Kirke- og undervisningdepartementet (1969). *Innstilling om lovregler for spesialundervisning.* Oslo.

KUF (2001). Nordisk undersøkelse viser: Skolen bedre enn sitt rykte. KUFAktuelt 2/01 Retrived June 16, 2001, from http://odin.dep.no.

Levin, B. (undated). Democracy and Schools: Educating for Citizenship. Retrieved July 6, 2002, from http://wwwa.ca/education/.

L97 (1999). *The curriculum for the 10-year compulsory school in Norway.* Oslo: The Royal Ministry of Education, Research and Church Affairs.

Mannheim, K. (1936). *Ideology and Utopia.* London: Routlede & Kegan Paul.

Nordahl, T (1998). Er det bare eleven? Rapport 12e/98 Norsk institutt for forskning om oppvekst, velferd og aldring.

Senge, P. (2000). *Schools that learn.* London: Nicholas Brealey Publishing.

Skrtic, T. (1995). *Disability and Democracy: Reconstructing (special) education.* New York: Teachers College Press.

Skaalvik, E. & Skaalvik, S. (1996). *Selvoppfatning, motivasjon og læringsmiljø.* Tano, Oslo.

Slagstad, Rune (1998) *De nasjonale strateger.* PAX Forlag AS, Oslo.

Speed, J. (1992 May 6). Barn blir dullet med. *I Vårt land.*

Stangvik, G. (1997). Beyond schooling: integration in a policy perspective. In S. Pijl, C. Meijer & S. Hegarty (Eds.), *Inclusive Education.* London & New York: Routledge.

The Royal Ministry of Education, Research and Church affairs (1999). *The Curriculum for the 10-year Compulsory School in Norway,* National Centre for Educational Resources, Norway.

Thomas, G. & Loxley, A. (2001). *Deconstructing special education and constructing inclusion.* Buckingham & Philadelphia: Open University Press.

Tjernshaugen, K. (2002). Åpner privatskolen I. *Dagsavisen.*

Torney-Purta, J., Schwille J., & Amadeo J. (2001). *Citizenship and Education in Twentyeight Countries: Civic Knowledge and Engagement at Age Fourteen.* Amsterdam: IEA.

UNESCO (2001). *International Conference on Education, Geneva, 2001.* Final Report.

Utdannings- og forskningsdepartementet (1989–90). St.meld. nr. 54. *Om opplæring av barn, unge og voksne med særskilte behov.*

Vestby, G. (2002). Barns medvirkning: En ung historie. I Barne og Familiedepartementet: Familia Nr 2–2002.

Yin, R. (1994). *Case Study Research,* London: SAGE.

COLLEEN CUMMINGS, ALAN DYSON & ALAN MILLWARD

4 PARTICIPATION AND DEMOCRACY: WHAT'S INCLUSION GOT TO DO WITH IT?

SOME PRELIMINARY QUESTIONS

In the first part of this chapter, we want to raise what we hope are pertinent questions about the way inclusive education is currently conceptualised and, in particular, about its relation to notions of participation and democracy. Our argument is that, although inclusive education is broadening its scope in terms of the range of marginalised groups with which it claims to be concerned, it is failing to make the shifts in thinking that are necessary if it is really to address the situations in which those groups find themselves. We hope to demonstrate this by considering the preliminary findings of a research study in which we are currently engaged which is investigating the role of schools in the regeneration of disadvantaged areas.

It may be useful to remind ourselves of the theme of the symposium out of which this book arose, as articulated by Julie Allan in her original circular to participants:

> The Scottish Colloquium meeting will examine inclusion in relation to the kinds of educational goals which are appropriate for individuals and their communities. It will seek to articulate the nature of participation and democracy which might be achieved in inclusive settings and the consequences for all concerned. These consequences relate to the kinds of educational, social and personal experiences which are acceptable, and are distinctively different from the narrowly defined performative *outcomes*.

This theme, the circular makes clear, looks beyond the narrow conceptualisation of educational outcomes as attainments, which appears to dominate government thinking in England (and, to a lesser extent, perhaps, the rest of the UK). Instead, it will focus on broader goals, understood in terms of participation and democracy.

Such a focus, we would suggest, is characteristic of a concern amongst many inclusion advocates to develop a form of education which will be participatory and democratic in itself and which will in turn contribute to the development of a more participatory and democratic society. This concern is evident not only in the work of commentators such as Skrtic (1995); Thomas (1997); Thomas et al, (1998); and – in an earlier meeting of this symposium – Ballard (1995), but also in UNESCO's highly influential Salamanca Statement (UNESCO, 1994). Barton (1997) is, perhaps, typical in the sorts of arguments that he advances:

> Inclusive education is part of a human rights approach to social relations

49

J. Allan (ed.), Inclusion, Participation and Democracy: What is the Purpose?, 49-65.
© 2003 *Kluwer Academic Publishers. Printed in the Netherlands.*

and conditions. The intentions and values involved are an integral part of a vision of the whole society of which education is a part. Therefore the role inclusive education plays in the development of an inclusive society is a very serious issue ... [It] involves a serious commitment to the task of identifying, challenging and contributing to the removal of injustices. Part of this task involves a self-critical analysis of the role schools play in the production and reproduction of injustices such as disabling barriers of various forms. Schools therefore need to be welcoming places. It is more than mere questions of access that are at stake here. It is a quest for the removal of policies and practices of exclusion and the realisation of effective participatory democracy. It also involves a wider concern, that of clarifying the role of schools in combating institutional discrimination in relation to, for example, the position of disabled people in society (p. 234).

This passage is worth quoting at length because it indicates both the complexity and the limitations of the arguments in this field. That complexity seems to stem from the recursive nature of the inclusive school-democratic society relationship. On the one hand, inclusive schools are a manifestation of a wider human rights approach to social relations and conditions. On the other hand, the creation of welcoming schools involves rooting out 'institutional discrimination' within the school and transforming the school from a producer of such discrimination into a means of realising effective participatory democracy. Such arguments are difficult to resist. However, they do leave some important questions unanswered. For instance:

- Apart from being welcoming, what else will these schools be like? What will children learn in them? How will they ensure that all children learn? What sorts of outcomes will they produce and how will they ensure that these are equitable?
- Likewise, apart from being characterised by effective participatory democracy, what else will society be like? How will it manage its economy? How will resources and social goods be distributed? How will power and interests be managed?
- What, precisely, is the link between inclusive schools and an inclusive society? Given the powerful structural forces which produce exclusive practices in schools (Tomlinson, 1995), how will inclusive schools emerge and survive – and, equally, if they do survive, how will rooting out 'institutional discrimination' within the school impact on society as a whole in the face of these countervailing forces?

What these unanswered questions reveal is what seem to us to be systematic absences and silences in the inclusion literature. We have argued elsewhere (Clark, Dyson, & Millward, 1998; Dyson & Millward, 1998, 2000) that the literature is stronger in the critique of traditional special education than in fleshing out the details of inclusive education, that it focuses on the organisational characteristics of inclusive schools rather than on the substantive issues of pedagogy, curriculum and educational outcomes and that it has a somewhat weak model of the relationship between schooling and society. We have also argued, along with Booth (1998), that some of the characteristics of the literature – including, therefore, both its strengths and weaknesses – can be attributed to the role which disability issues have played in its development (Dyson, 1998).

The arguments advanced by Barton are a case in point. Viewed from the perspective of the politics of disablement (Oliver, 1990), those arguments make considerable sense. Faced with the continuing production of 'disabling barriers,' it makes good sense for disabled people to expose and seek to dismantle those barriers wherever they arise. Schools are a good place to start because barriers there go on to generate both discriminatory attitudes and the more material forms of discrimination which arise from the denial of opportunities for accreditation, employment, social interaction and so on. The focus, therefore, is not on curriculum, pedagogy and outcomes per se, but on those structures and practices in schools which prevent disabled children from participating on the same terms as others. No particularly sophisticated model of school-society relationships is then needed to see that tackling these barriers in schools has to be part of a wider attack on 'institutional disablement' wherever it appears. Struggles for inclusive education (Vlachou, 1997) are part of a greater struggle for the recognition and valuing of diversity in society and the establishment of what Barton (1997), following Phillips, calls 'a vision of democracy through difference' (p. 235).

However, it is now becoming increasingly common to see inclusive education as concerned with the education of all children and to see children with disabilities and/or 'special educational needs' as simply one amongst many historically marginalised groups. As Barton himself puts it: 'It is not merely about placing disabled pupils in classrooms with their non-disabled peers ... Rather, it is about how, where and why, and with what consequences, we educate all pupils' (p. 234). This being the case, the question arises as to how the underlying assumptions in the inclusion literature apply to groups whose marginalisation is unrelated to disability and, specifically, to those whose marginalisation is related to social, economic and cultural disadvantage.

It is clearly important for children in such groups to be 'welcome' in schools and for barriers to their participation to be removed. However, this scarcely seems enough given the massive disadvantages which some of these children experience. A recent report for the Council of Europe, for instance, certainly argues for 'equal treatment ... the removal of discrimination against socially excluded groups' (Furlong, et al, 2000, p. 27). However, it also argues for 'Equal opportunity strategies [which] operate *upstream* against inequalities in society within which education is rooted: inequalities in terms of income, family background, health, access to culture etc.' (p. 25). These are to be supported by 'equal outcome' strategies: 'Based on the understanding that equal treatment of less privileged pupils is not enough to overcome social exclusion, equal outcome strategies focus on *positive discrimination*' (ibid, p. 29). Such strategies include placing additional resources into schools, developing alternative curricula and teaching methods, establishing 'second chance' schools and so on.

The aim of all this, clearly, is not simply the creation of an 'effective participatory democracy' or a 'democracy through difference,' in which individuals are welcomed and valued for who and what they are. It is to do with overcoming disadvantage and reducing the material inequalities in society. As the Council of Europe report concludes: 'purely educational measures are unlikely to offer a lasting solution. Educational failure has to be seen in the context of inequalities in society, the selective operation of the labour market and the unequal distribution of employment' (Furlong et al., 2000, p. 31)

None of this is, of course, incompatible with the notion of inclusive education, particularly in its extended form. However, it requires a different vision of what 'counts' as inclusion in schools – one which addresses the issue of equal opportunities and, particularly, equal outcomes, as well as of equal treatment. Such a vision has to be concerned not just with 'barriers,' but also with issues of curriculum, pedagogy, resourcing and achievement. Likewise, it requires a different – perhaps richer – analysis of the relationship between school and society, one which understands how social and economic disadvantage produces educational 'failure', how educational interventions support social and economic interventions to create a more equal society and what such a society might look like. These are huge issues which, we suggest, inclusive education has scarcely begun to consider. We cannot resolve them here. However, in the remainder of this paper, we will report on some research which is located at the centre of these issues.

THE SCHOOLS AND AREA REGENERATION PROJECT

In recent years, there has been considerable concern in the UK about the state of urban education (Ofsted, 1993, 2000), as part of a wider concern about the state of poor urban areas (Social Exclusion Unit, 1998). This has resulted, amongst other things, in a strategy for how such areas can best be 'regenerated' which involves a wide range of policy concerns impacting on urban issues (Social Exclusion Unit, 2000). Education has a major part to play in this strategy, not least through the developing 'schools plus' initiative (DfEE, 1999a), which encourages schools to place themselves at the centre of their communities and sees them as central to the delivery of multiple community services and to the creation of 'learning communities.' In many ways, this simply renews the efforts at family involvement and community education which have historically characterised many UK schools (Ball, 1998; Dyson & Robson, 1999). The difference now, however, is that schools are increasingly within the context of a wider regeneration strategy and their work with families and communities is understood as a contribution to broad social and economic policy goals.

In order to explore this new policy direction, we have been undertaking a project, sponsored by the Joseph Rowntree Foundation, which is studying the relationship between schools and their communities in two areas characterised by social and economic disadvantage. Our investigation, *The Role of Schools in Area Regeneration*, is located in two areas of social housing in the north of England – Senlac and Forest Villas – which are characterised by high levels of social and economic disadvantage. Both areas were built in the first half of the twentieth century to provide housing for working families. However, the heavy industries (steel manufacture, ship building, engineering and so on) in which those workers were employed declined significantly during the last quarter of the last century, creating high levels of unemployment, particularly amongst men. At the same time, changes in housing legislation meant that new residents in these and similar areas were increasingly drawn from the poorest families and/or those with the greatest problems. Not surprisingly, therefore, both areas are characterised by classic indicators of disadvantage – high dependency on state benefits, low incomes, poor health, high crime rates and low levels of educational attainment.

As a response to these problems, both areas have been subject to a range of 'regeneration' initiatives, aimed at improving social and living conditions. The housing in both areas has been (or still is being) refurbished. In Forest Villas, particularly, there was a large-scale refurbishment programme in the 1990s which was accompanied by an attempt to 'diversify tenure' – that is, to introduce some privately-owned and housing-association owned properties alongside a reduced stock of council (local authority) rented properties. As part of the regeneration programmes, a community centre was built in each area to act as a focus for community activity and to support the work of local community groups. Both statutory and voluntary agencies have been active in supporting families and communities in each area and there has been a wide range of employment, education, youth work, parenting and health promotion projects. In both areas, there are Education Action Zones (DfEE, 1999b) and Senlac is part of an Excellence in Cities (DfEE, 1999c) area – initiatives aimed at targeting additional efforts and resources into raising attainments in local schools. Moreover, in Senlac in particular, the local authority has attempted to play a strategic role in co-ordinating regeneration and involving the local community in the process.

Our study is focusing on the schools which educate the majority of children from these areas (one secondary and three primary schools in Senlac; two secondary and three primaries in Forest Villas). Our concern is the extent to which these schools can or might support the ongoing regeneration initiatives. We have completed a 'baselining' phase, where we have attempted to characterise the areas and the current roles of schools through analysing documentary evidence and interviewing key 'stakeholders' (teachers, local government officials, community members) in each area. We are now focusing more closely on particular initiatives being taken by schools, particularly through the Education Action Zones, in order to evaluate their impact on the local community. We have also begun to analyse performance data from the schools to try to determine how successful they are being in raising attainments for students from our study areas.

Preliminary findings

Although our research is not yet complete, some preliminary findings are already beginning to emerge.

The challenges of urban schooling

Whatever the commitment of our case study schools to notions of inclusion (and that commitment is, inevitably, somewhat variable), they face a set of common issues which arise, not from whatever internal barriers they may or may not set up, but from the challenging nature of the social contexts in which they are located. Many children, as one might expect in such disadvantaged areas, enter these schools with low educational attainments, limited learning skills and poor adjustment to the demands of formal schooling. They live amidst high levels of crime and drug abuse, high levels of (particularly male) unemployment and poor health outcomes. Many come from families experiencing considerable economic pressure, inter-generational unemployment and, in some cases, significant stresses in terms of inter-familial relationships. In Senlac, for instance, we were told that levels of social services involvement are particularly high and that 'five per cent of families undergo family therapy at some point' (Primary headteacher, Senlac). Senlac, we were told, has some of the highest teenage pregnancy rates in the country, large numbers of young mothers and a high proportion of lone parents. There are, according to some interviewees, consequent problems in parenting in the area: 'some families on the estate do not know how to bring up children. They do not possess the necessary skills' (Local councillor, Senlac). This interviewee also pointed to 'cases of parental abandonment where the children are being brought up by their grandparents.' A school representative commented that: 'There does not seem to be any evidence of play in the area. One does not see parents accompanying their children. The children grow up too soon and swear too soon too' (Chair of governors, Senlac). The consequence is that schools struggle to manage the behaviour of some children, to drive up their educational attainments and to meet their wider social and learning needs. This is a particular issue for schools in England where the current accountability regime in England means that pupils' attainments are a major indicator whereby the 'success' of a school is judged publicly and has an increasing impact on the career prospects of individual teachers and headteachers.

In other, more advantaged, areas, schools would be able to count on the support of parents in pursuing these educational goals. However, our schools report that they find it somewhat difficult to enlist such support. Parental attendance at meetings with school staff tends to be low, as is the participation of parents in extra-curricular activities or in the direct support of their children's learning. Sometimes, the lack of support from parents becomes subversion or even outright hostility. For instance, teachers report that some parents condone their children's truancy from school or try to imbue their children with attitudes and values which contradict those promoted by the school. A common point of conflict is when schools outlaw physical retaliation but parents tell their children that they must 'stick up for themselves,' with violence if necessary:

> Sometimes the expectations of children held by the school differ from those held by some parents. There are difficulties around dealing with fault and consequences and it is hard dealing with confrontation and conflict ... This

emerged clearly when the school tried to implement a behaviour policy which
stated that pupils should not hit each other. We discovered that some parents
had instructed their children to hit back (Primary headteacher, Senlac).

Most headteachers are able to report incidents where parents have come into school
angry at some action the school has taken and threatening violence towards the staff.
They also report arguments and violence between parents on school premises:

> Parents occupy different camps and this can be divisive. Occasionally there
> are outbreaks in school. There has been an attack by one parent on another
> in school and another attack on the way to school. One parent is now afraid
> to send her daughter to school (Primary headteacher, Forest Villas).

Under these circumstances, teachers and headteachers find themselves having to
move into what they describe as a 'social worker' role. They may, for instance,
have to spend time managing children's behaviour, resolving conflicts that have
arisen in the playground, or dealing with the upsets and disturbances which children
bring with them from the home. Moreover, although relations with parents are not
always smooth, headteachers particularly report a succession of parents appearing
at school with personal and family problems which they are unable to manage
and turning to the headteacher as a professional who might be able to find help
for them: 'Some parents use me as a mediator. This is not something to do with
me personally but is related to the job. I fulfil more roles than might be expected'
(Primary headteacher, Senlac).

These additional demands create particular problems for schools, given the
pressure they are currently under to 'raise standards' for all their pupils and the
lack of resourcing for a wider community or social work role. Most of them see
meeting these demands as an unavoidable part of their activities and as a necessary
precursor to any educational achievements. However, without specific resources,
they inevitably divert time and energy away from the business of teaching in the
classroom. Instead, therefore, of seeing a wider social support role as part of their
core educational function, schools are often compelled to see it as standing in
contradiction to that function.

A further complication for all of the schools is that, although some of their
children and families need additional support, others do not. Playing a wider social
role, therefore, diverts resources from children who are likely to do relatively well
in educational terms and who consequently will make the school appear to be more
successful. This dilemma is particularly acute for those schools (the majority in
our sample) which educate children from our case study areas alongside children
from other, less disadvantaged areas. In these circumstances, schools cannot simply
develop a single strategy to meet social needs as a pathway to meeting educational
needs. They must also find ways of increasing the educational progress of those
children who are starting from a higher level of educational attainment and social
resource.

Different conceptualisations of the role of schools

Given these complex demands, it seems not enough for schools to be 'participatory' and 'welcoming' in a classic inclusionist sense. The characteristics which many children and families bring with them are ones which are significantly disadvantaging in the education system and, crucially, beyond it in terms of individuals' life chances. Nonetheless, they are, potentially at least, able to be overcome or ameliorated though vigorous educational intervention, particularly if that is allied to wider social change. The relationship between children's educational difficulties and the family and community context within which they live, however, presents schools with a dilemma. Should they work with family and community in educating the child, or should they seek to insulate the child against negative family and community influences?

For some, the educational and community agendas are one and the same. The headteacher of the secondary school in Senlac, for instance, made it clear to us that he regarded an exclusive focus on educational 'standards' as a short-sighted policy, doomed to ultimate failure: 'The standards agenda cannot work by itself but needs the support of other initiatives. If this can be achieved the schools will win on added value.'

Only an approach which reaches out to the community and deals with children's social support needs is, he told us, likely to be successful in the longer term in raising attainments. Similarly, one of his primary colleagues expressed a commitment to using his school as a means of offering support and enhanced opportunities to parents, regardless of whether this has an immediate payback to the school in terms of increased support for the school's educational agenda: 'Anything that changes the life chances of families, that changes parents' aspirations and hopes for their children is top of my agenda.'

At the other extreme, one of the secondary heads serving Forest Villas sees his school less as a resource for the community than as an escape route from the community. In his view, Forest Villas is characterised by crime, drug abuse and family turbulence. His school has to act as a sanctuary, offering a different and better set of values and behaviours. If, he believes, he can maintain this more stable environment in the face of external turbulence, he can offer pupils opportunities to learn, to gain accreditation and ultimately to move out of the area in which they currently live.

These differences are paralleled in local authority (LA) policy. Both LAs are committed to the regeneration of the fabric and the social conditions of their most deprived communities. Both, too, are committed to economic regeneration and accept the argument that education is crucial to the development of a skilled workforce which can both contribute to and benefit from greater employment opportunities and, hence, prosperity. However, they differ significantly in how they see the relationships between these different aspects of regeneration. In Senlac's authority the educational development of individuals is seen as inextricably bound up with family and community development. Schools are encouraged to take on a community role and headteachers are appointed, in part at least, because of their commitment to community involvement. In particular, schools are seen as having a key role in taking forward the health improvement agenda and some, like Senlac's secondary school, are seeking to become 'full service' schools (Dreyfoos, 1994) with this in mind. School buildings are well-equipped with parents' rooms or other community facilities. Moreover, in Senlac itself and across the authority as a whole, there is a strategic investment in early years education and in family outreach, on the assumption that such intervention is the best – perhaps, only – way of raising children's attainment in the face of significant social disadvantage.

In Forest Villa's authority, on the other hand, although education is seen as having a clear economic role, the relationship between schooling and community development is a somewhat distant one. Schools are encouraged to focus tightly on driving up the attainments of their pupils and not to dissipate their energies by trying to involve themselves in wider community issues. Indeed, the strategic view of regeneration articulated by the LA's chief executive is that successful economic regeneration might well sound the death knell for some communities as schools drive up the attainments of their more capable young people, enabling them to become socially mobile and hence to leave the area.

In both areas, however, the issue for schools and LAs is not one that can be understood simply in terms of welcoming and valuing children, or removing sources of discrimination – important as these might be. The task is to take the limited educational resources which children bring with them and to transform them so that their attainments rise, their chances of gaining employment increase and their life chances become proportionately greater. What differentiates approaches in different areas and different schools is the judgement that is made about whether that transformation can be most effectively brought about by developing the social capital of the family and community, or whether it requires a tighter focus on the human capital of individual students.

The complexities of community

The views which schools can take of their relationships with families and communities are not entirely a matter of values and principles. They are also mediated by the geography and demography of the areas they serve. Senlac is a large, clearly-defined and relatively homogeneous area of mainly social housing. The schools we are studying are located within Senlac itself and overwhelmingly educate children from the area. In the primary schools, where children come from other, neighbouring areas, those areas share many of the characteristics of Senlac itself and are not perceived by residents as being significantly different. Even the secondary school, which serves a much wider area, has its intake dominated by Senlac children. This has two consequences. The first is that the schools see themselves as having a clear and uncomplicated relationship with the area; they are 'Senlac schools.' The second is that, although there is inevitable competition for pupils between the schools (and between them and neighbouring schools), the level of that competition is relatively low. Since the area is clearly defined and homogenous, there are no gross differences between schools around which competition might arise. In the words of one headteacher, they engage in 'co-operative competition,' where the emphasis is on the co-operation at least as much as on poaching each other's pupils.

Forest Villas, on the other hand, is a much smaller area. It forms part of a larger housing estate, 'The Manor,' but residents have always seen it as distinct from (and less desirable than) the other part of the estate. The housing regeneration programme of the 1990s operated only in Forest Villas itself (which was renamed at the time to mark the change). Moreover, the attempt to diversify tenure created divisions within the newly renamed estate, since it involved creating an area of owner occupation, distinct from an area of housing association properties, distinct again from a residual area of local authority housing. It is indicative of these divisions that, although a community centre was built in the middle of Forest Villas, it is overwhelmingly used by the housing association tenants from the surrounding streets and hardly at all by the residents of the unrefurbished Manor estate. Indeed, some residents of other parts of the Manor that we have spoken to regard many of their counterparts in Forest Villas as a somewhat dangerous and feckless bunch, with precious little concern for their children's behaviour and education.

The small size and internal divisions of Forest Villas have implications for local schools. Only one school, a primary, takes the majority of its pupils from the Manor as a whole and even then the proportion it takes from the area has declined from over 90% to nearer 60%. As the headteacher explained:

> There was new build of private and housing association accommodation. As a result of this re-modelling there are now less large families. Many of the families who moved out did not come back. The new families in Forest Villas are using other schools; families in the private and housing association housing send few children here. The families in this housing do not identify with Forest Villas. In general the population is shrinking and all schools are feeling the effects of this. As a result, nearby schools have surplus places and are taking children from outside of their catchment area.

For all other schools, Manor children – and, particularly, Forest Villas children – constitute a small minority of their intake. In one of them for instance:

> The school is seen as serving [a surrounding private] estate but in reality only 49% of their intake lives there. The remaining 51% come from approximately four other communities with approximately 18 to 20 % coming from Forest Villas (Primary headteacher, Forest Villas).

To complicate matters further, none of the schools serving Forest Villas is located on the estate and each also serves areas that are considerably more advantaged. Of the two main secondary schools serving the area, the one in whose catchment area Forest Villas notionally lies is actually further away than the other, with the result that they divide the estate's older children roughly equally between them.

This situation creates considerable dilemmas for schools. The head of the nearer secondary school, for instance, is keen to develop links with the Forest

Villas community. However, despite his relative proximity, he shares a campus with a primary school that takes relatively few Forest Villas children and his own school is located in an area of mixed private and social housing separated from Forest Villas by a main road. As he explained, it is much easier to work with the neighbouring school and with his immediate neighbourhood than it is to work in Forest Villas or with the one primary school located on the Manor. Likewise, the head of a primary school explained to us the difficulties she experienced in relating to Forest Villas. Most of her pupils come from areas of private housing or from a large area of social housing some distance away. She has had experience, not only of having to deal with feuds between different Forest Villas families, but of objections from other parents when she has tried to favour those families. In a context of competition between schools and the public reporting of assessment results, she is very concerned about attracting more Forest Villas pupils and driving away (as she sees it) her 'other' families.

The ambiguities of national policy

This last point brings us onto the impact of the wider policy environment. Much has been written (by ourselves also) about the anti-inclusionist tendencies in much recent education policy in England and the rest of the UK under successive governments (Booth, Ainscow, & Dyson, 1998; Dyson & Slee, 2001; Riddell & Brown, 1994; Rouse & Florian, 1997; Thomas & Dwyfor Davies, 1999). The critique chiefly relates to the supposedly exclusive impacts of an education quasi-market, in which schools compete with each other to attract students, of the central prescription of curriculum and (increasingly) pedagogy, reducing schools' flexibility to respond to individual differences and of a punitive accountability system which leads schools to meet centrally imposed targets and comply with centrally-mandated practices, even if this is at the expense of some of their more vulnerable students.

We have seen above some indications of these negative effects. However, policy is actually more complex and more ambiguous than critics sometimes suggest. Under New Labour governments since 1997, there has also been a major focus on the role of education in overcoming 'social exclusion.' The rationale for this approach was set out most clearly by David Blunkett, then secretary of State for education, in a series of speeches in the late 1990s (Blunkett, 1999a, 1999b, 2000). In simple terms, the government sees education as the key to both economic development and social cohesion. On the one hand, an 'effective' education system is the means of creating a highly-skilled workforce able to compete in a globalised economy. On the other, an education system which drives up the attainments and skill levels of all young people is the means of ensuring that vulnerable individuals and groups are themselves able to compete in the labour market and hence avoid the dangers of social exclusion. Crucial to this vision is the notion that vigorous intervention is needed in the case of 'at risk' individuals and groups to prevent their missing out on what is expected to be a significant hike in attainments across the school population (and lifelong learner population) as a whole. Hence, marketised, target-driven policies are accompanied by heavily interventionist strategies, many of them targeted on disadvantaged areas.

The consequences for schools in such areas are complex. They cannot, of course, escape the standards agenda or the education market place in considering how to relate to their communities. This means, as we have seen, heads have to be acutely aware of how their actions will impact on the school's ability to meet performance targets and to market itself in the area. It is not surprising, then, that some decide to take only those initiatives in relation to families and communities (such as parenting courses or involving parents in developing their children's reading) which seem likely to have an immediate feedback in terms of children's attainments, or, indeed, to reject community involvement entirely as irrelevant to their 'core business.' As one told us unequivocally: 'I do not think that the governors or the parents see it as the school's role to be involved with the community' (Primary headteacher, Forest Villas).

At the same time, they are, whether they welcome it or not, involved in a series of area-based initiatives aimed at addressing educational and wider social disadvantage. As we noted earlier, the Senlac secondary is formulating its bid to move towards full service status as part of the 'Schools Plus' (DfEE, 1999a) initiative, offering a range of non-educational support services to the local community. Senlac, moreover, is the site of a Sure Start initiative (DfEE, 1999d), aimed at providing multi-agency services for vulnerable young children and their families. The Senlac schools as a whole are part of an Excellence in Cities mini-Education Action Zone (DfEE, 1999b), in which they work together on common issues around raising standards in return for additional government funding. The Forest Villas schools are likewise part of an older form of Education Action Zone (DfEE, 1999b) with similar aims.

These initiatives themselves mirror the ambiguities which critics see in the government's policies. The proposal for the Forest Villas EAZ, for instance, started with a strong community orientation, but was reshaped by DfEE (latterly, DfES – the government's education department) into a much more standards-oriented initiative. The community-oriented secondary school head who was the driving force behind the proposal has thus been left without a vehicle through which to realise his community ambitions:

> Schools ought to be taking a greater role in the community. Schools recognise the problems in the communities they serve but are unable to do anything about them. The EAZ plan wanted to include high levels of community involvement, especially of the ICT facilities. It was hoped that local comprehensive pupils could use the facilities in primary schools for their homework. But, the DfEE have now given standards priority.

One of his primary counterparts, head of the school serving the most disadvantaged population, also told us somewhat wryly that the EAZ was originally planned in order to 'cut a swathe through disadvantage in [the area].' However, its small-scale and piecemeal efforts are instead benefiting a few individuals but having little impact on the problems of the community as a whole. Latterly, a similar issue has arisen in Senlac. Its EAZ, like Forest Villas, was conceptualised as having a strong community orientation and has been implemented as such by a group of headteachers who, as we have seen, make little distinction between developing families and communities on the one hand and driving up the standards of attainment of 'their' pupils on the other. However, the attainment outcomes from the first year of the Zone's operation have been disappointing and already DfES is putting pressure on the LEA – and the LEA in turn on the schools – to focus more clearly and more narrowly on 'standards.'

It is tempting to see these ambiguities with which schools are grappling as yet more evidence of central government undermining their attempts to become more inclusive. Whatever the truth of this, however, the central aims of government policy – to raise the attainments of all students in order to improve the life-chances of all – are shared by all those we have interviewed in and around schools. The issue for them is not about the aims of government policy, but around the balance in the means of realising those aims between more – and less – community-oriented approaches.

IMPLICATIONS: BEYOND INCLUSIVE EDUCATION?

There is, no doubt, much in our case study schools that can be understood through the analyses of participation and democracy that tend to be found in the inclusive education literature. The difficulties which children from these disadvantaged areas experience in school and the problematic relations between those schools and their families and communities are undoubtedly indicative of some form of what Barton (1997) refers to as 'policies and practices of exclusion' and 'institutional discrimination' (p. 234). Indeed, such an analysis is confirmed by some quite vitriolic accounts we have been given by students and parents of the discriminatory way they feel they have been treated by schools. We can also see how the relentless pursuit of the standards agenda, particularly in Forest Villas, means that, if parents and children are to participate in local schools, they have to do so almost entirely on the schools' terms. Democracy, in the sense of any real student or community control of decision-making, is simply not an option in these schools. The ceaseless quest for 'standards' inevitably means that children and families are judged overwhelmingly in terms of how they support – or, in many cases, fail to support – that quest. Even if schools wish to escape from this deficit view, their efforts to develop in other directions are, as we have seen, constantly undermined by national policy.

However, there is also much that such an analysis does not explain. The children and young people of Forest Villas and Senlac find themselves in a position where their life chances are significantly dependent on the extent to which they are able and enabled to take advantage of educational opportunities. The difficulties which many of them experience in doing this and which they present to their schools may well be compounded by unwelcoming attitudes and institutional discrimination, but they are real enough in any school serving similar areas (Levacic & Woods, 2002;

Ofsted, 2000; Thrupp, 1999; Woods & Levacic, 2002). Even if such schools could rid themselves entirely of discrimination and escape their overwhelmingly deficit-oriented perspectives, they would still have to overcome the real disadvantages which their students bring with them. Creating welcoming schools in which all could participate and whose relationships were democratic might well be highly desirable, but it would not in itself change the social and economic situation of their students, or significantly change young people's life chances, or bring about the regeneration of the areas where they and their families live.

Under these circumstances, the question arises as to what, precisely, schools could and should do to achieve these aims. We seem to have on offer, in national policy, local policy and school-level approach, two possible models. On the one hand, there is the individually-focused drive for 'standards' that characterises the government's dominant education agenda and is reflected particularly in the school and local authority approaches in Forest Villas. The assumption seems to be here that a relentless focus on the attainments of individual students which protects them from the chaotic and ultimately destructive influences of their families and communities offers them their best chance of escaping the social and economic conditions into which they were born. On the other hand, the government's area-based initiatives and the approaches adopted in Senlac would appear to be based on the assumption that individuals cannot simply be detached from their families and communities in this way. The development of the one, therefore, is seen as intimately dependent on the development of the other.

To a certain extent, these differences reflect politico-ethical differences in terms of how the relationship between individuals and communities is understood. One might be taken to indicate a neo-liberal, individualistic view of society in which 'democracy' is seen simply as a means of freeing individuals to maximise their advantages. The other might then be seen to derive from some notion of an 'inclusive society,' in which individuals are bound together in their development and are required to respect and value each other and to act collectively in removing the barriers and injustices which they experience. However, there are also more pragmatic issues in play. The schools in Forest Villas, unlike those in Senlac, simply do not have a large, coherent community to which they can relate. Moreover, the question of which approach is the more effective is, to an important extent, an empirical rather than a philosophical one. There are outcomes for young people in terms of attainments, progression and life-chances which can be identified and measured. It is, therefore, by no means impossible that the relatively 'hard-nosed' approach of the Forest Villas schools and of the government's standards agenda will produce better results than the superficially more sympathetic approach in Senlac.

We do not claim at this stage that any satisfactory resolution of these issues is readily available. Amongst other things, the situation in the two areas is considerably more complex than we have presented it as being here. Moreover, the ethical, political and empirical questions which our work raises are also much more complex than we have been able to suggest. Despite considerable efforts over recent years, we are still well short of understanding fully what approaches are most effective in raising attainments in disadvantaged areas. We do not really know (for all the government's confidence) whether raised attainments actually translate into improved life-chances. We have little idea what an education system would look like which responded to the real difficulties and disadvantages which individuals and groups experience, but which nonetheless did so without resort to deficit perspectives.

The point is, however, that these are real issues with real implications for marginalised children, young people and communities. Yet, for all the attempts to broaden the scope of thinking about inclusion, they are issues that the inclusion literature has very largely declined to address. There is, we suggest, a significant shift in thinking that needs to take place when the focus moves from the politics of disablement to the politics of social and economic disadvantage. There is a further shift when schools begin to be seen not simply as a microcosm of a 'participatory democracy,' but as engines for change in the lives of disadvantaged individuals and communities. The danger is that, in broadening the scope of inclusive education to encompass more groups – indeed, to encompass all students – without making these shifts in thinking, we run the risk of imposing thinking developed in one context on other contexts for which it is much less appropriate. It is just possible that inclusion may in the end turn out not to be the 'big tent' which many envisage and within which all the marginalised and disadvantaged of our societies can shelter. If this is indeed the case, we may need to move rapidly to find alternative discourses before too much damage is done.

REFERENCES

Ball, M. (1998). *School Inclusion: The school, the family and the community.* York: Joseph Rowntree Foundation.

Ballard, K. (1995). Inclusion, paradigms, power and participation. In C. Clark & A. Dyson & A. Millward (Eds.), *Towards Inclusive Schools?* London: David Fulton.

Barton, L. (1997). Inclusive education: Romantic, subversive or realistic? *International Journal of Inclusive Education,* 1(3), 231–242.

Blunkett, D. (1999a). *Excellence for the Many, Not Just the Few: Raising standards and extending opportunities in our schools.* The CBI President's Reception Address by the Rt. Hon. David Blunkett MP 19 July 1999. London: DfEE.

Blunkett, D. (1999b). *Social Exclusion and the Politics of Opportunity: A mid-term progress check.* A speech by the Rt. Hon David Blunkett MP. London: DfEE.

Blunkett, D. (2000). *Raising Aspirations for the 21st Century.* Speech to the North of England Education Conference, Wigan, 6 January 2000. London: DfEE

Booth, T. (1998). The poverty of special education: Theories to the rescue? In C. Clark & A. Dyson & A. Millward (Eds.), *Theorising Special Education.* London: Routledge.

Booth, T., Ainscow, M., & Dyson, A. (1998). England: Inclusion and exclusion in a competitive system. In T. Booth & M. Ainscow (Eds.), *From Them to Us: An international study of inclusion in education.* London: Routledge.

Clark, C., Dyson, A., & Millward, A. (1998). Theorising special education: Time to move on? In C. Clark & A. Dyson & A. Millward (Eds.), *Theorising Special Education.* London: Routledge.

DfEE. (1999a). *Schools Plus: Building learning communities. Improving the educational chances of children and young people from disadvantaged areas: a report from the Schools Plus Policy Action Team 11.* London: DfEE.

DfEE. (1999b). *Meet the Challenge: Education Action Zones.* London: DfEE.

DfEE. (1999c). *Excellence in Cities.* Retrieved July 1, 2001, from http://www.standards.df ee.gov.uk/library/publications.

DfEE. (1999d). *Sure Start: Making a difference for children and families.* London: DfEE.

Dreyfoos, J. (1994). *Full-Service Schools.* San Francisco: Jossey-Bass.

Dyson, A. (1998). Professional intellectuals from powerful groups: Wrong from the start? In P. Clough & L. Barton (Eds.), *Articulating with Difficulty: Research voices on inclusive education.* London: Paul Chapman Publications.

Dyson, A., & Millward, A. (1998). Theory and practice in special needs education: Current concerns and future directions. In P. Haug & J. Tossebro (Eds.), *Theoretical Perspectives on Special Education.* Kristiansand, Norway: Hoyskoleforlaget AS – Norwegian Academic Press.

Dyson, A., & Millward, A. (2000). *Schools and Special Needs: Issues of innovation and inclusion.* London: Paul Chapman Publications.

Dyson, A., & Robson, E. (1999). *School, Family, Community: Mapping school inclusion in the UK.* Leicester: Youth Work Press for the Joseph Rowntree Foundation.

Dyson, A., & Slee, R. (2001). Special needs education from Warnock to Salamanca: The triumph of liberalism? In J. Furlong & R. Phillips (Eds.), *Education, Reform and the State: Twenty-five years of politics, policy and practice.* London: RoutledgeFalmer.

Furlong, A., Stadler, B., & Azzopardi, A. (2000). *Vulnerable Youth: Perspectives on vulnerability in education, employment and leisure in Europe.* Strasbourg: Council of Europe.

Levacic, R., & Woods, P. A. (2002). Raising school performance in the league tables (part 1): Disentangling the effects of social disadvantage. *British Educational Research Journal,* 28(2), 207–226.

Ofsted. (1993). *Access and Achievement in Urban Education.* London: HMSO.

Ofsted. (2000). *Improving City Schools.* London: Ofsted.

Oliver, M. (1990). *The Politics of Disablement.* London: Macmillan.

Riddell, S., & Brown, S. (Eds.), (1994). *Special Educational Needs Policy in the 1990s: Warnock in the Market Place.* London: Routledge.

Rouse, M., & Florian, L. (1997). Inclusive education in the market-place. *International Journal of Inclusive Education,* 1(4), 323–336.

Skrtic, T. M. (Ed.). (1995). *Disability and Democracy: Reconstructing (special) education for postmodernity.* New York: Teachers College Press.

Social Exclusion Unit (1998). *Bringing Britain Together: A national strategy for neighbourhood renewal.* London: The Stationery Office.

Social Exclusion Unit (2000). *National Strategy for Neighbourhood Renewal: A framework for consultation.* London: The Stationery Office.

Thomas, G. (1997). Inclusive schools for an inclusive society, British Journal of Special Education, 24(3), 103–107.

Thomas, G. & Dwyfor Davies, J. (199) England and Wales: Competition and control – or stakeholding and inclusion? In H. Daniels & P. Garner (Eds.), *World Yearbook of* Education 1999: *Inclusive education.* London: Kogan Page.

Thomas, G., Walker, D. & Webb, J. (1998) *The Making of the Inclusive School.* London: Routledge.

Thrupp, M. (1999). *Schools Making a Difference: Let's be realistic!* Buckingham: Open University Press.

Tomlinson, S. (1995). The radical structuralist view of special education and disability: Unpopular perspectives on their origins and development. In T. M. Skrtic (Ed.), *Disability and Democracy: Reconstructing (special) education for postmodernity.* New York: Teachers College Press.

UNESCO. (1994). *Final Report: World conference on special needs education: Access and quality.* Paris: UNESCO.

Vlachou, A. D. (1997). *Struggles for Inclusive Education: An ethnographic study.* Buckingham: Open University Press.

Woods, P. A., & Levacic, R. (2002). Raising school performance in the league tables (part 2): Barriers to responsiveness in three disadvantaged schools. *British Educational Research Journal,* 28(2), 227–247.

KARI NES

5 WHY DOES EDUCATION FOR ALL HAVE TO BE INCLUSIVE EDUCATION?

EDUCATION FOR ALL: WHO ARE 'ALL?'

A fundamental aspect of democracy in education is students' access to schools and centres of learning. Education is a basic right for everybody, and is not dependent on social class or academic or physical ability. Article 1 of the World Declaration on Education for All spells this out:

> Every person – child, youth and adult – shall be able to benefit from educa-tional opportunities designed to meet their basic learning needs ... The scope of basic learning needs and how they should be met varies with individual countries and cultures (From World Declaration on Education for All, Article 1, WCEFA, 1990).

Many children of the world still have no or only a minimum of education. Primary enrollments in school in countries of the south increased enormously throughout the 1980s. In Africa as a whole they tripled, but African countries south of the Sahara experienced a fall in enrollment ratios. In most of the countries in question, educa-tional expenditures were cut. The budget in Tanzania, well known for its developed school system from the Nyerere era, was cut by 60%; in some countries it was cut by even more. Completion rates and educational attainment also fell. Against the background of such alarming descriptions, participants from 155 governments and almost as many non-govermental organisations met at the World Conference on *Education for All* in Jomtien,Thailand in March 1990. UN-organisations (UNESCO, UNICEF, UNDP) and the World Bank sponsored the conference.

'All' in the education context rarely literally means everybody (Damsgaard & al, 1982). Before studying the development after the world conference in 1990, let us take a look at who 'all' were at Jomtien. It was named a 'world conference,' but its target for the proposed initiatives was clearly not all countries, but the 'third world' countries, with the aim of using Northern research and advice to implement changes in the South. The rights of disabled learners and female learners were not clearly stated in the original documents of the conference, although sign ficant changes were made to improve the position of these groups in the final declaration. The content of education was also a somewhat neglected issue. Many African contribu-tors to the conference were particularly concerned about the part of education in preserving the culture – norms, values, traditional practices and historical identities. But as we shall see, these aspects were not given priority.

67

J. Allan (ed.), Inclusion, Participation and Democracy: What is the Purpose?, 67-80.
© 2003 *Kluwer Academic Publishers. Printed in the Netherlands.*

Education does not only take place in schools. It happens in informal settings
such as in the home and at play, and also goes on in organised ways in non-formal
settings, for instance in a voluntary organisation or in the workplace. Basic education does not apply only to children and youth. Even if this chapter mainly refers
to schools in a more traditional sense, it is limiting to refer to schooling only when
talking about education for all, especially for countries of the south (Kallaway 1998,
Booth & Black-Hawkins, 2001). When people's basic needs concerning food and
health are unmet, this is where education has to begin, the students being children or
adults, in or outside schools. In many countries in Africa it is impossible to ignore
the threat of HIV/AIDS when educational goals are set up, as this programme plan
from Uganda illustrates:

> To promote full cognitive and psycho-social development of children and
> adolescents within a supportive family and community environment which
> is conducive to education for all, prevention of HIV/AIDS/STDs, adequate
> care and protection of children and adolescents from birth to adulthood.
> (UNICEF, 1995).

In Jomtien, a main recommendation was to strengthen basic education in order to
increase general participation in education. What happened in the nineties after the
united efforts of the governments, the organisations, UN and the World Bank were
mobilised? Brock-Utne (2000) suggests that progress has been limited. Globally,
the number of children not attending school has been fast growing during the last
decade, in 2000 there were 34 million children more without schooling than in 1990
(UNESCO, 2001). In most sub-Saharan countries this is also the case. Generally
reduced welfare and growing poverty for many people is the main reason for this.
Even if education is free, supported as it is by the helping agencies and donors from
all over the world, not everyone can afford to attend. The requirement to pay fees
for secondary education has reduced the number of students gaining access, which
in turn impoverishes African academic standards, perpetuates Western domination
and in turn reduces the chances of getting well-qualified teachers.

Education for all? Examples from sub-Saharan Africa and Scandinavia.

Brock-Utne (2000) describes a typical situation in some sub-Saharan villages in
the nineties. In a village of rondavels (round huts) one building is quadrangle; that
is the school. The teachers employed have a rudimentary teacher training, if any
at all. For economic reasons, one has accepted the offer of free textbooks from
publishers in the former colonial power. The language of instruction is only to a
very limited extent the local language(s). Ability tests and exams are in British or
French. Even if the school is free, only half of the children of compulsory school
age in the catchment area attend, and none of these are disabled. Most of the
students are boys. Absence rates are high. According to Brock Utne, the so-called
education for all in sub-Saharan countries seems to be in reality western primary
schooling for some.

Kallaway (1998) is worried by the impact on African education of new education policy imported from the western world, based on human globalisation and economic efficiency, such as 'human resource development' or 'outcomes based education.' These new educational discourses arise from the needs of global policy and ignore the fact that 80% of the population in South Africa still live in the local village. Africa has relevant educational traditions of its own, risen in the post-independence discourse of democracy, equity, development and human rights. What happened to the African experiences in education built on the needs of people under the circumstances they actually live in, like 'education for self-reliance' in Tanzania and rural education in South Africa? Kallaway thinks the 'selective amnesia' comes from a widely held perception that this notion of education was hopelessly romantic and did not relate to the realities of the market, or it was dismissed altogether as socialist failures. South Africa, after apartheid, is introducing a new curriculum, Curriculum 2005, with intentions of education brought closer to real life, with less mechanistic forms of learning. But Meerkotter (1998) fears that this is only on the surface and the previously white schools will benefit the most from the implementation of the reform. Special support of English, science and mathematics will continue in these schools as before, along with programmes in art, ballet, athletics, rugby and leadership. This will inevitably reproduce further inequalities.

Looking at Scandinavian schooling, in contrast, the picture at first glance is very different from the African scene. Compulsory schooling lasts 9–10 years and is free, regardless of where you live. Parents are required by law to send their children to school. No child stays home because they have to work or because they do not have proper clothes, or because of an impairment. Schools are generally not allowed to reject any student. They are obliged in principle to give all their learners equal or equitable treatment according to their needs, independent of gender, abilities, social class or ethnicity. But realisation level is not the same as formulation level. What happens in practice within the school for all may be quite contrary to ideas of participation and inclusion, as is easily seen when you look at some of the more vulnerable students, ethnic minority students or students considered to have special educational needs. Even if formally included, some students appear to be out of class most of the time. In a study by Tössebro (1999), for example, a majority of students with learning difficulties spent less than five hours per week in their class. The school attainments of the students from ethnic minorities are much poorer than the majority students' results, in Norway as well as in other countries. In one Norwegian study for instance, 27% of the pupils from language minorities were judged by teachers to have learnt nothing at all in the subjects of natural and social science (Özerk, 1992).

When we look back – to the sixties and seventies – at the situation of the minority or indigenous populations in the far north of Scandinavia, we find parallels with the African village presented above. Hoëm (1976), for example, reveals that the Sámi students were not equally accepted along with the Norwegians, were prevented in using their first language, and were under-achievers. Niemi (2000) writes in his novel based on his schooling in a Finnish minority in north Sweden:

It was an upbringing of deficiency. Not in lack of material things – we had what was needed – but in lack of identity. We were nobody. Our parents were nobody. Our ancestors had meant nothing to Swedish history. Our surnames could not be spelt, far less pronounced by the few deputy teachers who came up from the real Sweden ... We did not have manners. We kept our hats on indoors. We never picked mushrooms, avoided vegetables and never had crayfish parties. We could not converse, not recite poems, not wrap up presents properly or make a speech ... We had Finnish accents without being Finnish, we had Swedish accents without being Swedish. We were nobody. (pp. 49–50)

Education for all and inclusive education

A school for all will not be possible if it is not based on principles of inclusion in education (Kisanji, 1998). Inclusive education is integral to a democratic society (Lipsky & Gartner, 1999). The international Salamanca-conference in 1994, which followed on from the Jomtien-conference about education for all, focused specifically on special education. The Salamanca Statement was:

informed by the principle of inclusion, by recognition of the need to work towards *schools for all* – institutions which include everybody, celebrate differences, support learning, and respond to individual needs. As such, they constitute an important contribution to the agenda for achieving Education for All and for making schools educationally more effective (Federico Mayor, preface to the Salamanca Statement, UNESCO, 1994).

In Dakar in 2000, The World Education Forum met in order to follow up the Jomtien declaration about 'education for all.' The Dakar Framework for Action stated more clearly than in Jomtien that successful educational programmes require, among other things 'a relevant curriculum that can be taught and learned in a local language and builds upon the knowledge and experience of teachers and learners' (UNESCO, 2001). This goal is as much in place for the north-Scandinavian villages as for the sub-Saharan.

The main task of inclusive education is overcoming barriers to learning and participation for all (Booth et al, 2000). All members of the school's communities must engage in a process of reducing exclusions within and from education and increasing learning and participation (UNESCO, 2000). The cultures, policies and practices of schools have to respond appropriately to the variations among the students.

The Index for Inclusion (Booth et al, 2000) was first published in the UK in 2000 as a tool for evaluation and a guide for school development processes towards a more inclusive practice. A set of indicators is listed to show what an inclusive school may be like. 'Community resources are known and drawn upon' is one of the indicators. Suggested questions to be asked to investigate this indicator include:

• Is there a regularly updated record of resources in the locality that can support

teaching and learning? This might include local businesses, local religious centres, politicians.
* Do members of the local communities contribute to the curriculum in school?

In discussing this indicator with representatives from India, South Africa, Brazil and England, it became clear that the irrelevance of what is taught can be a major barrier to inclusion and ought to be further emphasised. Additional questions were proposed by the members from these countries (Booth & Black Hawkins, 2001):

* Are learning materials culturally relevant?
* Is the content of lessons relevant to the background an interests of learners?
* Are children encouraged to make use of locally found material as a resource for learning?

These questions are fundamental to the establishment of education for all.

Identity. A model for socialisation in schools.

Valuing the identities which students bring to school is a key aspect of education for all. In Niemi's school, however, the teachers could not pronounce the names of the children. From Africa, Booth and Black-Hawkins (2001) report that the black participants in a South African workshop said that 'no white person ever had the intention of pronouncing their name correctly' (p.30). According to Hoëm (1978), it is a major socialisation task for schools to nourish and shape the identities of the children. Drawing on Mead, he shows how identity includes an 'I' with personal capacities, but also a feeling of belonging to a 'we' with reference to the cultural context. Shared values between school, and the learners and their homes is necessary.

In Hoëm's model there are four possible outcomes of socialisation in school:

1. Previous socialisation is reinforced
2. Previous socialisation is weakened (de-socialisation)
3. New socialisation takes place (re-socialisation)
4. Previous socialisation is unchanged (non-socialisation).

In the case of reinforcing socialisation, interests, as well as values, are shared between homes and school. De-socialisation takes place when there are shared interests, but a conflict of values, between the school and the families. If de-socialisation is the case and the students instead adopt the school's values to create their identity, then a re-socialisation takes place and the learners move away from the home identity. When there are neither common values nor interests between home and school, the outcome is non-socialisation, according to Hoëm. The school as a 'foreign world' seems to be of no use and has no influence on the child's development of identity.

Tate, The Chief Executive of the Schools Curriculum and Assessment Authority for England and Wales, is not concerned about the identity of the students, but about the curriculum helping society to maintain its identity (Ross, 2000). He proposes a strong emphasis on the established majority history and culture in the curriculum in order to create a national identity and maintain continuity within society. Ross, however, points out that regional identities are denied in Tate's scheme, as are those relating to gender, ethnicity or class.

Let me insert here a note on foreign aid and its influence on identity. It is no surprise that the support of donors in Africa and elsewhere sometimes contradicts the expressed aims of the projects (Brock-Utne, 2000). But aid has an impact in the donor nations too and the discourse of foreign aid is one of the most important ways in which basic social normality and identity in Norway manifests itself. It maintains the 'us' and 'them' way of thinking. Thus the 'aid trade' is a separate force that must not be underestimated in maintaining exclusionary practices.

COMMUNITY EDUCATION AS ALTERNATIVES

What would the alternatives look like when the efforts of providing education for all largely went wrong in many countries of the south? First and foremost, education for all should not be reduced to schooling for some, excluding others because of poverty or illness, or because of alienated styles of teaching and learning.

Since the 1960s, many attempts have been made in Sub-Saharan Africa and Scandinavia to increase relevance of the school by shaping its content closely related to the actual environment the students were living in, especially in rural areas. These community education based approaches (Pinar et al., 1995) include indigenous customary education (Kisanji, 1998), rural education (Kallaway, 1998), local-oriented school (Högmo et al., 1981), education for self-reliance (Nyerere, 1968), and cultural analysis (Engen, 1989). The local-oriented school in Norway probably had its basis in the 'Lofot-project' from fishing villages in the north, where the schools' content and methods were developed in relation to local culture and working life (Högmo et al.,1981). The background was an analysis of the school's standardised curriculum as conveying to a large extent urban middle class values. One outcome of the project has been local textbooks developed by teachers, parents and professional authors: 'Lofoten yesterday – today – tomorrow.' Another effect was improved contact between school and communities. A critique raised against the Lofot-project was that it showed a too homogenous picture of the communities. Haavelsrud (1997) asks where the gender or the social class perspectives were. These are issues that have to be included when curriculum is on the agenda: 'Any discussion of curriculum reform must address issues of representation as well as issues of unequal distribution of material resources and power outside the school.' (McCarthy, cited in Pinar et al, 1995, p. 867)

Indigenous customary education

In the traditional African village, everyone was included in a relevant education programme, formal as well as informal. Let us take a look at the traditions of customary education in the south – with a glimpse to the north as well – to see what might be there for today's situation. Kisanji (1998), referring to Ociiti's introduction to indigenous education in East Africa explained that: 'Indigenous customary education can be best conceptualised as the process of socialisation, child-rearing and formal/informal/non-formal learning, occurring at any time and place, and affecting any person living in a given culture or society' (p. 56). In this education 'elements of all the resources of the family, community and the society do contribute to the total education of the learners – be they children, young or adults' (Ociiti, cited in Kisanji, 1998, p. 57). Joseph Kisanji grew up himself as partially sighted in a Tanzanian village. He sums up four characteristics of the indigenous customary education:

1. Absent or limited differentiation in space, time and status, thus allowing for individual differences. Kisanji refers here to an absence of what I conceive as organisational differentiation (in specific classes, hours or groups), but on the other hand a comprehensive pedagogical differentiation is implied in the way that every learner takes part according to his or her particular abilities.
2. Relevance of content and method. The natural, social and cultural environments intertwined with religion are the foundations of indigenous customary education. Kisanji tells how he learned by doing growing up in the village – ploughing, planting and harvesting in the fields, cooking, listening to stories or assisting craftsmen at work by the huts, dancing and celebrating some occasion in the village centre. Every scene was a scene of learning, throughout all waking hours. Many of the adults were involved as teachers, and more competent or elder children were 'teacher assistants.' The three-stage teaching/learning process consisted of demonstration, practice and feedback. No child was excluded from this education. The individual adaptation to their needs was perceived as a natural thing, and there was an attitude of kindness in which help was given freely.
3. Functionality of knowledge and skills. Knowledge, attitudes and skills in the customary curriculum needed to be essential, relevant and useful (Baine, cited in Kisanji, 1998) and included social, as well as academic, skills. For people with disabilities, making these priorities was particularly important.
4. Community orientation. All education took place in the community and was based on the way of life in the community. No child was sent away for education somewhere else. But even the traditional African village was continuously changing and the content of education, developed accordingly.

What relevance does Kisanji's vision have to modern, complex societies, where literacy is central and the flow of information vast and traditional family values rank low? Homogeneity is illusionary, a fact that has to be mirrored in the curriculum. In many places, conditions of co-existence for survival no longer exist; thus the obvious legitimacy of indigenous customary education is no longer there. Even if giving priority to principles of a community education, the locality cannot be the only frame of reference for learning, as those who grow up need a competency to live in the greater society as well. They also need a shared knowledge base across the diversities.

Kisanji lists a number of conditions undermining indigenous customary education in African countries: industrialism, nationalism, cultural oppression through mission and aid, urbanisation, multi-culturalism, and breakdown of the traditional extended family pattern. In spite of this, he finds that the principles from traditional community education are crucial to really making school a school for all. Inclusion is also an essential component of the school for all. Since Western education is so competitive in nature, the principles are harder to implement in the west but should apply everywhere. In some non-Western countries which have no parallel system of special schools, inclusion goals can be approached more easily than in countries which have. The issue of how exclusionary practices are constructed and maintained in many societies, for instance according to gender, disability, religion, ethnicity, social class or age, are not discussed in Kisanji's article, but the author acknowledges the necessity of doing so.

The curriculum for the 10-year compulsory school in Norway

The curriculum reform of compulsory education in Norway of 1997 (L97) contains three elements of relevance to the school for all, namely community education, acknowledging cultural diversity and inclusion. The curriculum formally has community orientation as one of its main approaches to learning. This is formulated in several ways in the curriculum, for instance: 'A sense of local roots and identity is a basis for broader understanding of what different living conditions have in common, regardless of where people live' (L97, p. 64). The students should be able to bring into the classroom their experiences from the community and their local dialect. Each school or community can make local adaptations of the curriculum, allowing for local context-based education. But the formal limitations to making these adaptations were so substantial that a change was made and local control increased from 2000.

The reform also has as a major aim to bring about knowledge about 'other cultures' and sees ethnic and religious diversity as potentials for enrichment of the educational environment for all. The new non-denominational subject called 'Christian knowledge and religious and ethical education' replaces the former Christianity. In the Sámi region, functional bilingualism is a goal for pupils having Sámi as a first language and Sámi as a second language (Todal, 1999). There is a Sámi curriculum in all subjects for the Sámi townships, and the representation of Sámi culture has increased in the curriculum for all.

The curriculum encompasses the perspectives of relevance and functionality by stating that being part of an inclusive school means that everyone participates in the social, academic and cultural community. A further elaboration of what participation in these three equally important communities in school might mean is warranted.

Participation in the social community basically has to do with students' opportunities to play active roles in activities along with the others in school, in lessons, breaks, on excursions, and in the playground. It is not just a question of quantity of participation, but of quality: for example, do adults and students respect and help each other? Is anyone being bullied? Do students have any influence on decisions concerning themselves in school?

Participation in the academic community means being in class in lessons along with other learners. Even if this is the main rule, all students, not only those with a minority language or a disability, may from time to time profit from lessons organised in other ways, for example in smaller groups. Academic participation also means access to a common content in the curriculum. The quality of the participation should be continuously observed and the content and methods have to be suitably adapted. Students' different background should be looked upon as a resource for the learning environment of all.

Participation in the cultural community overlaps the social and the academic community. In this context, the cultural community indicates a school where common values based in L97 are made explicit, when at the same time minority cultures and values are appreciated and their views are represented in the lessons. All who live in the school's catchment area should be seen as natural participants in the school community.

There is an expressed intention, within the curriculum reform, of taking the local community into account. But which comes first, school or community?

> Good working habits developed at school have benefits well beyond the range of education. In addition to the intrinsic value for the learner, education aims at preparing the young to take on the tasks of both working and social life. The school must therefore stay in close interchange with the surrounding community and gradually expose learners to it and prepare them for active engagement in professional, cultural and political life (L97, p. 20).

In community education and indigenous customary education, the local context is the point of departure for what education should be about – community comes first.

There are intentions of local freedom in the curriculum, but freedom is still very limited. Another intention of the reform – establishing a national knowledge canon – may be undermining the local initiatives. One also may ask if the urge to bring about the national canon is a threat to the representation of a variation of cultures that is intended elsewhere in the curriculum.

CULTURAL ANALYSIS FOR CONSTRUCTING
A RELEVANT CURRICULUM

Social anthropology offers an understanding of culture which may be useful when you want to analyse a culture for curriculum purposes. All societies have to meet the basic needs of people and the means of doing so constitute the culture. In his definition of culture, Klausen (1999) lists four basic needs that have to be satisfied in any society and these are accompanied by some key questions to be explored:

1. A need for energy to maintain life. How do people use available resources for their livelihood? What kind of technologies and social organisations exist for this?
2. A need to carry on with life. How adequate are the social structures, for example in relation to family, kinship, housing child care and health?
3. A need to protect life and other values. How are decisions made and how are politics, justice and defence maintained?
4. A need to explain life and death. How do social structures enable life and death to be accounted for? How are basic human conditions of life and death interpreted through religion, beliefs, science and art?

Can a relevant content for modern education which takes local considerations, but also pays respect to national – and global – guidelines, be built on a cultural analysis in these four areas? Aasen and Engen (1994) hold the view that this is possible and have suggested a model for educational planning to be used in early childhood and primary education. The cultural, as well as the natural and social, context of the children guides the work, rather than the individual dispositions of the child or the traditional school subjects. The first stage of the planning process, the cultural analysis, deals with the 'what' questions in the curriculum. The 'how' and 'why' questions constitute further steps in the model, but these will not be discussed here. The approach to cultural analysis requires a primarily inductive investigation of the local environment, based on the four basic needs, as listed by Klausen above. Detailed cues for the analysis follow, and relate to cultural variations in, for example, religion, art and science. Comparative elements are also asked for and finally, language and literary expressions are registered (Aasen & Engen, 1994).

Ideally, the staff, children and their carers collaborate in the cultural analysis and fill in the form in accordance with the cues for each need. Professionals in different fields may be asked to support the investigation. The work can be done on a community or local educational authority level as well. An aim of this work is to approach a level of shared interests and values. The analysis – which continuously has to be updated – is a source for the schools or teachers to make well-founded choices for further work. It is not meant to be the only source; material built on deductive analysis of the national curriculum, like text-books, will often be used as well. There is some anecdotal evidence that working with the cultural analysis has contributed to increasing the self-esteem of people, especially in 'deprived' areas, where negative feelings about the locality were prevailing.

In a pluralist society, education for only a local community or a certain minority group is of course not satisfactory, but neither is a one-sided qualification for the society at large. A solution suggested by Engen (1989) is a double qualification for the local community as well as the larger society. The notion of a double qualification is derived from Park's concept of 'the marginal man,' used to describe the immigrant personality in American cities. Park believed that by being part of two cultures, the immigrant had a unique opportunity to see things from a distance, to actually develop social and cultural objectivity. He was able to take the role of the other culture in looking at himself, a highly desirable capacity not available for the average citizen. A Norwegian author in the nineteenth century, Vinje, spent a year in England and had a parallel experience. He wrote that the view of another country taught him better how to think about his own.

Engen (1989) suggests that bilingualism is likely to enhance the possibility of achieving a double qualification. The successfully socialised bilingual person has the strength of mastering two languages just as well as the monolingual in each of the languages, and has the same capacity as the 'marginal man' of seeing things in a double perspective. The work in school with the overall ambition of double qualification should be based on a methodological principle of cultural comparison. Cultural comparison is in accordance with the principle of making diversity visible – and appreciated – in inclusive education. The cultural analysis may be useful local background material for this comparative work.

Building on Hoëm's socialisation model with its four outcomes, Engen claims that a fifth possibility has to be conceptualised to meet demands in a multicultural society (Engen, 1989; 1994). This involves an integrating socialisation, combining reinforcing socialisation and re-socialisation. By necessity, there will be conflicting values between school and the diversity of cultures and sub-cultures represented in it, and there will often be a need for re-socialisation in certain fields. But all parties should endeavour to find certain shared values, so that the children will be able to experience aspects of school which support their 'cultural baggage.' The plan for the new cross-religious subject of religion in the curriculum may have the potential for the development of a double qualification.

A comment on social anthropology in education

Some community education projects – as well as other educational approaches – explicitly make use of social anthropological thinking and this aspect is present in two of the projects we have been looking at in Norway. The 'Lofot-project' sees the planning process in school as a result of choices made by the actors in given situations, based on the generative planning model of the social anthropologist Fredrik Barth (1972). Social and cultural patterns grow out of these choices and cannot be defined in advance, even if values and general ideas of what direction you want to go in have to be clarified. The analysis along the way must identify elements that create or maintain undesired patterns. Inclusion is the means as well as the ends (Slee, 2000) and therefore all members of the school's communities have to be included in the planning of the education, with a special concern that weaker voices should be heard. The strong emphasis in some anthropological traditions on taking the perspectives of the actors and collaborating in an open-ended process may well be a contribution to inclusive school development.

The cultural analysis draws on a social anthropological definition of culture in its planning model, as well as other theory traditions (Engen,1989). Understanding cultural diversity is vital for inclusive education in its intention to value all pupils equally and to let them use their various potentials. Social anthropology may offer support to schools in their efforts to explore culture in practice. The approach in social anthropology is, in an unprejudiced way, to describe and understand cultures in their own right. Teachers' consciousness that we are all carriers of culture will help prevent ethnocentric attitudes. Questions of what is right or wrong, true or false, may have several answers, and the teacher as a professional must be aware of his or her own answers as well as those of others. But even if the definition of culture underlying the model of cultural analysis is a descriptive one, that does not mean that education should avoid the normative questions. One pitfall for this kind of cultural education might be a romantic and uncritical appraisal of traditions. Existing conflicts as well as possibilities for development and change must also be part of the curriculum in an inclusive school (Engen, 1989; Sand, 1999; Haavelsrud, 1997).

CONCLUDING REMARKS

In a project undertaken by Usti (cited in Hirvonen, 2001), teachers in Sámi areas were asked about their knowledge of the Sámi stories, such as the one about how the mosquitoes came to Finnmark. Mosquitoes occur in vast numbers and are a terrible nuisance in the far north where most Sámis live. But in traditional ways of life connected to reindeer and fishing, the mosquitoes are also of some use, for instance as nourishment for fish, and they are able to help hunting the reindeer. Stories like this are important for maintaining identity. They have a place in the efforts of schools to acknowledge the culture of the students. The village schools we have heard about in the far south and the far north should ask for the stories in their environment, about the local customs and about the names of people and places – even if they are difficult to pronounce. They should open the doors in their quadrangle school houses and start finding out about housing in their locality. How are they built? How was it in earlier times? How was it other places, for instance with the circular rondavels in the south or the lavvos (Sámi tents) in the north?

By this we are into the process of increasing the relevance of content and functionality of knowledge and principles in indigenous customary education. Cultural analysis is on offer as a means to start the work. How do we make this approach work in a complex and pluralist classroom with multiple identities? The teacher cannot possibly know all the stories when she has children from several ethnic groups and cultures in the class, but perhaps someone else in the community does? If education is really going to be for all, it must be inclusive not only legally, but in the sense that the content is relevant and accessible to all.

REFERENCES

Aasen, J. and Engen, T. E. (Ed.), (1994). *Didaktikk og læreplanarbeid i barnehage og skole.* Vallset: Oplandske Bokforlag.

Barth, F. (Ed.), (1972). *The Role of the Entrepeneur in Social Change in Northern Norway.* Oslo: Universitetsforlaget.

Booth, T., Ainscow, M., Black-Hawkins, K., Vaughan, M., & Shaw. L. (2000). *Index for Inclusion.* Bristol: Centre for Studies on Inclusive Education.

Booth, T. and Black-Hawkins, K. (2001). *Developing learning and participation in countries of the South. The role of an index for inclusion.* Paris: UNESCO.

Brock-Utne, B. (2000). *Whose Education for All? The Recolonization of the African Mind.* New York & London: Falmer Press.

Damsgaard, B., Jorde, E., Skogen, K. and Tangen, R. (1982). *Hvem er alle? Hvem er så de andre?* Oslo: Universitetsforlaget.

Engen, T.O. (1989) *Dobbeltkvalifisering og kultursammenligning.* Oplandske Bokforlag, Vallset, Norway.

Engen, T.O. (1994). oppdragelse for det flerkulturelle samfunnet. dobbeltkvalifisering og kultursammenlikning. In J. Aasen & T. Engen (Eds.), *Didaktikk og læreplanarbeid i barnehage og skole.* Vallset: Oplandske Bokforlag.

Haavelsrud, M. (1997). Perspektiv i utdanningssosiologi. Tromsö: Arena forlag.

Hirvonen, V. (2001). *Innføring av samisk språk og forståelse i den samiske skolen.* Kautokeino: Research project, unpublished.

Hoëm, A. (1976). *Yrkesfelle, sambygding, same eller norsk?* Oslo: Universitetsforlaget.

Hoëm, A. (1978). *Sosialisering. En teoretisk og empirisk modellutvikling.* Oslo: Universitetsforlaget.

Högmo, A., Tiller, T. and Solstad, K.J. (1981). *Skolen og den lokale utfordring. En sluttrapport fra Lofotprosjektet.* Institutt for samfunnsvitenskap, Universitetet i Tromsö

Kallaway, P. (1998). Whatever happened to rural education as a goal for (South) African devlopmen? In W. Morrow & K. King (Eds.) *Vision and Reality, Changing Education and Training in South Africa.* Cape Town: University of Cape Town Press.

Kisanji. J. (1998). The march towards inclusive education in non-Western countries: retracing the steps. *International Journal of Inclusive Education*, 2(1), 133–151.

Klausen, A.M. (1999). *Kultur – variasjon og sammenheng.* Oslo: Gyldendal.

L97 (1999). *The curriculum for the 10-year compulsory school in Norway.* Oslo: The Royal Ministry of Education, Research and Church Affairs.

Lipsky, D. and Gartner, A. (1999). Inclusive education. a requirement of a democratic society. In H. Daniels & P. Garner (Eds.), *Inclusive Education, World Yearbook of Education.* London: Kogan Page.

Meerkotter, D (1998). The state of schooling in south Africa and the introduction of Curriculum 2005. In W. Morrow & K. King (Eds.). *Vision and Reality, Changing Education and Training in South Africa.* Cape Town: University of Cape Town Press.

Niemi, M. (2000). *Populärmusik från Vittula.* Stocholm. Mån Pocket.

Nyerere, J (1968). Education for Self-Reliance. In *Ujamaa: essays on Socialism.* Dar es Salaam: Oxford University Press.

Özerk, K. (1992). Tospråklige minoriteter. Sirkulær tenkning og pedagogikk, Oslo: Oris forlag.

Pinar, W.F., Reynolds, W.M., Slattery, P. and Taubman, P.M. (1995). *Understanding Curriculum.* New York: Peter Lang.

Ross, A. (2000). *Curriculum. Construction and critique.* London & New York: Falmer Press

Sand, S (1999). Oppgaven er kulturformidling – interkulturell kompetanse og pedagogikk. In *Nord-Syd. Udviklingspædagogisk tidsskrift*, 18. Copenhagen.

Slee, R. (2001). *Talking Back to Power. The politics of Educational Exclusion*. Keynote speech at the International Special Education Congress 2000, Manchester. (CD-rom).

Todal, J. (1999). Minorities with a Minority: Language and the School in the Sámi area of Norway. In S. May (Ed.), Indigenous Community-based Education. Clevedon, Philadelphia, Toronto, Sydney: Multilingual matters Ltd.

Tössebro, J. (1999). Epilog – refleksjoner over status innen norsk forskning om spesialundervisning. In P. Haug, J. Tössebro & M. Dalen (Ed.) *Den mangfaldige spesialundervisninga. Status for forskning om spesialundervisning*. Oslo: Universitetsforlaget.

UNESCO (1994). *Salamanca Statement on Principles, Policy and Practice in Special Needs Education and a Framework for Action*.

UNESCO (2000). *Overcoming Exclusion through Inclusive Approaches in Education. A Challenge and a Vision*. Conceptual Paper for the Education Sector.

UNESCO (2001). Dakar Framework for Action. Expanded Commentary. Retrieved May 8, 2002, from http://www.unesco.org/education/efa.

UNICEF and the Government of Uganda (1995). *Country Programme 1995–2000. Basic Education, Child Care and Adolescent Development Programme Plan of Operations*. Kampala.

World Conference on Education for All (1990). *World Declaration in Education for All*. Jomtien 1990.

PART TWO

CHALLENGING UNDERSTANDING

DORA BJARNASON

6 THE SOCIAL CONSTRUCTION OF ADULTHOOD WITH A DIFFERENCE IN ICELAND

INTRODUCTION

Icelandic society is a modern, democratic, Nordic type welfare state, with a high standard of living, and virtually full employment. Both men and women are active in the workforce, and Icelandic families, like families in most western countries, have undergone significant changes in the latter half of the 20th century, with a growth in rates of divorce, remarriage or cohabitations, falling birth rate and a high rate of children born outside wedlock. The population of Iceland is tiny, only 286,000, two thirds of which live in or around the capital city of Reykjavík, and the remainder in fishing villages or on small farms, around the country. Due to the scale of the population, social interactions are typically more 'face to face' than is the norm in most other modern societies. Many families are still close knit, and even when that is not so, people constantly run into each other in all walks of life. Icelanders, therefore, typically have some sense of community.

THE STUDY

The study that began in 1998, seeks to understand the world of young disabled adults in Iceland, the first generation to grow up with the ideology of inclusion as the law of the land. The study focuses on the experience of being a young disabled adult (16–24 years old) in upper-secondary schools, university or equivalent educational settings, in the job market and in society. The study explores the situations and experiences of disabled individuals that lead to exclusion; how they see themselves; and how they are perceived by parents, friends and teachers. The study also considers how different disability labels are attributed and experienced by young people and how the choices made for them by their parents influence their experiences. The study includes a variety of young disabled Icelanders, people from urban and rural sectors, from different socio-economic backgrounds and people with a broad diversity of disability labels (Table 1).

Two broad preliminary questions guide this study. First, what do these young disabled adults, their parents, teachers and friends, believe hinders them most in pursuing their learning, working or participating in society as adults, and what is most helpful? Second, what are the young adults' hopes and expectations for their future as adult members of society?

83

J. Allan (ed.), Inclusion, Participation and Democracy: What is the Purpose?, 83-103.
© 2003 *Kluwer Academic Publishers. Printed in the Netherlands.*

Table 1: The young disabled adults' home, school and workplace in 1998

School Type		Home		Workplace		Region	
Special school	0	Parental home	23	Regular work	4	Reykavik and gr. Rvik area	16
Special class in high school	12	Own flat/living alone/living with partner	8	Sheltered workshop	7	Towns and villages	16
Regular high school/Tertiary ed/University	11	Group home	5	Unemployed but available to work	1	Farms	4
Adult education for disabled learner	4	Other	1	Farms	1		
TOTAL	27	TOTAL	37	TOTAL	13	TOTAL	36

Three questions, no less broad, have emerged from the data. These are:

1. What does it mean to be a disabled adult in Iceland?
2. How do young people see themselves reaching that milestone when they have significant disabilities, and how do they negotiate adult status?
3. How is the adulthood achieved by young disabled people related to the parenting they receive, including parents' actions, choices, social status and approach to social service bureaucracy? Does the parents' influence vary according to the young person's age, type of impairment and need for support?

Exploring these questions raises new themes related to the interconnected pattern of parenting over time and the young adults' view of their personal situations and future prospects within general and special community settings. Furthermore, the study also looks at how parenting, schooling, work, hobbies, friendships, love and sexuality coincide with the young disabled adult's perception of his or her personal situation and future prospects. Lastly, the links between the individual, his or her family and society (Mills, 1959) are explored. It is underlined elsewhere (Bjarnason, 2002a) that decisions made by parents and their disabled children, often without much support from professionals, can contribute substantially to the inclusion of the children in general society. The main goals of the study are to make visible the important, but not always acknowledged, perspective of young disabled people about their own situation and future possibilities as adults; to explain the impact of choices made by parents and children through childhood and adolescence on their situation as young disabled adults; and to explore how parents, professionals, and the young disabled persons' social relationships play an important role in framing their experiences and their expectations about adulthood.

One metaphor in particular has helped to frame the analysis of the data. It is the metaphor of the young disabled people of the study, as either travelling along two roads (mainstream or special), or wandering about like nomads in the wasteland in between. The highway travellers (Group A), 14 young disabled people, are seen to travel alongside the rest of us. A few travel in the fast lane, and others move more along the middle of the road, but at a slow pace. Another set of travellers (Group C), 15 young disabled people, is seen to travel along a much narrower special lane for labelled people. Finally, the nomads (Group B), seven young disabled people, are seen to wander about in the wilderness between these two roads, sometimes aiming for the one and sometimes the other, but belonging to neither.

Modes of inquiry

This study used qualitative methods largely influenced by grounded theory and hermeneutics (Glaser & Strauss, 1967) and located the work within the interpretivist paradigm (Ferguson & Ferguson, 1995). The Fergusons characterise the methodology associated with the interpretivist paradigm 'as the systematic collection and analysis of the stories people tell about how they interpret reality' (p. 105). The primary method for collecting data was interviews. This author's professional and personal experience over the past 20 years as a university teacher and a researcher of sociology and disability studies, and as a single mother of a son with severe impairment, inform and focus the research.

The sample, 36 young adults with a variety of disability labels, were interviewed, as well as one or both parents or support persons of 30 young adults (44 individuals), 12 teachers, and 12 friends (Table 2).

Table 2: Key young adults' primary disability labels

Disability Labels	Number
Cognitive	18
Multiple	2
Physical	7
Sensory (3 deaf, 1 visually impaired)	4
Emotional (autism)	2
Physical illness/accident	3
TOTAL	36

Almost all the young adults were identified as significantly disabled according to the Icelandic Disability Pension regulations and all were entitled to disability pension paid by the National Social Security Bureau. Many had been given many additional disability labels. In most instances the primary label was 'mental retardation' or 'physical disability,' sometimes with an additional condition or a particular syndrome, such as cerebral palsy, seizure disorder, sensory problems, or physical illness. The most common label of 'cognitive disability' referred to a broad variety of conditions that were included.

A team of three students and an anthropologist helped at different times with the interviews of teachers and friends of the young adults and with some of the coding and data analysis. The interviews were in-depth and semi-structured, lasting from 45 minutes to over two hours. A young woman of 20, who uses a wheelchair and has experienced both segregated and general services for disabled persons, helped me overcome communication difficulties and understand the colloquialisms of youth and helped with most of the interviews with the young people. The interviews were carried out in my office or in the parents' or young persons' homes. The parents' education, social class, and geographic backgrounds were diverse.

The study started with a broad focus on the young people's experiences and interpretations of their present and recent past at home, in school and leisure, and the perspectives and interpretations of their parents, friends and teachers. A constant comparative method, in which the data collection and data analysis proceeded together, was adopted. Analysis was ongoing during fieldwork. Additional information was gained from statutory laws and regulations, policy documents, workers within the local and state welfare services, high school principals, and staff from the Ministry of Education and the Ministry of Social Services. Everyone involved in this study was promised anonymity, although hiding people in a society the size of Iceland is difficult. Names, places and facts that do not alter the content of the data have all been changed.

The social construction of typical young adulthood

Adulthood is described as a social construction, taking its meaning and content from the culture and socio-economic structure of society. Arnet made the point that transition to adulthood, as perceived by young Americans, is individualistic and emphasises qualities of character, primarily accepting responsibility for one's self, making independent decisions and financial independence (Arnet, 1994). These relate to Ferguson & Ferguson's (1993; 1996) three dimensions of adulthood, the personal dimension, the cultural dimension, and the familial dimension of the meanings of adulthood.

The personal meaning of adulthood implies gaining personal autonomy and the ability to make choices about living, working, travelling and leisure. Such choices are, of course, never completely free. They are mitigated by the person's social class, religious beliefs and other economic and social circumstances, psychological aptitudes, interests and peers. Figuring out who one is and what one wants is ridden with pitfalls, takes time, and is anchored in the webs of relationships that construct culture.

The cultural dimension of adulthood involves a more symbolic dimension. It goes beyond the personal circumstances to citizenship with its legal, political and social rights and obligations (Marshall, 1973). The prevalent individualism of the Icelandic culture engulfs Icelandic youth. The opportunities for most typical youth to work during school holidays from their early teens, and to do part-time work along with upper-secondary schooling, provide a fertile ground to foster Arnet's three basic qualities of the character of typical youth and young adults. Responsibility for one's self is highly valued in Icelandic socialization and nurtured both in formal education and informal upbringing in the home (Kristjánsson, 2001)

The familial meaning of adulthood is a simultaneous translation and merger of the personal and the cultural dimensions into a family definition of adulthood (Ferguson & Ferguson, 1996) This involves a process of gradual change in the relationship between that person and his or her parents and family, resulting in increased independence and self determination for the individual and fewer daily responsibilities and involvement for the parents. There is some indication that this gradual change may start from an earlier age in Iceland than in many other European countries and may be somewhat less restricted (Edelstein, 1988).

There is a difference between coming of age and achieving adult status. Symbolic communication certifies that a person has been endowed with the status of adulthood. Bates (cited in Ferguson & Ferguson, 1996) defines adulthood as: 'part of a tacit exchange of complex information through the interactive elements of language, social context and cognitive interpretations of relevant information about age (e.g.the appearance, voice size and so forth)' (p. 52). Bates' definition involves a communication process via symbols (language, social context and cognitive interpretations). Typical Icelandic youth are able to start that communication in their early or mid-teens, while not officially obtaining the legal status of adulthood until 18 years of age. This communication process is woven into the webs of the young persons' relationships. (Coleman, 1961; Nielson, 1991; Edelstein, 1988; Gudmundsson, 1984). Even though most people get through adolescence and young adulthood prepared to take on the rights and duties of adult life, for some, the pursuit of adolescence and young adulthood, can become tricky, painful, lonely or even life threatening. (Nielsen, 1991; Gudmundsson, 1984; Óskarsdóttir, 1995). But most of us get to become adults, and are recognised as such by others. In taking on the social status of normative adulthood, most of us soon discover that it is accompanied by rather more duties than we anticipated, and rather fewer rights than we hoped for, but most of us deal with that.

Summary of findings

Fourteen young disabled people, a group of travellers on the highway (group A) seemed to be on the same road as the rest of us, that is the road of mainstream society. One or two travelled at high speed at the middle of the highway, succeeding in school and leaving most of their non-disabled peers behind. Most of the travellers on this road went at a much slower speed nearer to the edge, faced with having to overcome a variety of access problems – access to buildings, school curriculum and school and wider community life. Many of the youth suffered bullying at compulsory school. The flexible general school, co-operative teachers, and a planned approach to class curriculum increased the disabled students' opportuni-

ties for participation and reduced their danger of getting bullied. Most traditional
general schools and typical classes, particularly at the upper secondary level, were
found to be organised in such a way as to create exclusionary processes, despite
the efforts of some teachers and other school staff to minimise this. This was most
noticeable at the upper-secondary level where student-teacher interaction is marked
by bureaucratic rules and a certain level of indifference towards all students. In such
situations, friends and peers were of utmost importance in supporting the disabled
youths' participation in the school curriculum and community.

The experiences of each of the young people had been characterised by high
levels of parental involvement. Their parents had made a number of choices on their
behalf and received support to sustain these choices. The young disabled people
had been in mainstream schools for many of their school years and were mostly
in typical classes. They had learned to become effective self-advocates. They had
at least one real non-disabled, as well as disabled friends, but many spent much
time alone and lonely, or trying to fit in with 'hi friends,' people who stop and say
'Hi, Johnny,' but not much more (Högsbro et al, 1999). All but one of these young
people had in common the firm belief that they would eventually become fully adult,
slowly but surely. One young man, knew that he was likely to die soon and would
not, therefore, become more adult than he was already. Two women had set up their
own homes, had found work, or had acquired the status of a wife, home-worker and
a mother, and looked upon themselves as fully adult. Both relied significantly on
family support. The mother, who was labelled with cognitive disabilities, was also
supported by her local social services. Unlike most typical wives and mothers, she
lived in fear of having one or more of her children removed by the authorities if she
failed to please the social service officials. (Booth & Booth, 1996; Sigurjónsdóttir
& Traustadóttir, 2000). The remaining young people on the highway (group A)
saw themselves as reaching adulthood within the near future if they worked hard
enough at realising their dreams, finding a home, a job, and maybe a partner. Most
hoped to get married and some to have children of their own.

The second group of travellers (group C) in the 'special' lane, fifteen in all,
travelled at a slower pace, receiving more segregated services than the group on
the highway (Group A), and had fewer demands placed on them. Many enjoyed
the safety, understanding and direction of staff and the companionship of disabled
peers. Professionals, particularly special education teachers, were found to be
both gatekeepers and important allies of this group of disabled youngsters. For
example, some of the special teachers interviewed leaned towards paternalism in
the application of their expertise, reducing the young disabled peoples' possibilities
of taking risks and building relationships with typical peers in general community
settings. In one special unit of an upper-secondary school, however, special teachers
worked enthusiastically and focused on group inclusion. These young people were
involved in a transition plan intended to secure them supported work in the general
job market upon their graduation.

With only two exceptions, these young people felt themselves to be years
younger than their chronological age indicated. They had in common parents who

were more likely to react or adapt to the rules and regulations prescribing the special services to which they and their children were entitled. Many reported that they had little or inadequate support from the system or from their close networks. Sometimes they felt that all support systems had failed them dismally. These parents took pride in playing by the rules and managing on their own when the rules did not fit. They shared a belief in the system's duty to meet the needs of disabled people and their families and argued for their child's rights to special services. The choices they made for their disabled children reflected this. Only one young disabled man from this group reported that he had tried to break away from some of his parents' control. He and his girlfriend dreamt about getting married one day and having children. He rebelled without success when his mother decided he should get sterilized or stop seeing his girlfriend.

More of the young adults in the special lane (group C) than those on the highway (group A) were labelled as cognitively disabled, but the group also included people labelled with physical or sensory disabilities. They had all been to special schools or special classes, accepted their disability in a fatalistic manner, and tried to fit into the system. Many of these young people were very content with their lives and led a rich social life inside their particular special group. This contrasts with the experiences of the young adults on the highway (group A), many of whom felt somewhat lonely and isolated. Most of the members of group C had only disabled friends and primarily associated with them in segregated settings. Some of these young people had been together since the special pre-school. Some had, in addition, non-disabled 'paid friends'(paid support people of their own age), who took them to the cinema or to other leisure activities, and a few had only 'paid friends' and 'hi friends.' Their dreams were similar to those of the young people in group A, but the fulfillment of those dreams was seen to be a long way away, if at all feasible.

Thirdly, between these two groups were seven young people, the nomads (group B), wandering about in the wasteland between the roads. Two of these young people were labelled autistic. The others carried a variety of labels including deaf, cognitive disability, physical disability, mental and physical illness, and impairment arising from disease, or accident. These young people experienced a variety of school situations from being outstanding students in general schools before the onset of their disease or accident, to being students in special schools and special or mainstream classes in general education schools. The parents of these youth resembled parents of the young people in both groups, except there is some suggestion that there was less agreement between fathers and mothers about how to tackle family activity settings (Gallimor et al, 1989) and professional involvement, than between the parents of the other travellers.

What characterised these young people is how they seem to roam around from one road to the other without belonging with either group of travellers. They had no real friends, but some had 'paid friends' or 'hi friends' only. Some saw lots of acquaintances, while others remained more or less isolated apart from their communication with their families. They sometimes advocated for themselves, but more often took a fatalistic attitude, finding it difficult to accept that adulthood could apply to them. Not all wanted to become adults. For some of the nomads, the road to adult- hood may pass through a period of 'wandering about in the wasteland,' as a part of their growing up, similar to that when non disabled youth 'drop out' for a while, to return to mainstream society in due course. Others seemed in a state of anomie or of feeling powerless to affect their own destiny. These young disabled people seemed in search of a meaning in their lives or appeared to have lost such meaning.

Those young disabled participants in the sample who allowed themselves the luxury of dreaming shared a similar vision. For all of them, their vision of their adulthood was the same as the normative adulthood of non-disabled young Iceland- ers. This vision involved living in their own home, having a job and meaningful leisure or a hobby. Most hoped for a partner and maybe a child. Neither disability labels nor a disabling society managed to stifle that dream, which they shared with most other young people (Oliver, 1990; Shakespeare et al, 1996; Barnes et al, 1999). For the young disabled people on the highway (group A), some kind of supported adulthood based on interdependence rather than independence was well within reach or had already been achieved. For young disabled people in the special lane (group C) adulthood remained a far-away dream, obtainable sometime in the future. Finally, for the nomads (group B) there was much greater uncertainty as to whether they would reach adulthood at all or whether they aspired to this status.

THE SOCIAL CONSTRUCTION OF DISABLED ADULTHOOD

In what way does the social construction of young adulthood differ for young disabled people? The broad picture, as painted by this research, suggests some im- portant differences on all the three dimensions of adulthood, as defined by Ferguson & Ferguson (1996), between the coming of age for typical and disabled persons. The individual (medical) model of disability dominates both professional and lay peoples' perceptions of the problems facing children and youth with disabilities. That approach depicts disabled children and youth as sick, pathetic and incomplete beings, in need of care, kindness and training from professionals, and as a source of sorrow, stress and toil to their families. The welfare state, its special schools and special classes in general education schools, leisure and work establishments for disabled people are organised from within that paradigm. Disabled children and youth, are consequently stigmatised and are often (more or less) barred from normative participation in general settings, paternalistically 'for their own good.' Parents, the young people themselves, friends or professionals frequently need to struggle with the bureaucracy to ensure necessary support and to to access generic services and participation in mainstream society. For these reasons, normative adulthood and normative adult status in Arnet's (1994) sense, encompassing full responsibility for self, for decisions and finances may not be fully within the reach of many disabled persons. Following the social model of disabilities (Reindal, 1998), it is argued that this is to be understood in terms of hindrances structured and perpetuated in society, rather than in relation to the individuals' impairment.

Yet interdependent adulthood with a difference could be made accessible to all the young participants of the study.

The personal dimension of adulthood

The personal dimension of adulthood implies gaining personal autonomy and the ability to make significant choices about one's personal life (Ferguson & Ferguson, 1996). It is also concerned with personal identity and the sense of who one believes one is. Portrayals of four young disabled peoples lives will serve to sketch out how each of the dimensions of adulthood are experienced by different young disabled travellers.

Thór was seen to travel in the fast lane on the highway of mainstream society. Thór was 21 years old, and came from a farm. He was one of four siblings, born with a disease that resulted in quadriplegia. His body was significantly impaired, and he needed help with most daily personal tasks, including turning over in the night. No special services were available in his part of the country when he was growing up, and his parents obtained what specialised advice they could find in Reykjavík, adapted what they felt they could use to their every day life, managed a small business, and ran a big home with their children, workers, other family members and friends. Thór joined the tiny local school for the first six years of his schooling, then moved to a larger school for his last three years at compulsory education school as a boarder. The teachers and kids treated him mostly 'like an ordinary guy.' He said:

> I have always known that I am impaired, different from the other kids, and I cannot do all the same things as they. As a child I did not think about that much. It was how it was, but I was and will be who I am. It is a bother sometimes, but no big deal.

Thór's father made sure that all the schools he joined were as accessible as possible, and he even built ramps himself in some of the schools, and became an expert advocate for his son and for other disabled children and youth in his area. Despite Thor's complex needs, he managed to get necessary support from friends and peers, became popular with his schoolmates, found lasting friendships, and became an excellent student. He went abroad with his friends upon graduation from the upper secondary school and tried some risky leisure activities with his most trusted friends, including diving. While at school and then at university, he learnt to advocate for himself, although he continued to encounter barriers within the system. Recently, he had some problems getting the system to replace his wheelchair:

> Thór: My old [wheel]chair was ruined, useless, but it was still a problem to get a new chair. The system apparently did not intend me to get one. This called for much letter writing and bother.

> Dóra: How do you feel when you get into such problems over such self evident needs?

> Thór: Of course, I simply become more determined, I rise to the challenge
> and figure out how to solve it.

At the time of the interview, Thór had been doing well as a university student, was living in his own flat with his best friend as his helper and flat mate, and had some other paid help. He had a strong sense of his identity and was both self-reliant and supported by his family and friends. When asked about his future he remained optimistic, but also concerned:

> Thór: I have thought a lot about my future. It is a bit unclear to me. My friend
> is graduating and moving out soon. I don't know my life will be ... who will
> help me then? I don't know if I can stay in this flat ... I am a bit scared, but
> I think it will be OK. I have been lucky, things have always managed to sort
> themselves out in the end.

Thór's friend moved out for a few years, and Thór managed to find different flat mates and helpers, but then his best friend and former flat mate returned for a while with his fiancé. Thór dreamt of finishing his studies, travelling abroad, buying a car, finding a challenging job, studying more later, finding a woman to love, have a home and perhaps children. Yet when he talked about his dreams, he kept telling me that this was 'just a dream.' He said: 'One must try and remain realistic, when one does not envisage how all the obstacles will get solved. Well I am sometimes a little hesitant whether or not they can all be solved.' Thór's identity was firm and his will to try and fulfill his dreams was crystal clear, but he was also a 'realist,' as he put it, and clear about the social obstacles he has had to overcome in the pursuit of his dreams.

Björg was a young woman of 18, the youngest of three siblings, and labelled with significant cognitive disabilities. She provides a good example of a traveller in the special lane. She and one of her older brothers lived with their parents in a comfortable villa in one of the suburbs of Reykjavík; her other sibling had moved from home. Her parents were well to do by Icelandic standards; her father had his own import-export company and her mother was a trained teacher. Her parents said they wanted the best available professional help for her and chose special services when available. Björg attended special school, did special sports, had the same respite family for 10 years, and she had gone regularly to summer camp for disabled children and youth. She spent much of her leisure time either with her family or in organised special activities for disabled children and youth. She had also travelled extensively, both in Iceland and abroad, with her parents and siblings. At the time of the interview, Björg was in a special class in a upper secondary school, alongside her boyfriend and closest female friends. She described herself as very happy at school and content with her life. When asked about her becoming an adult, she seemed surprised, explained that that was a long way away. She said: 'If I become a grown up, I want to move away from home, live with my love, and work at home.' She thought that she might get a job 'somewhere indoors.' She wanted her boyfriend to work in the same place, but at a different job. When I asked her if she wanted to have children of her own, she said: 'I am not sure if I want that. I am disabled. I don't think I want ... I will not be very good [at motherhood].'

Like Thor, Björg was secure in her identity, but in contrast with him, she saw herself as a very young teenager, who may or may not become grown up for a long while yet. She said she was 'a good and obedient girl most of the time,' a statement confirmed by her parents and teachers. She foresaw a long future with other disabled friends ahead of her, but this would be under the secure surveillance of protective adults.

Finally, Margrét, and Jóna provide different examples of young disabled people who are here identified as nomads in the wasteland. Margrét appeared sometimes to be striving towards the highway and sometimes towards the special lane. She was 20 years old, and identified as hard of hearing. She lived in a fine villa in Reykjavík with her younger sibling and her parents, who were affluent and educated professional people. Margrét's schooling had been varied: she had attended Deaf school, general education school, and a special class for Deaf students in a mainstream school. She had no friends, but many acquaintances, and she had experienced living a broad for extensive periods of time due to her father's job. She had a history of substance abuse that she said was behind her now, and spoke of periods of depression, anger, high activity, and spells where life did not seem worth living. She had recently returned to upper secondary school after dropping out, worked at a part time job, and worked to strengthen herself in the hope of gaining more access to the mainstream, while at the same time she wanted to be able to drop in on to the Deaf world from time to time. Neither felt comfortable at that stage in her life. She had a hard time figuring out her identity and aspirations for the future. When asked about her future she said:

> I find it fun to work and help people, but I have been so torn, trying to be strong. I have witnessed a suicide attempt. I saved my friend. I have been so depressed and now I don't know where I am heading. I want to go abroad, learn to help people, kids, but now I just take a day at the time.

Jóna, a young woman of 20 was another such nomad, but was in rather different circumstances. She became significantly physically impaired and lost her ability to talk, because of an accident in her teens, said she was terrified of meeting new people. She was the only child of a couple who worked as unskilled workers. The strain of the accident and a subsequent, fight first for Jóna's life, then for support and financial help, broke up their home. Her parents split up, and her mother stayed with Jóna almost day and night for a long time.

Before her accident, she had been a popular student, the president of her class at school and had had a boyfriend. After the accident, her old friends had almost disappeared. She described her life, with the aid of a spelling board: 'I live in my own flat. Most of the time I do little. Occasionally I go to the cinema, or meet friends on the internet. I am always on the internet.' She communicated with strangers and with former friends using a chat box on the internet. Her mother said she spent much of her time at her computer. Jóna said: 'I only live on the net.

I find it [that] wonderful, because there I can be myself.' Jóna's fear of meeting new people and her disappointment with former friends and helpers showed in her relationships. Her helpers at school complaneed that they had problems reaching her, and that she was unco-operative or hostile in her interaction with them. A helper said: 'She drives her chair into our legs out of spite. I help her, but she is no friend. I don't like her ... I did try, but I cannot'

When Jóna was asked about her hopes, dreams and expectations for the future, she said she did not want to become an adult. She had been moved from house to house against her will, occasionally forgotten for hours on end by negligent service staff, and had tried to go back to school without adequate support. Finally she had given up on most of her dreams: 'I will wait for a cure,' she said. She had fought a tough fight, and had even sat her compulsory school exams during the many months she was in hospital after her accident, but had given up for the time being at least due to formidable social barriers, and because she knew who she used to be, but had problems finding out who she had become.

The formidable disabling processes within society, together with the vulnerability of many of the young people, make reaching adulthood an uphill struggle. It takes work opportunities and wages, access to general schools and typical peers, (or an empowering disability sub-culture) and technical support, for young disabled people to be able, in accordance with the personal meaning of adulthood, to claim full personal autonomy. Most of the young disabled people in this study had graduated (or were about to do so) with few marketable skills into low paying jobs, sometimes in a sheltered workshop with token pay, or to no work. That and the low disability pension, does not hold much of a promise for full financial independence, in a country where the cost of living is among the highest in the world. Even a research participant, who graduated from a university with good grades and highly marketable skills, was unemployed for a year until he finally found a low paying part time job, with the assistance of his father, friend and other advocates.

Furthermore, in the case of young people labelled with significant cognitive disabilities, it takes supportive non-paternalistic relationships to bring and sustain the relevant symbols of adulthood to the individual (Ferguson & Ferguson, 1996). Many of the young people with cognitive disability labels, were educated partly or fully in special schools or classes, and spent much of their time at home with parents, or in segregated settings organised around their special needs as they were defined under the individual (medical) disability model. This restricted their access to typical experiences with age peers and the possibility of building a variety of relationships with persons outside these settings.

The cultural dimension

The cultural meaning of normative adulthood may not be fully within the reach of most persons with significant disabilities of any type, and certainly not without supportive empowering relationships and access to social goods and symbols of an adult status. Some of the research participants had the option of joining a disability sub-culture, but very few had accepted that offer so far. Ferguson (2001) warns against essentialistic over-generalizations in talking of a 'culture of disability' and of 'inclusion.' He argues, however, that it may make perfect sense to talk of a 'Deaf culture' (Andersson, 1997), a 'Blind culture' or a 'Physical Disability culture' as valid options. They are available for groups of disabled people, to replace or resist the suppression, exclusion and stigmatization of general culture. Such sub-cultures are constructed and reconstructed by the members, often in opposition to general culture, and to celebrate 'disability identity' and 'disability culture.'

A sub-culture of this kind has both positive and negative aspects. On the one hand, the need for mutual support and the celebration of difference is likely to empower individuals and groups that have been rejected by mainstream society. But on the other hand, it can be argued that if people learn to accept and respect each other's difference, a foundation is built for a more tolerant and a culturally richer society. In a tiny society like Iceland, both the benefits and shortcomings of such sub-cultural membership for the individual with a difference are likely to become highlighted. In Iceland, where the members of each such sub-culture are bound to be few, it is also likely that the group will exercise firm social control over the insiders of such outsiders groups (Gustavsson, 1999). Further, the variations of perspectives and experiences within tiny sub-cultures may be uncomfortably uniform or narrow. In such a case, membership in a tiny sub-cultures may become stifling, rather than empowering, for the individual. Disabled people join sub-cultures by choice. In contrast, as Ferguson (2001) points out, that choice is not available in the same way to people with significant cognitive disabilities, and such individuals are unlikely to be able to create and sustain a sub-culture adorned with the necessary communication of symbols. He suggests that 'For most the choices have involved movement between alternative and mainstream culture. For people with cognitive disabilities the choices have involved movement from no culture to some culture' (p. 17).

For persons with cognitive disabilities, such choices have been made by others in the individual's social network, for example parents, professionals, staff or advocates. Ferguson (2001) describes the congregation of persons with cognitive disabilities, as placing them in 'a professional or bureaucratic sub-culture that engulfs people with mental retardation' (p. 16). Furthermore, he argues that at worst, such segregated settings for persons with cognitive disabilities, may result in what he calls a 'ghettoization of people with the most significant cognitive disabilities on the margins of both the disability community and mainstream culture' (ibid, p. 18). He suggests that: 'At most people with cognitive disabilities have been offered the options of a fragile assimilation into, or paternalistic parodies of, dominant culture' (ibid, p. 17).

Thór's story provides a good example of the limited options available. Despite his impairment, he managed with support from friends, family and paid staff, to engage in culturally ascribed age appropriate adulthood. He did most of the things other young men of his age engage in, but less often and only with support. He had attained the fragile assimilation into dominant culture which Ferguson & Ferguson (1996) refer to. Björg, on the other hand, moved along the special lane. Despite

her age and her vitality, she was getting more and more locked into a special world
for disabled people, dominated by bureaucratic professional structures. Within that
structure, she had found her particular gemeinshaft of friends and companions. The
fact that she could only see them at organised activities for special people, or when
parents were available to drive her, irritated her somewhat, but she accepted that as
a fact of life. The young disabled people referred to as nomads had a much harder
time fitting into the culturally prescribed dimension of adulthood, but for different
reasons; Margrét (and her parents) had made a number of different choices that some
times directed her towards the highway and sometimes away from it. Margrét's personality and her thirst for trying all kinds of new things and testing new boundaries
made it difficult for her at the time of the interview to settle on her journey on the
highway. Due to her very different experiences from those of many Deaf children
and youth in Iceland, and because she did not identify wholly with the Deaf culture,
it was also hard for her to find acceptance. Jóna, on the other hand, had tried her
best, supported by her mother, to get back into the highway, but because of a lack
of support from the service system, her attempts had been in vain. Her reactions had
been anger, despair, and at the time of the interview, near capitulation.

Ferguson & Ferguson's (1996) relational approach provides a more nuanced
way of thinking about the coming of age for people with cognitive disabilities.
Perhaps their reasoning can be stretched a little to include people with other significant disabilities who have been more or less locked into the individual model
of disabilities and segregated services for much of their childhood and youth. The
cognitively disabled youth in the research, both those who managed to stay on
the highway, and the many more like Björg, in the special lane could all boast
some of the essential symbols for claiming adulthood. All, for example, were in
the possession of language.

It is sometimes hard to distinguish between what can be rightfully described
as joining a sub-culture by choice, and joining a 'bureaucratic' or 'professional'
sub-culture, populated by professional staff and the group of disabled clients. Some
of the young participants in the study who came from segregated schools or classes,
such as Björg, said that they had a preference for special, rather than general,
settings, because that was where their friends were. Can it be said that they made
their choice in full knowledge of what the alternatives might be? Sometimes such
a choice was determined by what was available, and amounted to a choice between
some service and no service.

The familial dimension

The familial meaning of adulthood takes on distinctly different forms and processes
in families of most disabled youth, than it does for typical children and youth and
their families. Different families deal differently with disability (Turnbull, and Turnbull, 1997, 1978; Sætersdal, 1985, 1994). However, at least two elements seem to
impact on family relationships where there is a disabled child, which distinguishes
them from such relationships in most families of typical children and youth.

The first aspect concerns the physical work involved in caring for disabled children and youth, the bulk of which is done by mothers (Traustadóttir, 1992), creating a dependency and interdependency between the parent(s) and the child. Obviously, different individuals and different disability labels call for different types and intensity of parental work. Parental responsibilities change over time but they seldom diminish with the disabled child coming of age. Some of the work can be farmed out to paid or non-paid helpers, but parents continue to feel responsible (Ferguson, & Ferguson, 1996; Sætersdal, 1985).

A second factor relates to the typical gradual change in the relationships; a shift towards increased independence and self determination for the youth, and the reduced level of daily responsibility of the parents, negotiated as the person reaches adulthood, can become difficult to achieve in families with disabled children and youth. Parental love and concern and the routines built into family activity settings (Gallimore, et al, 1989), so necessary in the disabled child's childhood, can lock both the parents and the person with disabilities into a harmful paternalistic mode of interaction and interdependence. (Sætersdal, 1994).

Parents, as in Thór's case, who managed to build negotiations in to their relationship with their disabled child, inviting both 'dignity of risk' and the gradual increase of independence and self-determination, could support their sons' or daughters' transition to adulthood, and equip them with access to the symbols of an adult status. (Ferguson, and Ferguson, 1996). This involves encouraging and rewarding choice, empowering the disabled child to advocate for his or her own needs, attending to age appropriate interactions, and respecting the person's coming of age. In the case of Björg, parental supervision appeared to have changed much less, than in Thórs' experience. In her case, and in the case of many of the other young disabled people in the special lane, parents, in consultation with professionals, made many important and relevant decisions on behalf of the young person. As mentioned before, Björg described herself, and was described by her significant others as a 'very good girl.'

Margrét and Jóna were differently situated regarding the family dimension of adulthood. Margrét felt that both her parents were not equally behind her, one of her parents did not feel comfortable in using sign language, and Margrét confessed that she felt at times ignored, but at other times over dominated, by that parent. This had created problems in her home, spurring Margrét on to test her boundaries within her family. In Jóna's case, the shock of becoming needy like an infant, witnessing the split up of her parents, and feeling let down by the service system, disempowered her. She said that it had been almost intolerable to need help with simple activities, that she had been able to do for herself, before her accident. Having to rely so much on her mother was difficult for her, and at times she felt further disempowerment. She said that for a time she and her mother began to quarrel a lot, but that their relationship had improved again when her mother moved out of their joint home. The mother agreed with this, laughing, but explained her bitterness at how the system had failed to provide necessary support, and had shifted her daughter from one place and one service routine to another. Those people categorised as nomads indicated that they had been a burden to one or both parents, or in one case that the parents had failed them.

Interdependent adulthood and the importance of relationships

The social construction of disabled adulthood differs from that of typical adulthood along the three dimensions, personal, cultural and familial, in the relational aspects on each of these dimensions. All of the participants in the study needed support to embrace interdependence (rather than independence) to access and adopt personal and cultural symbols of adulthood. Such support must be relationally anchored to membership on the highway of mainstream society and possibly also in a disability culture of their own free choice. The young people with physical or sensory disabilities needed access to non-patronising support, to educational and economic resources, and to technical aids, in order to embrace their interdependent adult status. The young people labelled with cognitive disabilities also needed to have the symbols of adult status brought to them in an age and culturally appropriate way, through interpretations and reinterpretation. In this study, a socially constructed adulthood with a difference was within the reach of each and every one of the participants, but not everyone had the relational support at the time of the study to access that status, on the personal, cultural or familial meaning dimensions of adulthood.

Supports and hindrances on the roads to adulthood with a difference in the Icelandic culture and society

Families move and change, as the lives of their members take on new meanings, tasks and forms. When a disabled child arrives on the family stage, the life of all the members changes in significant ways from then on. New decisions have to be made, and some decisions had consequences that were more likely than others to help or hinder the disabled child reaching out for his or her adulthood. Parents have to decide, for example, whom to trust amongst experts or own social network, what resources and support to apply, and what kind of pre-school, school and summer camp to select for one's disabled child.

The parents of the young disabled people in this study had varied experiences, values and beliefs. Some had bought more fully into the individual (medical) model of disability than had others. All had been through the painful labelling process of their child's (or children's) problems (Booth, 1978), and all had been seen by professionals from within different professional paradigms. The most important forms of support were found within empowering relationships of the young person's immediate social network of family, friends and professionals. Such relationships were flexible, and changed with the disabled child's coming of age. Adequate information on rights, and on how to obtain support from the social service system and from schools were also very important. There was a need to work with professionals who had the ability to listen, and who were seen to try to help find solutions that the family and the young person were content with. Such professionals needed to care, to empower the young disabled person and his or her family, and to tread the fine line between paternalism and indifference. For some of the families in the study, however, there appeared to be some difficulties finding such a balance (Kirkebæk, 2002)

Some parents of disabled children found it difficult if not almost impossible, to change the balance of parent-child relationship over time. Some of the parents interviewed found this particularly difficult to deal with their disabled 'child' reaching milestones such as confirmation, starting upper-secondary school, becoming sexually active, finishing school, entering the world of work, and moving from the parental home. In such cases, the parental love and concern appeared at times transformed into paternalism, restricting the adult child's possibility to develop, expand his or her experiences and partake in age-appropriate activities in mainstream society or in a disability sub-culture of his or her choice. In such instances the disabled person may not have had sufficient access to the symbols involved in the communication of adulthood.

Paternalism involves a dimension of governance like that of a father wanting the best for his children. Disempowering to the disabled child or youth as that may be, the alternative extreme of indifference is worse. The balance between parental support and paternalism changes over time and from one domain to the next in their and their children's lives. It is difficult to pinpoint exactly when parental actions or attitudes stray from being supportive to becoming paternalistic. Indications of parental manipulations of grown-up children as paternalistic are in this study taken to be incidents when parents make important decisions in what they see as their child's best interests. These include decisions parents made, either behind the youth's back, or against his or her explicit will, for example decisions to have their disabled child sterilised, setting up stringent rules about their sons or daughter's interaction with friends or lovers, or withholding most or all of their sons' or daughters' money. Each of these actions inevitably reduced their child's opportunities for accessing normative relationships or activities.

The data contain some evidence of how parental love and toil get transformed into such paternalism, particularly in some of the narratives of parents' attitudes and actions concerning youth labelled cognitively disabled, but also in connection with persons differently labelled. The stories some parents told contained a mixture of love, bemusement over 'childlike' attitudes or deeds of their adult children, their trust in every body and the parents' fears of that trust being misused. These parents were particularly worried about sexual or physical abuse harming their children, and about their children's money and objects being used for foolish things or taken away. These fears are certainly not without real and scary foundations. The more the parents select from the segregated 'special service plate,' the harder it becomes for the young disabled people to embrace adulthood, in what is described as a normative way.

The gains for disabled youth enrolled mostly or only within segregated settings involved membership in the gemeinshaft of other disabled youth, at least as long as the school years and in some cases in adult services. The losses accompanied by such choices for these youth were the diminished opportunities to expand the web of relationships within general settings and experience the enrichment and stimuli from the broader culture. The data show that many of the young disabled participants in the research, who were travelling on the highway, and who were mostly or solely included in educational and other typical settings (Group A), felt isolated as they were approaching their mid teens. As Ferguson (2001) reminds us, inclusion may involve a fragile assimilation into dominant culture for at least some disabled people. The good professional should seek ways of making 'fragile' inclusion more robust, and of building or strengthening mutual interdependence between disabled and non-disabled persons. The group in the study characterised as nomads sticks out as having few important supportive relationships. Their reported sense of loneliness, powerlessness, being lost, or capitulation is heartbreaking. A quote from a young man labelled with autism sums up that group's bewilderment at the prospect of adulthood. He asked, with some surprise: 'can one become a grown up when one is autistic?'

Adulthood with a difference and the quality of life

Two overarching questions need some reflection: How does reaching adulthood with a difference relate to possible participation in mainstream society? and what are the prospects of enjoying quality of life for the young disabled participants?

The travellers on the highway were, at the time of the study, approaching adulthood with a difference and a fragile assimilation into dominant culture. The disabled people in the special lane were moving further along into a segregated protected sub-culture of the bureaucrats and the professionals, away from mainstream society. And finally, the nomads were depicted as either sitting down for a while, feeling a lack of power to determine their destination, or walking about sometimes towards the highway and sometimes towards the special lane. For the nomads, the possibility of joining the dominant culture is unclear. Out of the seven nomads, two or three seemed likely to join dominant culture eventually, but the others were unlikely to do so without massive support.

How far do these two roads, the highway and the special lane, or wandering in the wilderness, lead to a quality of life? Knowing who one is and what one wants, receiving adequate support to fulfill basic needs, and dreaming modestly are the building blocks of quality life. The interpretation of the data suggests that the interaction between inclusion and the strengthening of a disabled persons' identity go hand in hand. The young disabled people on the highway, many of whom had gone through difficult and lonely times, appeared to have a strong and normative sense of who they were as individuals. They identified with other young people with and without disability, in mainstream society. The young disabled people on the special lane, on the other hand mostly felt that they were much younger than their years. They identified with others in their special group, although some made a distinction between the talkers and the non talkers or between the wheelchair users and the ambulatory. The young people referred to as the nomads seemed much less clear about who they thought they were. Only one thing was expressed by all of them, and that was that they were a burden to their families, or a cause of difficulty and distress to their families. These young people's isolation and loneliness can be imaged as a bottomless pit.

The goals and ambitions for inclusion and full active membership in mainstream society are bound up firstly with inclusive schooling and school communities, where disabled and non disabled students learn to know each other, to share and to benefit from each others' mutual strength. After families, schools are the fountains for strong supportive social networks within the Icelandic society. Many, but not all, Icelandic children and youth find in school the threads of relationships and mutuality. By helping teachers to work towards more inclusive schools, more students will find themselves enmeshed within inclusive networks, so important to all, and so necessary for disabled students. Such strong and lasting networks are also basic elements of an ethical and democratic society.

The political and administrative focus should be altered to provide the practical and financial support necessary for disabled persons to make flexible use of available opportunities within the job and housing market, leisure and general community life. Such support must be individualised and tailored to the shifting and changing needs in individual and family lives. Commonly, available practical support provided by the Icelandic welfare system is defined in a static bureaucratic manner, or on the basis of average needs of groups of people seen to have similar syndromes or problems. Such support often ends up fitting no one well, or it is too little and too late to contribute to the quality life of disabled individuals.

Paternalistic attitudes, so often found within the special lane for disabled people, are likely to diminish when disabled people gain access to the mainstream via friends, family and other community members, and are seen to lead ordinary lives. Even the express travellers in the research could hardly hope for more than a fragile adulthood with a difference. Yet, they are great teachers to the community. They have learnt to refuse paternalism, and ask instead for relevant support to get on with their lives. The nomads can be pulled out from the wasteland on to the highway, through strong determined and supportive relationships and adequate practical support. The alternative is to remain where they are and watch their already fragile network dwindle.

The young disabled people, who at the time of the research seemed likely to remain in the special land of eternal youth, together with their parents, teachers and other professionals, require more role models of robust adult roles with a difference, to provide them with an incentive to dare step of from the special lane, and join the rest of us in the risky, but hopefully more inclusive, society. For the time being, they will be housed, looked after, fed and taken care of medically by the welfare system, as long as that does not crumble. Those who at some point in the future do not shift from the special lane are likely to have a life that is very vulnerable to changes in service ideology, personnel and co-habitants. Their freedom of choice will be more or less sacrificed in the interests of protection from the outside. For some, it may become a perfectly satisfactory life with a difference, as a childlike human being in a world, who reaches out to general culture in many ways, without becoming a fully fledged part of that world. For others, the dangers from inside that world, or the monotony of co-existing with others will make life difficult to enjoy.

REFERENCES

Andersson, Y. (1997). *Implementing inclusive education. OECD proceedings.* Paris, Organization for Economic Co-operation and Development.

Arnet, J. J. (1994). Are college students adults? Their conceptions of the transition to adulthood. *Journal of adult development,* 1, 154–168.

Barnes, C., Mercer, G. & Shakespeare, T. (1999). *Exploring disability: A sociological introduction.* Oxford, Polity.

Barton, L. & Armstrong, F. (2001). Disability, education and inclusion: Cross-cultural issues and dilemmas. In G. L. Albrecht, Seelman, K. D. & M. Bury (Eds.), *Handbook of disability studies.* Thousand Oaks: Sage.

Bjarnason, D. S. (1999). Heima er best: Thjónusta vid fatlad fólk sem býr á eigin heimili og tarf mikinn studning. *Uppeldi og menntun,* 8, 55–69.

Bjarnason, D. S. (2002a). New voices in Iceland: Parents and adult children: Juggling supports and choices in time and space. *Disability & society,* 17 (3), 307-326.

Bjarnason, D. S. (2002b). New voices in Iceland: Young adults with disabilities in Iceland: The importance of relationships and natural supports. *Scandinavian journal of disability research,* 4(2), 156–189.

Booth, T. (1978). From a normal baby to handicapped child: Unravelling the idea of subnormality in families of mentally handicapped children. *Sociology,* 12, 203–221.

Booth, T. & Booth, W. (1996). Supported parenting for people with learning difficulties: Lessons from Wiscounsin. *Representing children,* 9(2), 99–107.

Coleman, J. S. (1961). *The adolescent society: The social life of the teenager and its impact on education.* New York: Free Press of Glencoe.

Edelstein, W. (1988). *Skóli, nám, samfélag.* Reykjavík, Idunn.

Ferguson, P. M. (2001). Mapping the family. Disabilities studies and the exploration of parental reponses to disability. In . G. L. Albrecht, K. D Seelman, & M. Bury *Handbook of disability studies.* Thousand Oaks: Sage.

Ferguson, D. L. & Ferguson, P. M. (1993). The promise of adulthood. In M. Snell (Ed.), *Instruction of students with severe disabilities.* Columbus, OH: Macmillan.

Ferguson, D. L. & Ferguson, P. M. (1996). Communicating adulthood. *Topics in Language Disorders,* 16(3), 52–67.

Gallimore, R., Weisner, T. S., Kaufman, S. Z. & Bernheimer, L. P. (1989). The social construction of ecocultural niches: Family accommodation of developmentally delayed children. *American journal of mental retardation,* 94, 216–230.

Glaser, P. and Strauss, A. (1967).*The discovery of grounded theory:* Strategies for Qualitative Research. Chicago, IL: Aldine Publishing Co.

Gudmundsson, G. (1984). *Let's rock this town: Subcultural production of subjectivitet.* Copenhagen: Sociological Institute.

Gustavsson, A. (1999). *Inifrån utanförskapet: Oma at vara annorlunda och delaktig.* Stockholm: Johansson and Skyttmo förlag.

Högsbro, K., Kirkebæk, B., Blom, S. V. & Danö, E. (1999). *Ungdom, utvikling og handicap.* Copenhagen: Samfundsliteratur.

Kirkebæk, B. (2002). Det onde og det gode – om forholdet mellem paternalisme og ligegyldighed. In B. Sætersdal and K. Hegger (Eds.) *I den beste hensikt? 'Ondskab' i behandlingssamfunnet*Aknibe: Gjövik.

Kristjánsson, B. (2001). *Barndomen och den sociala moderniseringen: Om att vaxa upp i Norden pa troskeln till ett nytt millennium.* Stockholm:HSL forlag.

Marshall, T. H. (1973). *Class, citizenship and social development.* Westport: Greenwood Press.

Nielsen, L. (1991). *Adolescence: A contemporary view.* Florida: Holt, Rinehart and Winston Inc.

Oliver, M. (1990). *The Politics of Disablement.* Basingstoke, Macmillan.

Óskarsdóttir, G. (1995). *The forgotten half: Comparison of dropouts and graduates in their early work experience: The Icelandic case.* California: University of Berkley.

Reindal, S. M. (1998). *Disability, personal autonomy and the subject: A dilemma in special needs education.* Oslo: Oslo University.

Sætersdal, B. (1985). *Når veiene skilles: Samtaler med foreldre som har utviklingshemmede barn på institusjon.* Oslo: Universitetsforlaget.

Sætersdal, B. (1994). *Menneskekeskjebner i HVPU-reformens tid: Livshistorier og sosiale forandringer.* Oslo: Universitetsforlaget.

Shakespeare, T., Gillespie-Sells, K.&Davis, D. (1996). *The sexual politics of disability: Untold desires.* London: Cassell.

Sigurjónsdóttir, H. B. & Traustadóttir, R. (2000). Motherhood, family and community life. In . R. Traustadóttir and K. Johnson (Eds.), *Women with intellectual disabilities: Finding a place in the world.* London: Jessica Kingsley Publishers.

Traustadóttir, R. (1992). *Disability reform and the social role of women: Community inclusion and caring work.* New York State: Syracuse University.

Turnbull, A. P. & Turnbull, H. R. (1997). *Families, professionals and exceptionality: A special partnership.* Upper Saddle River, NJ: Merrill.

Turnbull, A. P. & Turnbull, H. R. (1978). *Parents speak out: Views from the other side of the two-way mirror.* Columbus, Ohio: Charles E. Merrill.

GWYNNED LLOYD

7 INCLUSION AND PROBLEM GROUPS: THE STORY OF ADHD

INTRODUCTION

This chapter considers an issue which challenges our thinking about inclusion. Attention Deficit Hyperactivity Disorder (ADHD) has become quickly accepted as a 'disorder' in Britain, with rapidly increasing rates of diagnosis and prescription rates, and follows a pattern well established in the USA and Australia. The chapter will discuss the presentation of ADHD in the press, in books aimed at parents, on the net and in academic books and papers. I will argue that the information and advice available to parents and teachers is often a crude simplification of a complex issue. This raises the question of how such complex issues can be represented to teachers and parents, so that they may develop a critical awareness of the broader context. I will suggest that the story of ADHD shows how medical and special educational policy is influenced by well organised pressure groups of academics, professionals and parents, often supported by the vested interests of pharmaceutical companies. Finally I discuss the challenge for thinking about inclusion when young people and parents assert their rights to have a medical diagnosis.

A NORMALISED CONCEPT

The existence of ADHD is now widely accepted in Britain. Large numbers of children and young people are identified as suffering from the disorder and are prescribed medication, often multiple medication (Kewley, 1999). Teachers, parents, classroom assistants, and educational psychologists all know about the condition. Articles, as well as jokes and cartoons, are found regularly in the press. Somehow, in just over a decade, it has gone from being an obscure term from an American Psychiatric lexicon, not used by professionals in Britain, to part of everyday discourse and a label that can be used by teachers to describe a child. One Scottish primary school teacher, for example, said: 'I've got a class of 20 with three ADHDs, one ADD and a Tourette's.' The normalisation of the concept can be seen from articles in the professional press. The Times Educational Supplement Scotland quotes the tragic case of a young person with ADHD who was permanently excluded from school and is now brain damaged as a result of hanging himself. An educational psychologist in the same article describes the approach in her authority, saying: 'It's a spectrum disorder and children with ADHD are all different.' An advisor is

J. Allan (ed.), Inclusion, Participation and Democracy: What is the Purpose?, 105-115.
© 2003 *Kluwer Academic Publishers. Printed in the Netherlands.*

quoted as saying: 'We're keen to get the message across that this is a disability, not a child who is trying to annoy you' (TESS, 2000). So it is a 'disability,' a 'disorder' its existence as a discrete, measurable phenomenon is accepted even though 15 years ago we had never heard of it.

An increasing consensus

In an article which analysed press coverage of ADHD (Norris & Lloyd, 2000), we argued that professionals speaking about ADHD, and quoted in the press, adopted three broad positions. The most frequently quoted were those who represent a unproblematic view of ADHD as a clear, measurable, clinical disorder, significantly under diagnosed in Britain, and manageable through medication. One of the most prominent is Kewley (1999), a consultant paediatrician who also runs a specialist clinic and who says that 'Attention deficit hyperactivity disorder is internationally recognised as a problem of brain dysfunction with associated educational, behavioural and other difficulties' (p. 23) He also claims that 'research shows that it is a genetic, inherited condition that can be effectively managed' (ibid, 2001, p. 1). Kewley argues that the evidence for a largely biological explanation is very strong and accepted by most experts, especially from North America and Australia and that, in the UK, very few children are being effectively managed medically for 'what is essentially a medical condition' (op cit., p. 27).

The second position is held by those who accepted some idea of ADHD or hyperkinetic disorder but who expressed caution about the risks of over diagnosis and over-prescription. US and Australian estimates of prevalence were not accepted. These are often British psychiatrists or paediatricians who are used to working with the idea of hyperkinetic disorder, previously the standard British diagnosis. Hyperkinetic disorder is listed in the World Health Organisation's International Classification of Diseases (ICD), which was predominant in Europe until recently. ADHD comes from the US classification of the American Psychiatric Association Diagnostic and Statistical Manual IV.

There has been a clear conflating of these two positions, with those from the more extremely 'pro' position strategically moderating their expressed opinion somewhat. In addition, the more moderate objections seem to have been swept away in the process of acceptance and professional normalising of the concept. This is quite apparent, for example, in the newly published British Psychological Guidelines on successful multi-agency working (BPS, 2000). A third group of commentators are those who are much more critical of the concept of ADHD and who have looked for broader reasons for this apparent epidemic and opposed the large-scale use of drug therapy.

In a recent issue of *The Psychologist*, the professional journal of educational psychologists in Britain, there was a 'head to head' debate between two exponents of different views, Paul Cooper and the late Steve Baldwin (Baldwin & Cooper, 2000). Cooper's position appears to be very moderate but somewhat disingenuous in that he argues against an oversimplification, but yet in the end he does not consider the broader criticisms and has also been associated, in print and on conference platforms, with many of its most uncritical proponents. Cooper has been by far the most prolific prominent academic writer on ADHD in education. He convened the working group and contributed substantially to the recent British Psychological Society Guidelines on multi-agency working (BPS, 2000). The recently edited volume, *ADHD Research, Practice and Opinion*, is almost entirely written by uncritical proponents, for example, Kewley and Detweiler, who contend that children are being let down by not recognising ADHD more and by not using medication (Cooper & Bilton, 1999). In the Psychologist debate, however, Cooper appears critical of supposedly over simplistic positions, making careful qualifications about research evidence. Whether the disorder develops and the nature of its development depend on the complex interactions between the molecular level, the cellular level and the organism in the external environment. This interaction makes it entirely disingenuous to frame a discussion around the simplistic dichotomy of whether 'ADHD is a biological brain dysfunction – this is inaccurate and misleading. ADHD is best understood as a biopsychosocial problem and the 'bio' is in there because the research evidence indicates that it is an important factor' (Cooper in Baldwin & Cooper, 2000, p. 599).

Baldwin, in contrast, suggests that the issue is really social control, not clinical intervention:

> There are no reliable scientific criteria for making an ADHD diagnosis. Judgements are made by parents, teachers and medical personnel using unreliable and invalid checklists ... In the UK psychiatrists, paediatricians and psychologists have colluded with the pharmaceutical industry to maintain the fiction that ADHD is a biochemical brain dysfunction best treated with amphetamines. (Baldwin in Baldwin & Cooper, 2000, p. 598)

Baldwin argues that the diagnosis of ADHD is based on subjective observation and that hyperactivity disorders are 'reversible, socially constructed conditions, optimally treated with psychosocial interventions and never with amphetamines' (op cit, p. 599). He refers to concerns about the prescription of powerful amphetamines to children, to the problems associated with multiple medication and to the reported side-effects. He quotes the North American psychologist Breggin, who has campaigned for an end to the mass identification of children with ADHD and drug treatment (Breggin and Cohen, 1999). Baldwin is critical of the 'biopsychosocial approach' of Cooper, arguing that all disorders have some biological component and that the real challenge is to provide effective psychosocial intervention alternatives that work for children and their families (Baldwin in Baldwin & Cooper, 2000).

According to Cooper and most of the current professional literature, there appears to be a carefully constructed professional consensus – it is a biopsychosocial disorder which should be treated using a multi-modal, multidisciplinary approach which may involve the use of drugs, but of course we are all aware of the dangers of over-prescription. A careful reading of the recent British Psychological Society Guidelines suggests that this careful professional consensus really conceals a considerable level of acceptance of a highly uncritical view. The Guidelines make the usual qualifications about there being disagreements over the concept of ADHD but then go on, for example, to make frequent reference to 'the nature of ADHD,' dismissing the criticisms.

The ADHD diagnosis refers to a social phenomenon of large-scale proportions with international estimates of prevalence ranging from one to six percent of the child population (Tannock, 1998). It has received widespread public attention and continues to be the subject of a great deal of controversy. Much of this is focused on aetiology and the diagnosis of ADHD as a distinct clinical category. This is despite the fact that there is a powerful body of research evidence to support the validity of the condition (BPS, 2000).

The reading list at the end contains none of the most critical publications from either the USA or Britain, but consists largely of articles and books written by well known proponents of ADHD. This contrasts withthe earlier publication by the BPS which referred in more open way to the idea of an evolving concept (BPS, 1996). It seems that the concept has rapidly evolved in the last 4 years into a widely accepted and used label.

Labels of forgiveness

According to Cooper and to the ADHD support organisations, there seems to be a simple choice between accepting the validity of the concept and diagnostic procedures of ADHD and blaming parents for bad parenting. At a more fundamental level, an informed diagnosis of ADHD challenges the deeply embedded and pernicious belief that deviant behaviour in young people is always either primarily volitional in nature or the product of neglectful or deviant parenting (Cooper in Baldwin & Cooper, 2000, p.5 99). This is often emphasised in the parent support organisation leaflets and on web sites, for example in this extract:

> *An excuse for bad parenting.*
> How many times in the course of trying to get help for our children do we come up against this old chestnut? Often, from the very people we have gone to for help! In actual fact, parents of ADHD children are often BETTER parents because of all the difficulties they have had face ... Often though, it is not the challenging behaviour which causes the greatest issues for us, it is the knock-on effects of the behaviour. For example, having to go into school repeatedly to apologise for the child's difficulties, trouble with neighbours who sometimes just have these children down as *bad uns*. Having psychologists and psychiatrists who we have gone to for help, doubt our word and listen, but not hear and understand what we tell them. If bad parenting causes ADHD, what then accounts for the fact that often there are other children in the same family who are perfectly well behaved and/or normal, who have never in their lives had any sort of behavioural difficulty? (ADHD – UK – support web-site).

The literature produced by these organisations and their conference presentations demonstrate the enthusiastic over-simplification of some of the language and the models of ADHD offered to professionals and parents. A report on the web-site of the Third Annual ADDISS Conference, *ADHD Across the Spectrum*, included an account by a nurse who attended the conference . I have included a great deal of it, as it seems to me to be a clear example of how the information is put across and understood by professionals at such conferences. My own observations are in square brackets. I intend no particular criticism of this writer, who is understandably reflecting what she has been told at the conference.

I'm Glad You Asked

Written by Jane Wood, Student Nurse, Lancashire

The conference on ADHD started with a dedication to a Scottish adolescent sufferer who only a few days before had been found hanging in his bedroom by his mum and was currently on life support. I went knowing nothing and I couldn't begin to tell you all the complexities I have learned about ADHD. I attended workshops and seminars relating to ADHD what it is and what it is not. Ritalin and other medications, what they are and how they work. The myths surrounding medication and why they are wrong.

[Definitions are apparently unproblematic – 'what it is'. Criticisms of medication are 'wrong']

The co-morbidities of ADHD of which there are many. The genetics involved in ADHD ... I learned about techniques for handling these children in school and home situations. I listened to parents, some who have one, two or even in one case, three children with this condition. I noticed how some were incredibly bitter with the support systems (health, social services, education, remand) while others were harnessing that energy and using it constructively. (This whole conference was a result of parent power.) I heard a member of the audience – a seventeen year old's – heart rendering accounts of struggling against an education system full of ignorant, prejudiced teachers who labelled and insulted her and how she succeeded against all odds to prove them wrong. (she's a small minority I bet).

[Brave parents and children struggling for a diagnosis against ignorant professionals]

The speakers were amazing. Paediatricians, Researchers, psychologists, parents, teachers from across the world. Australia is leading the field at the moment and they have really got their act together compared to England. Other countries do it right. Sophisticated interdisciplinary working structures are in place and used and help prevent parents from waiting years in frustration, feeling isolated and ostracised into the bargain, (until they finally get a diagnosis- 'ADHD' for their child, only to find that the average professional doesn't know what to do for the child with that condition (ADDISS, undated).

The conference presentation described by this nurse is very typical of the standard model for ADHD conferences. Definitions are represented as unproblematic – we know 'what it is.' Criticisms of medication are just 'wrong'. Brave parents are

described as struggling for a diagnosis against professionals who are ignorant, old
fashioned and unwilling to accept the clear weight of evidence – the facts of ADHD.
Other countries do it properly but Britain lags behind. So conferences like this set
out to inform relevant professionals about the 'facts' of ADHD and the 'myths'
– ie criticisms of drug use. Speakers tend to be from the USA and from Australia.
Several speakers from the USA contribute regularly to conferences in Britain; often
they are academics or psychologists who operate private consultancies in this field.
The constant suggestion is that the Americans and the Australians are getting it
right by diagnosing more children and prescribing more drugs.

What is missing from such accounts?

There is no mention of the range of criticisms made in those countries, or of the
US Drug Enforcement Agency and International Narcotics Control Board, both of
whom have frequently stated their concerns about over-prescription in the USA, or
that methylphenidate hydrochloride (MPH, often marketed as Ritalin) is frequently
stolen and sold and used illegally (Lloyd & Norris, 1999). The British press and
literature for teachers and parents does not mention the class actions currently in
process in three American states against the drug manufacturers. Equally there is
often no mention that, although there is much research evidence in the USA of the
short term efficacy of (MPH), that most organisations, even those which support
ADHD, admit the absence of wider long-term studies (NICE, 2000; McCubbin &
Cohen, 1999) Much of the research into the effectiveness of medication such as
MPH has been American. There is almost no discussion of the validity of import-
ing, not only a concept developed in a particular cultural context, but applying the
research findings to a different populations.

   The English National Institute for Clinical Excellence (NICE) guidelines on the
use of MPH, which are in general quite positive about its use, do make important
qualifications, but these are often ignored in the literature aimed at parents and
teachers. A large number of randomised controlled trials (RCTs) of methylphenidate
has been conducted. However, this evidence is predominantly from the US and
does not necessarily generalise to a UK context. (NICE, 2000). The guidelines
also say:

> 4.1 The ultimate measure of the effectiveness of methylphenidate is the over-
>   all long-term impact on the health and well being of children and their
>   families. In practice, this is difficult to measure, and no such data were
>   identified in the review of evidence that accompanied this appraisal.
>
> 4.7 Evidence from placebo-controlled clinical trials (n=1257) shows that
>   common side effects of methylphenidate are relatively mild and short-
>   lived, and that more severe side effects are very rare. However, these
>   data are based on treatment and follow-up of less than one year. None of
>   the studies included assessment of longer-term side effects or the risk of
>   addiction or abuse with methylphenidate (Section 4.2).

It is well established that manufacturers' and medical advice on the prescription and monitoring are often ignored in the USA and in Britain. In his study, Baldwin found children in their early teens who had been prescribed psychostimulants continuously for seven or eight years and other children who had been first prescribed MPH at three four or five in direct contravention of manufacturers' guidelines (Baldwin & Cooper, 2000).

There is a substantial critical literature in the USA, and now some in the UK, concerned about the validity of the concept, diagnosis and prescription rates, substance misuse, and the lack of monitoring (Wright, 1997; Baldwin, 2000). These concerns, however, are often ignored. The US study of intervention that is most often quoted is the MTA study, the Multimodal Treatment Study for ADHD sponsored by the National Institute for Mental Health. This study is claimed by proponents to be the definitive proof of the effectiveness of medication. At a Scottish conference in 2001, organised by a parents support group, speaker after speaker from the USA quoted this study with certainty. None of them acknowledged the very substantial criticisms made, for example by the US writers Breggin and Cohen, who identify substantial methodological flaws in the study. (Breggin, 2002; Breggin & Cohen, 1999). The bookstall did not feature their works.

The failure of many ADHD organisations and proponents to acknowledge criticisms is criticised by the North American writers McCubbin and Cohen (1999):

> An ethical analysis of intrusive interventions upon vulnerable persons is obligated, at the least, to acknowledge the counterclaims of those disputing the facts used to support the interventions. This is particularly true where those agents with resources to create and disseminate facts have a special interest in maintaining the viewpoint ...Today, resources and power to create and disseminate viewpoints regarding ADHD and MPH lie primarily in the hands of medical research, pharmaceutical and educational industries (p. 459).

The literature and information available to parents and to professionals in Britain today often fails to acknowledge the 'counterclaims' of a more critical perspective. They silence them by refusing to recognise that there is a debate, by asserting that the 'facts' are clear.

How did the normalisation of ADHD happen?

There is a complex range of factors to be considered in trying to make sense of the rise and rise of ADHD from the early 1990s (Lloyd & Norris, 1999; Norris & Lloyd, 2000). These include the campaigning of parents groups, their alliances with enthusiastic professionals, and the establishment of private clinics and consultancies offering diagnoses, support and information. Access to information about ADHD in the media and on the Internet has become much easier and information from US web sites is available to parents and professionals in Britain. This information often draws on US parent support groups, who are heavily funded by the manufactures of medication and the Internet removes an expert intermediary, such as a pharmacist or physician, from the physical, regulatory and scientific 'spaces' between individuals and medications (Cohen et al, 2001)

In the early 1990s, methyphenidate in the commercial form Ritalin began to be remarketed in Britain. At the same time, we saw the development of the quasi-market in education, pressures on schools created by league tables and an increase in the use of exclusion from school. The funding mechanisms in education authorities for special educational support often encouraged the identification of proper 'syndromes.' There is also evidence in professional practice of a confusion of discourses within mental health, educational and social welfare which leads to a loose labelling of pupils, in which terms are used without clear understanding or shared definition (Lloyd & Norris 1999).

Desperate parents looking for labels of forgiveness found that diagnoses offered support not blame and an associated entitlement to financial benefits, eg Disabled Living allowance if ADHD is medically diagnosed. From the 1980s onward, there had been an increasing diversity of social inequality in Britain and an increase in the numbers of children and families living in poverty. As in the USA, there was in Britain a growing use of illegal drugs by young people and by young parents. In Scotland, there has recently been a large increase in children referred to the Children's Hearing System, the welfare based decision making system, on the grounds of parental neglect, particularly associated with hard drug using parents. There is a particular contradiction here, of course, in the increasing medication of school children alongside a 'just say no to drugs' policy in the community.

CHILDREN'S VOICES

There is an enormous volume of research on ADHD, almost all of it within the medical or positivist psychological tradition including hundreds of, still not conclusive, controlled trials of drug treatment. There is very little research which expresses the voice of children and young people. There are some accounts, sometimes tragic in their focus, such as that written before suicide by a young man ('Frank,' 1999). However the accounts published tend to be those of 'sufferers,' selected to support arguments for increasing diagnosis. There is a growing research literature on childhood which sees children as active in the construction of their own social experiences (James et al, 1997). The literature on children with ADHD rarely represents them as active in the negotiation of their life, but more often as determined by a biological condition. If we can continue to be critical of the use in practice of the concept ADHD, then we need research of a different kind. We need the highly critical research that Baldwin and colleagues were engaged in, but we also need research that suggests we are listening empathetically to the voices of children and parents. We should be developing research that emphasises the children's humanity, explores their resources and their strategies in negotiating and influences what happens to them in school.

CONCLUSION

Whether or not the concept of ADHD exists as a discrete, measurable phenomenon, it is nonetheless clear that a lot of people want it to be. Some of these are professionals with axes to grind; some are pharmacological companies with profits to maintain; some are teachers looking for help or who wish to see children dealt with elsewhere; some seem to be parents who feel that the educational and medical support services were letting them down. Thomas & Loxley talk of 'the entrapment of children in a cocoon of professional help' (2001, p53). They and others argue that a confusion of psychological models leads to a supposedly therapeutic approach that is really about control, about the response of schools to unacceptable behaviour and the maintenance of order (Thomas & Loxley, 2001; Slee, 2001). The logic of this approach is to see ADHD as the stigmatising and medicalising of simply naughty behaviour in the interests of the school. This may be as simplistic as the claims of the ADHD lobby.

I am arguing for a continued effort to challenge the uncritical acceptance of a simple model of ADHD and the trend towards the medication of children with challenging behaviour in Britain. The difficulty for those who wish to make this challenge is that the medical approach is so apparently simple and uncomplicated. The more critical position argues for a greater complexity of factors in understanding why children's actions should be seen in this way and that is more difficult to explain to children, parents and teachers: at the moment this position is losing the argument. In making sense of the actions of an individual child or young person, of course, it may be helpful to consider individual developmental, family, school and other social and environmental aspects. To suggest that an understanding of how a child acts in school sometimes involves discussing with parents how the children are in their family is not necessarily to adopt a 'blame the parent' position. However, it is clear that many parents do feel blamed by educational professionals. An alliance of parents, professionals (mainly medical) and academics has been highly effective in promoting a disorder which appears to offer forgiveness, support and respite, but seems to point us in the direction of the USA where the behaviour of millions of children is explained in terms of psychiatric disorder and where many are treated through clinical intervention, particularly by the use of drugs. This has not, however, led in the USA to a school system free of disruption and violence, nor has it led to a reduction of the numbers of children requiring support. On the contrary, the rate of school dropout in many US states is increasing.

There is a critical challenge to our thinking about inclusion in the story of ADHD, where children may require a disordered identity in order to feel supported. Much literature on inclusion contrasts medical and rights discourses, which 'avoid pathologising individual's deficits' (Allan, 1999, p 16). Medical discourses are seen to be produced by self interested professionals and not in the best interests of the children. There is an uncomfortable paradox for us when parents assert the right to a label and to a medical diagnosis. Slee (2001) argues that:

> The problem for the school is one of working out how to fit different kids
> in with a minimum of disruption ...Teacher education needs to explore new
> forms of knowledge about identity and difference and to suggest new ques-
> tions that invite students to consider the pathologies of schools that enable
> or disable students (pp. 173–174).

Our goals for inclusion should not include a reproduction of the dividing practices
of special education but should be about identifying the pathologies of schools. They
should not deny the anxieties and fears of parents and children and the existence
of real personal troubles. In an analysis of the social processes of schooling, we
have perhaps denied the powerfulness of individual experience and feeling (Furlong,
1991) The literature on ADHD, in its offer of straightforward help, is attractive to
families and children who are experiencing difficulties.

An ethical approach to inclusion must recognise and acknowledge that some
children and families experience difficulties and are looking for support. At the moment, they are getting this support through an inappropriate medicalised approach.
The labels of forgiveness appeal in contrast with the punitive approach associated
with the label 'disruptive.' If parents and pupils themselves feel that they are
struggling and need help, then an inclusive school would respond to this. It must,
however, be possible to show parents and young people that there are significant
drawbacks and dangers in the medicalised route; that they are not being given the
full story of ADHD; that such labels do serve controlling purposes for institutions
like schools; that medication makes huge profits for the drug companies; and that
supportive schools need not resort to the old dividing practices of special education.
If we are to propose an alternative to medication, we must discuss how to help the
children. We need to develop an approach to supporting young people, as human
subjects, which recognises the drawbacks of an individualising approach – one that
acknowledges the social construction of deviance but which offers practitioners a
way to work children in difficulty.

Attention Deficit Hyperactivity Disorder is a simple, medical name for a
complex phenomenon, involving individual human beings in a web of knowledge
and information, labels and professional interests. At the moment, information for
parents and professionals is dominated by a simplistic view of ADHD as a condition
'cured' by medication. It is important that we acknowledge the complexity of factors
which underpin its rapid rise and that our explication of this process is helpful in
creating a critical perspective available to parents, young people and professionals.
We need to listen to their views and explore ways of supporting and helping them,
that acknowledge their troubles without over-professionalising them.

REFERENCES

ADHD (UK) Support Website (undated) An excuse for bad parenting. Retrieved on March
   1, 2002, from http://home.freeuk.net/theadhdgazette/recognise.html.
ADDISS (undated) I'm glad you asked. Retrieved on March 1, 2002, from http:
   //www.addiss.co.uk/Conference%20comments.html.

Allan, J. (1999). *Actively Seeking Inclusion: pupils with special needs in mainstream schools.* London: Falmer.

Baldwin, S. & Cooper, P. (2000). How should ADHD be treated? Head to Head. *The Psychologist,* 13 (12), 598–602.

British Psychological Society (1996). Attention Deficit Hyperactivity Disorder (ADHD). *A psychological response to an evolving concept.* Leicester: British Psychological Society.

British Psychological Society (2000). *Attention Deficit Hyperactivity Disorder: Guidelines and principles for successful multi-agency working.* Leicester: British Psychological Society.

Breggin, C. and Cohen, D. (1999). *Your drug may be your problem. How and why to stop taking psychotropic medication.* Cambridge MA: Perseus Books.

Breggin, P. (2002). A Critical analysis of the NIMH multimodal treatment study for Attention- Deficit Hyperactivity Disorder (The MTA Study). Retrieved February 18, 2002, from http://www.breggin.com/mta.html.

Cohen, D. McCubbin, M. Collin, J. & Perodeau, G. (2001). Medications as social phenomena. *Health* 5(4), 441-469.

Cooper, P. & Bilton. S. (1999). *ADHD: Research practice and opinion.* London: Whurr

'Frank, J' (1999). Struggles with an inebriated horse: The pain of having ADHD. In P. Cooper & S. Bilton *ADHD: Research Practice and Opinion.* London: Whurr.

Furlong, V.J. (1991). Disaffected Pupils: Reconstructing the sociological perspective. *British Journal of Sociology of Education,* 12(3), 293–307.

James, A., Jenks, A., & Prout, A. (1997). *Theorising childhood.* Cambridge: Polity Press

Kewley, G. (1999). *Attention Deficit Hyperactivity Disorder: Recognition, reality and resolution.* London: David Fulton.

Kewley, G. (2001) Personal paper: Attention Deficit Hyperactivity Disorder is underdiagnosed and undertreated in Britain. Retrieved November 16, 2001, from http://bmj.com/cgi/content/full/316/7144/1594.

Lloyd, G. & Norris, C. (1999). Including ADHD? *Disability and Society,* 14(4), 505 –507.

McCubbin, M. and Cohen, D. (1999). *Empirical, ethical and political perspectives on the use of methylphenidate.* Ethical Human Sciences and Services.

National Institute for Clinical Excellence (2000). *Guidance on the Use of Methylphenidate for ADHD.* National Institute for Clinical Excellence.

Norris, C. & Lloyd, G. (2000). Parents, professionals and ADHD. *European Journal of Special Needs Education,* 15(2), 123–137.

Slee, R. (2001). Social justice and the changing directions in educational research: The case of inclusive education. *International Journal of Inclusive Education,* 5(2/3), 167–178.

TESS (2000) Crying out for attention. Times Educational Supplement Scotland. 1 December. Retrieved on February 1, 2002, from http://www.tes.co.uk/scotland/news/.

Thomas,G. & Loxley, A. (2001). *Deconstructing special education and constructing inclusion.* Buckingham: Open University Press.

Wright, S. (1997). A little understood solution to a vaguely defined problem: Parental perceptions of Ritalin. *Educational and Child Psychology,* 14(1), 50–59.

LINDA WARE

8 WORKING PAST PITY: WHAT WE MAKE OF DISABILITY IN SCHOOLS

I'm telling people about a child in trouble. If it's pity, we'll get some money. I'm just giving you the facts. Pity? You don't want to be pitied? And yet you're crippled in a wheelchair? Then just stay in your house. (Jerry Lewis, Chairman and host of the Annual Muscular Dystrophy Association Telethon, the CBS Morning Show, May 20, 2001).

I am not asking for pity. I am telling you about impairment ... I am not asking for pity. I am telling you about disability (Eli Claire, author and poet, Exile & Pride: Disability, Queerness and Liberation, 1999).

Democracy demands wisdom and vision in its citizens (National Foundation on the Arts and the Humanities Act of 1963).

INTRODUCTION

This chapter describes one component of *A Collaborative Inquiry on Under-standing Disability in Secondary and Post-Secondary Setting*, a two year project funded by the National Endowment for the Humanities (NEH). Participants were introduced to humanities-based disability studies through structured activities that included a disability studies lecture series featuring well known disability studies scholars; six collaborative inquiry dialogues convened with university and secondary teachers; and a curriculum development component for secondary teachers. At the heart of the project was the belief that Mitchell and Snyder (2000) have articu-lated, based on the insights of Henri-Jacques Stiker (1999), that 'the query about disabled people's integration is not enough – we must press instead for recognition of disability as integral to cultural understanding' (p. 178). The focus here is on the development of a disability studies curriculum for secondary students, designed by teachers in a project inspired by scholarship emerging from humanities-based disability studies. Emphasis is placed on the K-12 educators' reflections on, and interactions with, the content, the development of curriculum and the forms of engagement and participation signaled by this project in support of inclusion. I begin with a brief overview of humanities-based disability studies followed by a description of the project. In the conclusion, I consider how inclusion, informed by humanities-based disability studies, will demand engagement with, and the embrace of ideas, rather than the application of skills and the implementation of prescriptive models.

J. Allan (ed.), Inclusion, Participation and Democracy: What is the Purpose?, 117-137.

LOCATING THE FIELD OF HUMANITIES-BASED DISABILITY STUDIES

Over the past several decades, disability studies has attained legitimate academic status amid ongoing and unresolved debates about its origins, purposes, and pursuits. Thus before I introduce humanities-based disability studies, I briefly consider the broader field of disability studies. Most scholars trace the origins of disability studies on both sides of the Atlantic to activism initiated by disabled people (Albrecht et al, 2001). Its academic home in the US was initially in the social sciences, where, despite strict adherence to normative methods and models, the field drew from a diversity of scholarship. Numerous overviews of the field exist, many of which explore the academic debates that continue to inform disability studies (e.g., Barnes, 1999; 2002; Gleeson, 1999; Linton, 1998a, 1998b; Longmore & Umanksy, 2001, Pfeiffer & Yoshida, 1995; Ware, 2001). For some, the need for precise language and definitions remains even though national boundaries, international debates, disability categories, meaningfulness of models, and cultural readiness to challenge disability-negative positions complicate such demands. The recently published *Handbook of Disability Studies* (Albrecht, Seelman & Bury, 2001) reveals the breadth of this scholarship in thirty-four chapters, with contributions from international and inter-disciplinary scholars in varied fields, including advocacy, anthropology, economics, education, English, ethics, film studies, literary criticism, philosophy, policy studies, political science, psychology, and sociology. Although no claims are made to suggest this is the definitive work, it does reflect current thinking about disability studies and the editors attempt to situate the field despite the 'diverse historical, theoretical, advocacy, political, and cultural forces [that] influence how disability is expressed and represented' (p. 3). The breadth of scholarship confirms that the trajectory of disability studies scholarship remains difficult to predict, given that it includes issues related to access, architecture, geography, employment, religion, identity, sexuality, representation, personal meanings of disability, and strategies for empowerment and activism, to name but a few.

HUMANITIES-BASED DISABILITY STUDIES

Humanities-based disability studies also thrives on interdisciplinarity and thus promises to deliver even greater complexity to the field of disability studies. Although some might suggest that greater complexity amounts to a threat, rather than a promise, as an educator who borrows from disability studies and humanities-based disability studies to inform education, I urge otherwise. Because education has similar roots in the social sciences, the appeal of humanities-based disability studies is that it affords the exploration of disability as a product of cultural, rather than purely biological, forces. That is:

> Unlike the social sciences, humanities scholarship provides the opportunity to better define and comprehend the lives of historically prominent disabled people and collective disability experiences. Likewise, it enables comparisons across histories and between cultures. Artistic and literary materials afford

ideal locations for re-tracing the divergent institutional and communal histories that inform what we recognised as disability today (Mitchell et al, 2002, p. 2).

Elsewhere, I suggest that educators have too often shuffled through the steps of poorly choreographed compliance routines in the absence of articulation of their own beliefs-in-action (Ware,1998; 2002a). As a consequence, disability is cast in the narrowest terms of human understanding – impediment, limitation, deficiency, dependency, needs – most of which connote pity. Today, educators must grapple with the larger meaning of social inclusion while simultaneously enacting personal beliefs in response to the mass relocation of previously segregated students into their classrooms. Their demands for skills, tools, and tricks underscore the fact that educators remain without moorings in the face of inclusion. Furthermore, in the absence of understanding disability as part of our shared human experience, more pernicious claims of privilege and entitlement often underwrite educators' assumptions for exclusion. That is, when arguments turn on the preservation of segregated systems because some students 'don't belong' or others pose 'too great a threat to the fair and equitable allocation of instructional resources,' it becomes evident that a significant shift in standpoint is needed to succeed with inclusion.

In this chapter, I describe how twelve teachers re-examined the meaning of disability through a humanities lens, one that challenges the hegemony of the dominant reductionist view of disability as deficiency. I suggest such an approach is a potential way to imagine disability otherwise, but caution that this shift in standpoint will not be easily attained. Reductionism has long served special education in its hunt for disability (Baker, 2002; Campbell, 2000), and special education has long served general education as the sorting mechanism to ensure that education be preserved for some, but not all, children (Barton, 1987; Sarason, 1996; Skrtic, 1991; 1995; Slee, 2001; Tomlinson, 1982). For Campbell (2000), the challenge amounts to nothing less than overcoming ontology as 'matters ontological (the thinkable and unthinkable) are inextricably bound up with the politics of inclusion' (p. 309). In her analysis, disability incites more than fear and apprehensiveness towards that which is foreign or strange – but rather a depth of fear that 'posits *disability* as negative space corporeally out-of-bounds – a deep-seated *misoanomalia* that places *disabled bodies* at the edge of the abyss, pushing the limits of human subjectivity – an outlaw ontology' (ibid).

HUMANITIES-BASED DISABILITY STUDIES AND EDUCATION

The promise of humanities-based disability studies is that it purposefully seeks to re-imagine disability by challenging our collective stories about disability. Because our earliest lessons begin in schools, retracing the divergent institutional and communal histories that inform the varied construct we recognise as disability ensures that schooling will be scrutinised. Although there are but a few scholars writing on disability studies in education, this scholarship challenges the overly deterministic discourses of cure, care, failure, impairment, perfection, and regulation as each relates to policy, curriculum, parenting, and cultural difference (e.g., Erevelles, 2000, 2002; Ferguson, 2001; Peters, 1993; Ware, 2001, 2002). More recently, Bernadette Baker (in press) considers the promise of disability studies to disrupt and 'disorganise' education in general, and curriculum in particular. Baker offers a typology of the tropes utilised in the disability studies literature, which she traces to four sites: historical, sociological, anthropological, and critical legal theory:

> Disability Studies presents convoluted and productive liaisons with and de-
> partures from existing curriculum studies scholarship, troubling traditional
> notions of curriculum planning in some ways, demonstrating similar ethical
> commitments and theoretical tools to curriculum history and Reconceptualist
> theorising in others, and contributing unique insights based on the specificity
> of the focus that have not arisen within the domains of curriculum history,
> curriculum theory, or curriculum planning (p. 3).

Further, in the instance of special education she criticises the unreflective development of IEPs for adjusting curricula to defect and contends that:

> Perceptions of *school* problems have to be adjusted to understanding how
> the constant refiguration of normativities in everyday activities creates
> perceptions of disability-negative ontologies, generate experiences that
> incite efforts to modify those perceptions in multiple ways, and produce
> unintended effects from well-intentioned approaches that in the end remain
> irreducible to simplistic definitions for the one *ethical* or *politically correct*
> strategy (ibid, p.23).

Indeed, if educators sully rather than 'clean up' the messiness such a conversation promises, there will be less likelihood of the re-appropriation of disability studies discourse in education. However, among special educators, an historical reluctance to 'sully' inherited assumptions, beliefs and practices has been linked to their unwill-ingness to engage in critical dialogue. According to Skrtic (1991; 1995) limitations imposed by allegiance to the ideology of functionalism and a strict conformance to beaucracy bar any potential movement of the field away from it's pseudo-scientific origins. Unless we confront the limitations of special education's basic assumptions, meaningful links to disability studies will probably be undermined. Slee (1996; 2001) expresses alarm at the 'alacrity with which special educators relocate their traditional knowledge and practice in new settings' (2001, p. 170). The resettlement process proceeds over time from special education to mainstreaming to inclusion with little more than a nod to the incommensurability of these initiatives:

> Traditional special educators demonstrate a remarkable resilience through
> linguistic dexterity. While they use a contemporary lexicon of inclusion, the
> cosmetic amendments to practices and procedures reflect assumptions about
> pathological defect and normality based upon a disposition of calibration and
> exclusion (ibid, p. 167).

Recovering humanity

Although disability studies holds great promise to 'disrupt' education in general and special education, in particular, I suggest here that even when humanities-based scholarship signals no overt connection to education, it is remarkably applicable for educators. Consider the following insight from Robert McRuer, an English professor and queer theorist who analyzes a fundamental ideological cultural demand he terms 'compulsory able-bodiedness.' This construct borrows from the highly politicised writings of Adrienne Rich and Judith Butler, in combination with Life As We Know It, a memoir by Michael Berube who writes about life with his son Jamie, who has Down's Syndrome. According to McRuer (2001):

> Berube writes of how he sometimes feel[s] cornered by talking about Jamie's intelligence, as if the burden of proof is on me, official spokesman on his behalf. The subtext of these encounters always seems to be the same: In the end, aren't you disappointed to have a retarded child? ... Do we really have to give this person our full attention?' (p. 180).

In his analysis, McRuer suggests two related questions drawn from Berube's experience and bound by the same common ground of able-bodied consciousness to tease out an important subtext at play in interactions between able-bodied and disabled people. These often-unarticulated questions are juxtaposed to make a critical point. In the end, wouldn't you rather be hearing? In the end, wouldn't you rather not be HIV positive? By his analysis, these questions are more alike than they are different and more reflective of the able-bodied culture posing the question than about the 'bodies being interrogated' (ibid, p. 8). The dialectic is one in which abelist culture uncritically assumes an 'affirmative answer to the unspoken question, yes, but in the end, wouldn't you rather be more like me?' (ibid). The significance of these questions is that of the able-bodied desire for neither people who are deaf nor those with AIDS to exist.

McRuer, like Baker, disentangles the underlying assumptions that inform abelist benchmarks used to inscribe the bodies, minds, and lives of disabled children and adults in contemporary society. Although neither scholar is located exclusively in disability studies, both draw upon this interdisciplinary scholarship, and both enlarge the concerns that are otherwise sidestepped when considering inclusion, disability, and education. Disability studies scholarship provides theoretical insights for educators to examine both societal attitudes, beliefs, and assumptions and the lived-experience of disability – a perspective that has thus far failed to influence either general or special education. For educators willing to seriously consider the cultural analyses emerging from this exciting field of inquiry, the possibilities to imagine disability otherwise are limitless. This project was developed with that goal in mind. In the section that follows, I present an overview and discussion of its three components: a lecture series, critical dialogues, and curriculum development. Then I describe the response of secondary teachers who interacted with this scholarship when planning their curricula.

PROJECT BACKGROUND AND OVERVIEW

Dialogue was the stated goal for the project in which university faculty and secondary educators met to consider the construction of disability in our culture and classrooms through the study of both archival representations and more contemporary accounts of disability. This two-year initiative was funded by the NEH – a somewhat unusual funding stream for disability related research. That is, at the time I submitted the proposal, disability was not among the explicit 'field of project categories' designated by the NEH. What would prove timely was the administrative support from the former NEH director, William R. Ferris, a folklorist who promoted more 'popular' programs to broaden public interest (Chronicle of Higher Education, 6 October, 2000, p. A30). This point is relevant background as the controversy that marked Ferris' tenure at the NEH (1997-2001) underscores both the shift in standpoint suggested by Stiker (1996) and the promise of disruption suggested by Baker (2002). Criticism of Ferris focused on his reallocation of funding from traditional disciplines and high culture. Endeavors such as work on a dictionary of the Sumerian language (the world's oldest written language) was slighted in favor of projects such as *Barn Again* – a travelling exhibition detailing the history of the barn that was viewed by tens of thousands of people. These changes prompted a flurry of elitist criticism from academe that targeted the NEH and its director as 'lacking a strategic view' of the humanities, and who possessed no 'vision of what the academic humanities are or where they fit' (Chronicle of Higher Education, 6 October 2000, p.A29). Entitlement, elitism, privilege, and exclusivity came into sharp focus as claims were made that the NEH was being 'dumbed down.' One scholar who received 60K annually to edit the letters of James D. Polk, the eleventh President of the United States joined many in public criticism of Ferris, claiming he would not submit for future funding from the NEH because he could no longer 'foresee success' (ibid, p. A31). Despite the criticism, Ferris countered such claims, insisting, 'If we do the same pattern of activity and the same policies we inherit, we're not securing the future of the agency' (ibid).

Without intending to do so, Ferris disrupted, if only temporarily, a fraction of the entitlement, elitism, and privilege that underwrite the assumption of 'inheritance' prevalent in academic institutions. Although academe and public schools espouse the rhetoric of goals to enlarge humanity, such intentions are quickly recast by the perceived threat to assumptions of entitlement. Elsewhere, I explore the interplay between the pernicious pillars of entitlement, elitism, privilege and exclusion enacted among faculty in a school of education forced to confront the reality of inclusion (Ware, forthcoming). Although another component of this project focused on higher education issues in response to disability studies, that discussion is not included here in any depth. While both university faculty and K-12 teachers were participants in the project, they interacted as audience members during the lecture series.

Disability scholars lecture series

Six well-known disability studies scholars presented a broad sampling of disability-related lectures in a series that was free and open to the public.

1. *Seeing the disabled: visual rhetorics of disability in popular photography*
   Rosemarie Garland-Thomson, Associate Professor of English, Howard University, Washington DC.

2. *Seeing invisible disabilities: reading the romantic body in medical practice*
   Stephanie Brown-Clark, University of Rochester, School of Medicine, Department of Medical Humanities.

3. *Representation and its discontents: the uneasy home of disability in literature and art*
   David T. Mitchell and Sharon L. Snyder, Professors of Disability Studies and Human Development, University of Illinois, Chicago.

4. *Cultures of piety and the moral meaning of disaiblity in the United States*
   Nancy L. Eisland, Assistant Professor of Sociology of Religion, Emory University, Atlanta, Georgia.

5. *Caring, justice and disability*
   Eva Feder Kittay, Philosophy Department, State University of New York, Stony Brook

6. *The withering away of the disability state: a possible future for disability studies*
   Lennard J. Davis, Professor and Chair, Department of English and Professor of Disability Studies and Human Development, University of Illinois, Chicago.

University faculty, graduate students, medical school students, educators, and community members attended the lectures and actively engaged the presenters in the question and answer discussion immediately following. Given the diversity of the audience, the range of interests in the lectures was equally broad. For example, in Seeing Invisible Disabilities: Reading the Romantic Body in Medical Practice, Stephanie Brown-Clark traced the history of the medical profession's desire to prove the scientific basis for pathological deviance. She introduced the notion of 'monstrosity' through the work of Ambrose Parre, Monsters and Marvels (1982), who explains:

> Monsters are things that appear outside the course of Nature (and are usually signs of some forthcoming misfortune), such as a child who is born with one arm, another who will have two heads, and additional members over and above the ordinary (p. 3).

Set in the context of medical science dating back to the 15th century, the lecture considered Sander Gilman's question, how do we learn to see disability? With an assortment of slides of historic images from medical texts and excerpts from contemporary film (e.g., Frankenstein, The Elephant Man) to support her arguments, Brown-Clark problematised the distinctions between physical and mental illness inscribed on the body over time. The multiple sources from which society has learned to see disability spanned several centuries into the present to impart to the audience the notion of inherited and unproblematised views of disability.

One aspect of the lecture by Rosemarie Garland-Thomson examined the relationship of disability to disease and included slides from the Breast Cancer Foundation that depicted an array of confusing cultural messages about the body in contemporary society. Teachers were confident their students would welcome this conversation because, in their view, youth were at the centre of the creation and perpetuation of confusing cultural messages. Further, one teacher offered that such an analysis might provide a useful vehicle to engage students who had personal experience with the disease. In an e-mail after the lecture, the teacher explained that his comment was motivated by concerns for his own daughter following his wife's recent mastectomy. Driving home after the lecture, he continued to ruminate and imagine how much more humane it might be to raise this topic, first, in a language arts curriculum, and later in a science class.

Representation and Its Discontents: The Uneasy Home of Disability in Literature and Art prompted a lively debate when the chair of the history department charged that Mitchell and Snyder's post-modern critique of disability and the 'esoteric' language used to construct their claims would fail to promote the necessary activism to engage populist concerns. Following the familiar volley of claims and counterclaims, one teacher, Mary, interjected: 'I don't mean to interrupt, but while I will go home and look through a dictionary to get the meaning of some of these words, I am pleased, very pleased to hear these issues discussed someplace other than in the medical field. My son has CP, he's twenty-seven, and I have never had a class – except in education – where his life concerns were worthy of consideration.' Like most of the participants, Mary expressed awe at the multiple interpretations afforded disability and its place in our lives.

Given that the lectures were held at the end of the school day, I initially wondered if the teachers would participate in the question and answer sessions, but quite to the contrary, the teachers were active participants, often commenting from personal experience rather than pursuing clarification of an academic point. Their engagement with the speakers, the audience, and with one another made for an easy transition to the dialogue component of the project.

COLLABORATIVE INQUIRY DIALOGUES

Six collaborative inquiry dialogues were organised in a seminar structure during the course of the lecture series. Initially participants included faculty from Art & Art History, Anthropology, Counselling and Human Development, English, Visual Cultural Studies, History, Modern Languages, Women' Studies, the School of Medicine and Dentistry, administrators from the Office of Disability Resources, and twelve teachers from four school districts. The dialogues sought to promote increased awareness of disability-related courses currently offered at the university; consider possible course revision to support greater coherence and interdisciplinary teaching of disability related themes; explore the most suitable vehicles for teaching relational content; and support secondary curriculum planning among teachers informed by the readings and collegial exchange following the lectures. The dialogues were tape-recorded and transcribed as research data in which key issues and themes raised by the participants were identified.

Initially, I proposed that the dialogues be inclusive of all participants, optimistic that broad representation would enrich the dialogue. However, early into the project, it became apparent that issues were participant specific. The university faculty was less concerned about pedagogy and more concerned about internal institutional structures to support interdisciplinary teaching. The high school teachers voiced concerns about pedagogy and relational issues as they, more than the university faculty, would teach this content to a constituency that included disabled students. Midway into the project, the dialogues were restructured so that each group met separately to enable the teachers to consider specific curriculum development concerns.

Secondary curriculum development

The curriculum meetings provided the teachers with additional time to address the topics raised during the lectures and dialogues, and to consider the development of curriculum units. There was no explicit expectation that the teachers would actually teach the content during the current school year; their task was to consider its merit. Our meetings were framed by questions such as: 'where to begin' 'what to teach' and 'how to develop' useful materials appropriate to their settings. Unlike my prior work over the past decade with teachers and administrators in support of inclusion, it was a welcome relief when no one raised the 'why' question. I have written elsewhere of the challenges inclusion poses to educators and school systems, chief among them is the enduring question: 'Why do we have to do inclusion?' (Ware, 1998; 1999; 2000b). Recently, when introducing a five year partnership I developed with one of the participating districts, I asked the audience comprised of school administrators: 'When will we come to understand, value, and teach disability?' The question perplexed the administrators for reasons it might perplex many in society who overtly and covertly author and accept disability-negative portrayals. In fact, the tension between disability-positive and disability-negative positions is most apparent in education where the discourse is exclusively behavioural and medical. Interventions and cure are celebrated, but rarely does the discourse celebrate 'values that place a more positive value on our bodies, our selves, and our lives' (Morris, 1991, p. 28).

My existing relationships with all but one of the participating districts was based on continuing support of inclusion framed through a 'cultural politics' approach (Corbett & Slee, 1999; Slee, 2001; Ware, forthcoming). The fourth district was unique in that the principal initiated contact after reading local media accounts about the project. He was intrigued by disability studies in general and felt his high school would make good use of the content, given their strong humanities programme. Furthermore, he was hopeful that the introduction of disability studies in his school would serve as a proactive way to address increasing inclusion pressures. In his view the 'why' question was rarely articulated publicly among his colleagues, although he sensed it was a lingering concern.

Sample texts for secondary teachers

Overall, the teachers came to the project with a vague sense of the meaning of disability studies, although they were familiar with a cultural studies approach to feminist, race, and queer studies. None recognised disability as an identity marker, and few had given thought to the hegemony of medical interpretations of disability inscribed by traditional special education policy and practice. A lengthy bibliography, from which they could select readings to inform their individual interests, included the following:

> *Life as we know it: A father, family, and an exceptional child*, by Michael Berube (1996). A father describes the life of his 4-year old son with Down's syndrome. Tracing his son's developmental stages, social experiences, and interactions with the professionals and the social system, Berube raises a number of critical issues germane to disability studies, including questions about the social construction of ability to disability law.

> *Exile & Pride: Disability, Queerness, and Liberation*, by Eli Clare (1991). This first-person account of disability, class, queerness, child-abuse, activism and other relevant topics appeal to readers who find alliance with Clare possible on many registers. This is not another account of how we 'other' but rather a poetic interpretation of the everyday practices of exclusion.

> *Staring Back: The Disability Experience from the Inside Out*, by Kenny Fries (1997). This collection of work by disabled individuals includes fiction, non-fiction, poetry and drama to inform understanding of disability as part of the human experience. The book is well regarded for the breadth of work collected by Fries.

> *Thinking in pictures: And other reports from my life*, by Temple Grandin (1995). An autobiographical account of the childhood of a woman with autism who thinks primarily in pictures rather than words. Grandin, who holds a PhD. in animal science, argues for consideration of the relationship between autism and genius.

> *Waist-high in the world: A life among the disabled*, by Nancy Mairs (1997). This well-published poet and essayist probes the familiar themes of responding to life changes in health, body image, sexuality, and issues of advocacy and social justice. These sometimes witty and other times raw accounts of living with disability provide contemporary insights on living life unbound by disability.

Moving Violations: War zones, wheelchairs, and declarations of independence, by John Hockenberry (1995). This collection is based on the life and work of this award-winning journalist and wheelchair user relies on humour and adventure to challenge status quo assumptions about living and working with disability.

Autobiography of a Face, by Lucy Grealy (1994). The author describes her decades old journey 'back' to her face after navigating a lifetime of 'uncensored stares,' known only as ugliness, and as a 'face' disfigured by cancer.

The Diving Bell and the Butterfly, by Jean-Dominique Bauby (1997). Following a stroke and diagnosis of 'locked in' syndrome this memoir is 'told' by blinking to select one letter at a time from an alphabet created for his use.

Films and documentaries

Breathing Lessons, by Jessica Yu (1996), recounts the life of this poet and journalist who contracted polio in childhood, and spent much of his life an iron lung. His poetry and spirited commentary provide a contemporary perspective on the rules of engagement when living with a disability.

When Billy Broke his Head, by Billy Golfus and David E. Simpson (1994), explores disability rights, the rights movement and the individuals who are involved, as narrated by Golfus, who has a traumatic brain injury.

In *Vital signs: Crip Culture Talks Back*, by David Mitchell and Sharon Snyder (1997), participants in a national Disability and the Arts conference discuss the politics of disability through their performance, which includes such texts as art, fiction, poetry, stand-up comedy, drama, and personal narratives. Behind-the scene conversations include those with cultural concerns for a shared approach to issues of access for all.

Locked-in Syndrome, by Jean-Jacques Beinex (1996). This documentary captures the final year in the life of Jean-Dominique Bauby (author of The Diving Bell and the Butterfly, above). It was filmed on location in France and includes interviews with individuals who remained close to the flamboyant and former editor of Elle.

King Gimp, by William A. Whiteford and Dan Kiplinger (2000). Documentary about Dan Kiplinger filmed over the course of 13 years beginning in his early school years through to the completion of college and the beginning of his painting career.

Audio Series

Beyond Affliction: The Disability History Project (Block, 1997) is an audio tape series that addresses four aspects of living with disabilities. These include: 'Inventing the Poster Child,' 'Tomorrow's Children,' 'The Overdue Revolution,' and 'What's Work Got To Do With It? The series host and co-producer, Laurie Block, is the mother of twin daughters, one of whom was born with spina bifida. Block's exploration into disability addresses many of the central themes integrated into this project as she explores the historicity of disability and living with disability in the present moment. The series is presented in a provocative style well suited to a general audience.

Poetry & Haiku

The teachers also considered poetry and haiku, including the following:

My Place

I don't want to live in bungalow land
On the outer edges of the urban sprawl
In the places designed for people-like-us
Kept safely separate, away from it all.
I want to live in the pulse-hot-thick-of it,
Where the nights jive, where the streets hum,
Amongst people and politics, struggles and upheaval,
I'm a dangerous woman and my time has come (Napolitano, 1996)

These and other first person accounts of living with disability were introduced to the teachers because they extended the lecture topics and served as potential instructional materials. The materials were unknown to all but one of the participants. In the section that follows, I describe how this content and the project components came together to influence the teachers and their development of curriculum. I make a distinction between the studied account of disability in schools informed by special education, the storied account revealed by the project's content, and the resulting layered account of disability that began to take shape during this project.

The studied, the storied, and layered meanings of disability

While I might want to claim that some grand research scheme guided the participants to the very ends I anticipated, I am unable to do so. In many ways, much of what occurred followed personal reflection on the lectures, or it surfaced in the readings outside of class, or in dialogue with one another – slowly shaped in the space between our inquiry meetings. Although the project attempted to enrich teachers' understanding of disability, in the process, our efforts revealed that the approach and the content would necessitate new forms of engagement that all but insured a collision with the studied story of disability – education's reductionist stance towards disability. Certainly, our interactions and the data I collected were informed by the teachers' individual and collective insights, but what I offer here are but a few layers of what might be made of disability in schools. I identify three relevant recurring themes in the data: confusion, contradiction, and complexity – by most standards, a far cry from the outcomes of a successful project.

Teacher reflections

The lectures, while not specific to education invited multiple ways for educators to examine societal attitudes, beliefs, and assumptions as well as the lived experience of disability. However, when augmented by the supporting materials, the combination overwhelmed the teachers. In turn, this deep immersion into disability studies, as one teacher characterised the experience, unexpectedly gave rise to doubts about their readiness to teach this content. In both their journals and in our dialogues, concerns surfaced about to a perceived lack of grounding in the content, their subsequent lack of preparation, and a general lack of prior knowledge from which to build instruction. Further, their claims invited concerns about pedagogic authority, entangled with issues of personal discomfort relative to the content. This was an unanticipated development in response to what I assumed was a well paced exposure to the content and ample time to work through the creation of new knowledge. The following excerpts from their journals appeared midway into the first year of the project:

> Before this project I never really thought about any of this.

> I leave our study group, mostly annoyed – why was this left out of my teacher training?

> The 'lens' I've been using as a special ed teacher has really fooled me into seeing disability as defect.

In discussion, some insisted that a new language was needed to convey this content to their students – one that included new vocabulary – but more to the point, 'safely' challenged their inherited views of disability. Another teacher explained, 'this is heavy stuff, it really doesn't come up in the curriculum anywhere.' His concerns were both content-based and relational, given the 'highly-charged' content. Initially, while some teachers found the lectures to be interesting, overt linkages to the existing curriculum proved difficult to identify. Some held to the unwritten requirement for objectivity and personal distance from the teaching of taboo topics in their classrooms; some insisted that new rigid directives for standardised curriculum barred the addition of this content into their curriculum; and some anticipated that, given the return of disabled students to their classrooms as a consequence of inclusion, additional discomfort might cloud the issues for the students. In addition, a few insisted that the disability content served to undo all that was meaningless about the curriculum.

In general, most expressed doubts that they could sustain this new perspective against the day-to-day demands of the institution and the narrative it maintained about disability: 'There's no box to check on the IEP for the development of disability cultural pride,' one teacher quipped. This prompted doubts about locating the necessary resources to supplement their teaching and more importantly, peer support for the ongoing development of these ideas outside their own classrooms. As the list of challenges grew, Mary assessed the situation as amounting to nothing short of large-scale brainwashing. She conceded that while the lectures provided valuable information, for teachers coming to this content 'raw' – the task was premised on unlearning: 'I think, for teachers, the principles will be far more difficult to apply than the concepts.'

Hearing the stories, grasping the principles

Given the expressed discomfort and growing doubts, it was remarkable that the teachers remained with the project. Although their engagement was uneven, most continued to consider the complexity of this content and to imagine the influence of a disability studies perspective on their teaching. Those who began the project eager to engage the lectures remained so, probing the materials for the nuances as if in testimony to their willingness to the unlearning process. For example, in his opening remarks, David Mitchell mentioned the challenge his non-disabled parents faced guiding him through life as a disabled child. His point was not to criticise his parents, but to remind the audience that in the absence of a shared identity, and unlike race, class, and gender, disability can mark an individual as an outsider even from inside the family. This insight prompted intense exchange among the teachers as none had previously considered this perspective. Some questioned the veracity of the claim, wondering what degree of 'consciousness' a child might possess versus the acquired consciousness of an adult reflecting back to one's youth. Others voiced outrage that Mitchell's perspective was challenged. This and other exchanges among the teachers revealed that the studied account of disability would not be easily displaced by a storied account of disability. Having so long invested in knowing disability through normalising discourses grounded in the biological, social, and cognitive sciences that shape education, the counter-narratives explored throughout this project marked a significant departure from that means of knowing. In time, it became apparent that in fact, there was only one interpretation of disability in schools from which to guide their thinking – that of disability as deficiency. Although some limited their focus to issues of pedagogic authority, others began to recognise the intricacies of reductionist hegemony in their everyday actions and how it shaped their standpoint in the example of disability. Indeed, as one teacher suggested, introducing disability from a humanities lens would require a whole new language – a language informed by honest reconciliation with what we 'make of disability in schools.'

Confusion, contradiction, and complexity

Rather than cast the themes from this research in terms that might seduce readers into believing that new layers of meaning unfurled one at time in safe tidy scenarios, I trace confusion, contradiction, and complexity back to the actual sites of struggle to reveal the subtle ruptures that signaled the collision with education's reductionist stance towards disability in schools.

The project, with its emphasis on dialogue, was structured to provide teachers with the time to consider the material and to accept or reject its merit accordingly. Such an approach to professional development is rarely afforded teachers who are expected to 'hear and adhere,' rather than to engage and reflect upon, new instructional material. Because this content demanded otherwise, the teachers initially launched into the curriculum to probe for existing linkages – seemingly unaware that their exchanges initially skirted the themes of personal issues raised in the question and answer sessions following the lectures. Working through the received messages authored by various institutions that had informed their professional training left them increasingly unwilling to confront the complexity of their individual response to disability. What began as a healthy give and take in earlier dialogues in time proved to be a recipe for confusion given the disorganising effects disability studies imposes upon the inherited conditions and curriculum in schools. That is, as Baker (2002b) explains:

> The tropes emanating out of Disability Studies reasoning can therefore be said to have disorganising effects, where disorganisation is both a positive and dangerous opening onto alternative, convoluted, and complicating orientations to educational processes (p. 72).

The teachers' deep immersion into disability issues gave rise to these same disorganising effects, although theorising their concerns was, in their view, less important than considering a course of action. While some accepted confusion as part of the process, others expected more direct guidance from me, and answers to some fairly simple questions such as, 'where do we begin?' My unwillingness to provide answers was consistent with my own approach to the content, but indeed, a difficult principle in practice when working with teachers – the default is to press for the 'right' way and for the steps to do so. Because identity concerns remained an enduring issue throughout the lectures – enhanced by the videos, poetry, and memoirs – the suggestion emerged that the theme of identity might be a useful starting point.

Applying the concepts

In the example of identity, earlier concerns of 'false consciousness' had by now given way to incredulity and awe that disability cultural concerns were in fact, excluded from the curriculum. These tensions slowly turned to frustration with each new lecture until finally one teacher asked: 'So where are we supposed to begin? Is this something my wife should teach her fourth graders – or do we wait till junior high?' In response, Mary wondered: 'why not earlier?' In her view, the aspects of stigma revealed by this project were probably enacted every time a student was called away for resource classes, therapies, or any other 'special' aspect of their day: 'We always think we are sensitive to that sort of thing, but you know, thinking back to what Professor Mitchell said, how can we presume to know what's in their little heads.' Another teacher concurred: 'it's not like we really ever ask young children what they think about their 'special' status. I know that by the time I get them in high school, they're pretty done with anything that reeks of special ed.' Chris, a middle school teacher pressed this point further, 'Or are they just done with what we've done? We name them different but special. They likely know earlier on, they're neither.'

This exchange signaled a subtle shift – a slow invasion of previously unquestioned assumptions about professional claims to authority. Months before, when

David Mitchell suggested his view of childhood stigma, some teachers concurred, while others rejected his insights, but on the whole, his interpretation was not completely disentangled. In contrast, the above exchange followed months of ongoing interaction with the assigned texts and with additional speakers. One teacher offered an analysis similar to the 'don't ask/don't tell' policy for gays in the military, suggesting that insights about living with disability were better left untold in our society where silence has long shaped society's fear. Another teacher wondered if schools, because they could essentially 'hear' only one story about disability, also perpetuated a 'don't ask/don't tell' approach to understanding disability. This exchange prompted Mary's suggestion for a potential unit on 'unasked and unanswered questions,' in which disability was but one part. Borrowing from Eli Clare (1999), she wondered if the liberation which Clare described might prove a good hook for disabled and non-disabled students prompted by the following excerpt:

> For as long as I can remember, I have avoided certain questions. Would I have been a good runner if I didn't have CP? Could I have been a surgeon or pianist, a dancer or gymnast? Tempting questions that have no answers. I refuse to enter the territory marked bitterness. I wondered about a friend who calls herself one of the last of the polio tribe, born just before the polio vaccine's discovery. Does she ever ask what her life might look like had she been born five years later? On a topological map, bitterness would be outlined in red (p. 5).

Mary explained that in addition to the above passage, the following passage offered openings into a brief overview of the theories and social models as a way into the political content:

> I thought about the model of disability that separates impairment from disability. Disability theorist Michael Oliver defines impairment as 'lacking part of or all of a limb, or having a defective limb, organism or mechanism of the body.' I lack a fair amount of fine motor control. My hands shake. I can't play a piano, place my hands gently on a keyboard, or type even 15 words a minute. Whole paragraphs never cascade from my fingertips. My long hand is a slow scrawl. I have trouble picking up small objects, putting them down. Dicing onions with a sharp knife puts my hands at risk. A food processor is not a yuppie kitchen luxury in my house, but an adaptive device. My gross motor skills are better but not great. I can walk mile after mile, run and jump and skip and hop, but don't expect me to walk a balance beam. A tightrope would be murder; boulder hopping and rock climbing, not much better. I am not asking for pity. I am telling you about impairment (pp. 6–7).

These excerpts were noteworthy, given their complete absence of pity or sentimentality, Mary reasoned. And because Eli Clare reads one of her poems in *Vital Signs: Crip Culture Talks Back* (Snyder and Mitchell, 1997) her vitality would be important for students to recognise as they assessed the power of her experience:

> Oliver defines disability as 'the disadvantage or restriction of activity caused by a contemporary social organisation which takes no or little account of

people who have physical (and/or cognitive/developmental/mental) impairments and thus excludes them from the mainstream of society.' I write slowly enough that cashiers get impatient as I sign my name to checks, stop talking to me, turn to my companions, hand them my receipts. I have failed timed tests, important tests, because teachers wouldn't allow me extra time to finish the sheer physical act of writing, wouldn't allow me to use a typewriter. I have been turned away from jobs because my potential employer believed my slow, slurred speech meant I was stupid. Everywhere I go people stare at me, in restaurants as I eat, in grocery stores as I fish coins out of my pocket to pay the cashier, in parks as I play with my dog. I am not asking for pity. I am telling you about disability.

I decided that Michael Oliver's model of disability makes theoretical and political sense but misses important emotional realities (Clare, 1999, pp. 5–7).

Mary held that the theme of 'unasked questions' would invite a deluge of issues many educators had likely masked in the process of following institutional policy. Informed by her experiences as a special educator and a parent, she realised the damage done by what we make of disability in schools, and in her view the task was rooted less to pedagogic authority than to engaging with disability. Her insights would prove invaluable to the project as contradictions continued to surface.

Educators have more frequent interactions with disability than do most other non-medical professionals as they are the front line workers who convey cultural meanings about disability – often in the absence of understanding the significance and implications of that role. A humanities approach to educating about disability as part of the lived experience invites, if not assumes, understanding of ourselves in relation to the other. It provokes questions about the self that were either formerly overlooked or silenced in both teacher preparation coursework and inservice training. This project was structured in the hopes that new knowledge would give rise to the necessary imagination needed to develop curriculum. I assumed an approach similar to that taken with other curriculum development projects, wherein new content would merge with their existing expertise and the curriculum would emerge. However, the need for teachers to locate themselves in relation to this content once again proved to be as significant in this project as it had in the pilot study. In that research, the teacher recalled midway through the project that his brother's disability experience might have motivated his own engagement with the content. He had rarely claimed the influence of that experience in a positive way either in his teaching or elsewhere, but was starting to make the connection. It was equally ironic that Mary came to a similar realisation when she suggested that her family had been robbed of knowing disability as a worthy aspect of their lives. That is not to say she viewed their lives as unworthy or lacking in any particular way, but external social affirmation or validity for the way their lives had been informed by disability was all but disavowed: 'Our lives aren't that different from other people's lives, well, in some ways – yes – but no matter how I try to approach telling about our experience, the response is often one of pity.' After reflecting on the 'don't ask/don't tell' approach attributed to the school setting, Mary found a similar response by society, offering that: 'I think we've all learned to read what is appropriate to tell in a social setting and what is better left untold.' The liberation Eli Clare claimed in 'telling' about disability would slowly unfold for Mary as she grew increasingly suspicious of her own silence.

The lectures, the project content, the dialogues, and Mary's life experiences, as she continued to reflect on their intersections, seem to operationalise MacIntyre's view that the starting point to shift one's standpoint relative to disability begins with a certain 'suspicion of ourselves' (1999, p. 4). MacIntyre is among a growing number of moral philosophers who have raised important questions about disability and its relationship to the 'common good.' Critical of the historical failure of philosophers to consider disability as a 'central feature' of human life, his latest book, *Dependent Rational Animals: Why Human Beings Need the Virtues* (1999) is intended to provide a correction to his earlier analysis of moral virtues specific to disabilities (MacIntyre, 1984). He hopes to reveal how much of a change in standpoint is needed to re-examine the role of disability and dependence in all our lives. Arguing that, although new knowledge and imagination will be essential in the creation of communities in which disabled individuals might thrive, these efforts cannot begin until we acknowledge our complicity with past constructions of disability that have clearly limited our view of humanity. In his discussion of the virtues necessary for self-making explicit to disability, MacIntyre urges that we revisit the meaning of human vulnerability and dependency, the origins of flourishing and alternative futures, and the necessity for exploring 'whose good' is included in the common good.

Mary, although she was steeped in prior knowledge on the ways of knowing disability outside the normative categories, recognised that she could tell a lot more than she had ventured to do thus far. Her journals evidenced more personal insights and elaboration on the materials. Late in the school year she was awarded recognition for her teaching. Her acceptance speech drew upon her family's experience with disability as a means to steering them through a life of experiences 'too often untold.' She also acknowledged the insights gleaned from the project that she continues to integrate into her teaching.

CONCLUSION

The curriculum initiated many conversations that continue to develop and although I cannot predict how these teachers will or will not re-imagine disability, my sense is that the content and our dialogues will stay with them for a long time. They are likely to continue to attempt to integrate this content, although whether it becomes a sustained conversation for them is difficult to say. As the project concluded, many of the teachers had yet to confront their own complicity in preserving the silence on disability inscribed by everyday practice. It was an initiative that some, but not all, would venture towards during the course of project.

This early experience is a beginning rather than an ending point. Institutional structures have long served to authorise particular narratives of disability, histories of deficiency, and the very language used to name disability experiences will not be easily disentangled. An equally troubling concern at this moment is that the parameters of policy fall short of an approach to understanding disability through a humanities lens where complexity is a given rather than a threat. As the field of disability studies continues to explore and invite multiple interpretations for understanding disability through a cultural lens, the promise remains for educators to explore the connections to curriculum and practice in pursuit of authorising more humane ways to name and know disability.

REFERENCES

Albrecht, G. L., Seelman, K. D., and Bury, M., (Eds.), (2001). *Handbook of disability studies.* Thousand Oaks: Sage.

Baker, B. (2002). The hunt for disability: The new Eugenics and the normalization of school children. *Teachers College Record*, 104(4), 663–703.

Baker, B. (in press). Disorganising educational tropes: Conceptions of dis/ability and curriculum. *Journal of Curriculum Theorising.*

Barnes, C. (1999). Disability studies: New or not so new directions? *Disability & Society*, 14(4), 577-580.

Barton, L. (1987). *The politics of special educational needs.* Lewes, UK: Falmer.

Bauby, J.D. (1997). *The diving bell and the butterfly.* New York: Knopf.

Beinex, J. J. (1996). *Locked-in Syndrome.* London, England: BBC Productions.

Berube, M. (1996). *Life as we know it: A father, a family, and an exceptional Child.* New York: Vintage-Random House, 1996.

Block, L. (1997). *Beyond Affliction: A History of Disability.* Straightahead Pictures Inc. Amherst, MA.

Campbell, F. (2000). Eugenics in a different key? New technologies and the 'conundrum' of 'disability.' In M. Crotty, J. Germov and G. Rodwell (Eds.). *'A race for place:' Eugenics, Darwinism, and social thought and practice in Australia.* Newcastle: The University of Newcastle Press.

Clare, E. (1999). *Exile & Pride: Disability, Queerness, and Liberation.* Boston: South End Press.

Corbett, J. and Slee, R. (1999). An International conversation on inclusive education.' In Armstrong, F., Armstrong, D. and Barton, L. (Eds.), *Inclusive Education: Policy, Contexts and Comparative Perspectives.* London: David Fulton. (1997). *The disability studies reader.* New York: Routledge.

Davis, L. J. (2002). *Bending over backwards: Disability, dismodernism & other difficult positions.* New York: New York University Press.

Erevelles, N. (2000). Educating unruly bodies: Critical pedagogy, disability studies, and the politics of schooling. *Educational Theory*, 30(2): 25–48.

Erevelles, N. (2002). (Im)Material citizens: Cognitive disability, Race, and the politics of citizenship. *Disability, Culture, and Education*, 1(1), 5–25.

Ferguson, P. M. 2001. Mapping the family: Disability studies and the exploration of parental response to disability. In G. L. Albrecht, K. D. Seelman, and M. Bury, (Eds.) *Handbook of disability studies.* Thousand Oaks: Sage.

Ferris, W. J. (2001). Interview: National Public Radio, Morning Edition. Retrieved June 20, 2001, from http://www.npr.org.

Fries, K. (Ed.),(1997). *Staring back: The disability experience from the inside out.* New York: Plume.

Grandin, T. (1995). *Thinking in pictures: And other reports from my life with Autism.* New York: Vintage.

Gleeson, B., (1999). *Geographies of disability.* London and New York: Routledge.

Grealy, L. (1994). *Autobiography of a face.* Boston and New York: Houghton Mifflin.

Golfus, B. and Simpson, D. A. (1994). *When Billy broke his head and other tales of wonder.* Boston, MA: Fanlight Productions.

Hockenberry, J. (1995). *Moving violations: War zones, wheelchairs, and declarations of independence.* New York: Hyperion.

Linton, S. (1998a*). Claiming disability.* New York: New York University Press.

Linton, S. (1998b). Disability studies/not disability studies. *Disability & Society,* 13(4), 525–540.

Longmore, P. K. & Umanksy, L. (Eds.), (2001). *The new disability history: American perspectives.* New York: New York University Press.

MacIntyre, A. (1999). *Dependent rational animals: Why human beings need virtue.* Chicago: Open Court Press.

McRuer, R. (2001). Compulsory Able-Bodiedness and Queer/Disabled Existence. In B. Bruggerman, R. Garland-Thomson, and S. L. Snyder, (Eds.), *Enabling the Humanities: A Sourcebook in Disability Studies.* New York: MLA Publications.

Mairs, N. (1997). *Waist-high in the world: A life among the disabled.* Boston: Beacon Press.

Mitchell, D. T. and S. L. Snyder (Eds.) (1997). Vital signs: crip culture talks back. In *The body and physical difference: Discourses of disability.* Ann Arbor: The University of Michigan Press.

Mitchell, D.T. and Sharon L. Snyder, (Eds.), (2000). *Narrative prosthesis: Disability and the dependencies of discourse.* Ann Arbor: University of Michigan Press.

Mitchell, D. T., Snyder, S. L. and Ware, L. (2002). *Integrating disability studies into secondary education curricula.* Institute proposal to the National Endowment for the Humanities, 15, April.

Morris, J 1991 Pride against prejudice: transforming attitudes to disability. London: The Women's Press.

Napotilino, S. (1998). *A Dangerous Woman.* Manchester: GMCDP Publications/ Carisbrooke.

Parre, A. (1982). *Monsters and Marvels,* trans. Janis L. Pallister. Chicago and London: University of Chicago Press.

Peters, S. J. (1996). 'he politics of disability identity. In L. Barton (Ed.), *Disability & Society,* 15, (4), 583–601.

Pfeiffer & Yoshida (1995). Teaching Disability Studies in Canada and the USA. *Disability & Society,* 10(4), 475–500.

Sarason, S. B., (1996). Revisiting 'The culture of the school and the problem of change.' New York: Teacher's College Press.

Skrtic, T. (1991). *Behind special education: A critical analysis of professional culture and school organization.* Denver: Love Publishing.

Skrtic, T. M. (Ed.), (1995). *Disability and democracy: Reconstructing [Special] Education for Postmodernity.* New York: Teachers College Press.

Slee, R. (1996). Clauses of conditionality: The 'reasonable' accomodation of language. In L. Barton (Ed.), *Disability and Society: Emerging Issues and Insights.* New York: Longmore.

Slee, R. (2001). Social justice and the changing directions in educational research: The case of inclusive education. *International Journal of Inclusive Education*, 5(2/3), 167–177.

Southwick, R. (2000). Scholars fear humanities endowment is being dumbed-down. *Chronicle of Higher Education*, A 29–31, October 6. 2000.

Stiker, H. J. (1999). *A history of disability*. Trans. William Sayers. Ann Arbor: University of Michigan Press.

Tomlinson, S. (1982). *A sociology of special education*. London: Routledge and Keagan Paul.

Ware, L. (1998). I kinda wonder if we're fooling ourselves? In T. Booth and M. Ainscow (Eds.), *From Them to Us: An international study of inclusion in education*. London: Routledge.

Ware, L. (1999). 'My kid and kids kinda like him.' In K. Ballard (Ed.) *Inclusive Education: International Voices on Disability and Justice*, London: Falmer Press.

Ware, L. (2000a). *A collaborative inquiry on understanding disability in secondary and post-secondary settings*. A research proposal to the National Endowment for the Humanities, April 2000.

Ware, L. (2000b). Sunflowers, enchantment and empires: Reflections on inclusive education in the United States. In F. Armstrong, D. Armstrong, & L. Barton, (Eds.), *Inclusive Education: Policy, Contexts and Comparative Perspectives*. London: David Fulton Press.

Ware, L. (2001). Writing, identity, and the other: Dare we do disability studies? *Journal of Teacher Education*, 52(2), March/April, 107–123.

Ware, L. (2002). A moral conversation on disability: Risking the personal in educational contexts. *Hypatia*, 17(3), 143–172.

Ware, L. (Forthcoming), Understanding Disability and Transforming Schools. In T. Booth, K. N;s, & M. Stromstad (Eds.), *Developing Inclusive Teacher Education*. London & New York: Routledge.

Whiteford, W. A. & Kiplinger, D. (2000). *King Gimp*. Boston, MA: Fanlight Productions.

Yu, J. (1996). *Breathing Lessons*. Boston, MA: Fanlight Productions

ALISON CLOSS

9 AN OUTSIDER'S PERSPECTIVE ON THE REALITY OF EDUCATIONAL INCLUSION WITHIN FORMER YUGOSLAVIA

INTRODUCTION: VEZE (CONNECTIONS)

I first encountered Yugoslavia and Yugoslavs as a student over forty years ago. Yugoslavia was a Communist-ruled country, albeit one with substantial freedoms. Tito's regime welcomed diversity, but only within the boundaries of its own form of political unity (Singleton, 1985; Pavlowitch, 1992). In many ways, my early relationship with the country and its people had some of the characteristics of a romantic affair. It also had some of the risks inherent in any idealising relationship – not least the dimming of critical faculties in relation to all that the loved one is and does. I loved the country's beauty, its diverse peoples' warm vitality, and the challenge of understanding its complex history and cultures. The professed multi-culturalism and international socialist non-alignment and the evident enjoyment of life seemed very attractive to a young person brought up in largely mono-cultural and calvinist Scotland during the Cold War of East and West. I visited the country frequently, learned the main language (Serbo Croatian), and built up a network of friends, and later of professional colleagues, across the country's six Republics and two semi-autonomous regions. Perhaps I was seeking to identify with a place whose prevailing ways of being complemented rather than replicated my own – I could feel both at home there and at the same time enjoy the strangeness. And it seemed so happy and safe.

With greater knowledge and age came greater criticism which I thought I could voice from what I perceived to be my privileged position of being, if not an 'insider,' then at least less of an 'outsider' than many other non-Yugoslavs. This confidence or arrogance diminished as I reflected more on my own shortcomings and those of my own country, recognising the strength and pull of my own roots and the kinds of bias they could generate. I also realised that direct criticism of that which one holds dear – whether a family member, one's workplace and colleagues or a country – very rarely effects change when it is based simply on subjective opinions derived from one's own personal experience and history. 'Criticising,' I have found, is most productive as a mutual activity, based on some degree of shared principles, aims and roots. Critical partners, to be effective, need to be self-critical and open to bilateral change, implying deep mutual respect.

My professional activities in former Yugoslavia and in the exchange visits that

J. Allan (ed.), Inclusion, Participation and Democracy: What is the Purpose?, 139-162.
© 2003 *Kluwer Academic Publishers. Printed in the Netherlands.*

took place prior to its destruction, therefore, took the forms of dialogue, mutual enquiry and enlightenment and exchanged experience. Sometimes we shared frustration and explored ideas and ways forward, for instance, in relation to the painfully slow demise of institutions for children and adults with learning difficulties in the UK – I worked in a 'mental handicap hospital' for over 1000 people from 1973 to 1978 – and their continuing existence throughout former Yugoslavia. I did not see myself as an advocate then for inclusive education in which I was only beginning to find my own feet. Even now I have to acknowledge some diffidence and ambivalence in relation to total or required inclusion and view militant international advocacy of 'any' cause with great caution.

This chapter is about the prospects for greater educational inclusion for children with special educational needs in the parts of former Yugoslavia most affected by the ten years of conflict between 1991 and 2001. It is contextualised within the socio-political, economic and educational – mainstream and special – circumstances of the area both before and during the ten years of aggression and disruption. It makes the case, cautiously, for inclusive education, not only for the sake of marginalised children themselves, but also as a possible contribution towards civil society. At various points throughout the chapter and at the end, I return to questioning my own motivation and role, and that of other 'outsiders,' in the educational and societal systems of other countries.

The end of Yugoslavia

I did not foresee the terrible violence that would end former Yugoslavia, although disintegration seemed inevitable by the late 1980s. Yugoslavs remembered the horrors of World War II and now enjoyed a comfortable way of life, albeit on uncertain financial means. There was a growing middle class, adequate service infrastructures and very many people in larger towns in Yugoslavia were inter-married ethno-culturally. In rural areas, different ethno-religious communities had lived side by side peacefully since 1945 (Donia & Fine 1994). Tito seemed to have succeeded in imposing a Yugoslav identity based on the pragmatic interests of the various peoples living in its constituent republics. However, the process of identification, as Hall and Du Gay (1996) remind us, ' is in the end, conditional, lodged in contingency. Once secured, it does not obliterate difference. The total merging it suggests is, in fact, a fantasy of incorporation' (p. 3). Although I was not so naïve as not to recognise continuing differences, I thought that identification with Yugoslavia, if not always with Communism, was perceived as a more practical solution than other alternatives to the majority of its peoples. And another war, I thought, was not an acceptable option to the people at large.

However, the following contributed to the violent end of Yugoslavia as an entity (Allcock, 2000; Woodward, 1995; Silber & Little, 1995; Donia & Fine, 1994; Popov, 1996):

• A lack of realistic transitional planning for the leadership, post-Tito

- The exploitation of patriotism and the use of nationalism as vehicles for greedy personal ambition among Yugoslav politicians, criminals and academics to enhance their own egos, advancement and purses; the exploitation by those profiteers of economic, religious and ethnic differences, imposing exclusive identities on willing or unwilling people
- The calling-in of the country's huge international debt, resulting in economic crisis
- The end of Communist rule in East Europe and the determination of the US and Western Europe to end Communism
- Serbia's and Croatia's re-emerging territorial ambitions in relation to Bosnia and to each other
- The Yugoslav People's Army's role in opposing the secession of Slovenia and Croatia and then, effectively in becoming the Serbian Army in Bosnia
- The gullibility of the various Yugoslav Republics' rural electorates
- The collective and individual market ambitions of Western countries
- The inept, ignorant and ineffective responses of Western Europe and the US as the crises developed successively.

The four Yugoslav Republics most affected were Croatia, Bosnia, Serbia and its two semi-autonomous regions of Vojvodina and Kosovo, and Montenegro; the first two by violent internal and external aggression and the latter two by international economic sanctions then by aggression in Kosovo and by the NATO bombardment of Serbia. Serbia and Montenegro now form an uneasily allied single country, confusingly called Yugoslavia. This chapter does not address either Slovenia or Macedonia.

VALUES, ATTITUDES AND EDUCATIONAL PRACTICES IN FORMER YUGOSLAVIA, PRE 1991

I felt critical of some aspects of Yugoslav society but was aware that Scots also shared some of its shortcomings. These include chauvinism towards women, racism towards their national neighbours, disdainful attitudes towards country cousins – *seljaci*! (peasants!) (Zukin, 1975), personal and media thirst for lurid non-factual reporting and *rekla-kazala* (rumour) (Thompson, 1994), willingness to argue and fight rather than debate, and excessive regard for 'strength' or 'power' whether in families, schools or society. These did not – to me – sit comfortably with *Bratsvo i Jedinstvo* (Brotherhood and Unity) any more than they did with 'We're a' Jock Thamson's bairns' (a Scottish phrase suggesting common parentage and therefore the social equity of all).

Mainstream education

My muted criticism of Yugoslav education also grew and paralleled my developing criticism of education at home. Much later, I perceived connections between its education system and the violent end of Yugoslavia (Closs, 1996). While obviously the education system cannot in itself be blamed for the war, neither did it equip the majority of its former pupils to recognise and resist those that led them into war. A gap between rhetoric and reality in societal values was evident in former Yugoslavia's mainstream education, especially in the three-tier selective system of mainstream secondary schools and the existence of many special schools and institutions. Former Yugoslavs persisted in valuing most highly their academic grammar schools, gimnazije, and the acquisition of 'book knowledge.' Again, there are parallels between the gimnazije, English Grammar schools and the previous existence of Scottish Academies, all of which were resistant to changes towards comprehensive education that, to me, seemed to offer wider opportunities to more children and young people, regardless of background and ability.

The Yugoslav Communist government tried to address some inequalities and to secure well-trained employees for industry and technology by attempting, largely in vain, to raise the status of technical and vocational secondary schools. The education system, common across most of East Europe and the Balkans and inherited from Catherine the Great of Russia, and its ideals of academia, remained secure. Their defendants argued that able young people from any background could win places in *Gimnazije* – as indeed some of the Communist leaders from disadvantaged backgrounds themselves had done. Yugoslavia still had a class system after the advent of Communism following World War II, albeit a political and war veteran elite rather than an inherited or land – or property – owning elite (Djilas, 1974). This elite had either come through *gimnazije* themselves or were determined that their children should do so. The education system conformed with Beane and Apple's later criticism of schools elsewhere (1999), that they 'largely reflected the interests and aspirations of the most powerful groups in the country and ignored those of the less powerful' (p. 13).

From my liberal Western and pro-comprehensive education stance, I identified other features of the system which discriminated against those not coming from this elite, with their access to wider knowledge and experiences, and deprived the non-elite of choice, inclusive experiences and opportunities to develop critique. These were:

* The issuing of single textbooks for curricular areas
* The large number of traditional academic subjects taught and the absence of many practical subjects and subjects such as modern and media studies (civics took the form of Marxism-Leninism)
* The use of traditional didactic chalk and talk, whole-class pedagogy, undifferentiated for varying learner need
* The associated and accepted power role vested in teachers in class
* Large classes
* Low pay and increasingly low social status of teachers, with many teachers being the product of pedagogical courses run in parallel with main subject choices

at University, often taken as an insurance policy against unemployment rather than as a vocational choice
- The existence of a large special education sector with its own separate profession of teacher-therapists.

Crick (2000) suggests that 'talk, discussion, debate and participation are the bases of social responsibility and intercourse and the grounding and practice of active citizenship' (p. 129). Such classroom activities were significantly absent in former Yugoslavia. Yugoslavia was committed to worker self-management (Djodjevic et al, 1982), yet there was little in the practice of school education that prepared young Yugoslavs for meaningful participation in this aspect of adult life.

However, Yugoslavs could point to a strong political and educational commitment to first language elementary education, resulting in areas such as Vojvodina in the north of Serbia printing basic texts in up to eight different languages to cover the most numerous minority ethnic and language populations – an expensive and admirable investment in linguistic plurality. Despite in-class authoritarianism, teachers and pupils often had warm and informal relationships out of class, frequently going on holiday together to the sea or the mountains. Education as a concept was and is valued in former Yugoslavia, and the existence of the large special education sector was, and is, defended – as here – as evidence of very substantial investment in the well-being of children with special educational needs.

There were also schools such as the *Prva Gimnazija* (First High School) of Sarajevo, for example, which educated its pupils not only academically but also holistically as citizens. Later, it was to remain courageously open alike to Serbs, Croats and Muslims, its staff modelling inclusion and valuing all students equally throughout the siege of Sarajevo (Salom, 1999). There were many students who not only survived Yugoslavia's educational system but thrived and distinguished themselves academically, nationally and internationally. For a small and relatively poor country, former Yugoslavia had many distinguished mathematicians, scientists, linguists, writers and artists. The numerous emigrants and refugee/asylum seekers with professional qualifications, who came to the West during and after the hostilities, have largely been warmly welcomed and found to be immediately employable. Students who found asylum often completed their studies with distinction.

Some young former Yugoslavs did recognise the early signs that preceded the violence and wars, courageously protesting against the nationalistic and racist movements. Perhaps, however, they owed their discernment and courage more to their families and social contexts than to their schools. Most young people also saw these signs, joined their respective armies willingly or unwilling'y and fought, sometimes viciously and with no regard for civilian life, for what they perceived to be their separate ethnic and religious identities and the liberation or separation of their previously federated countries. Have I any right to say, as I do, that they were 'wrong,' that they were misled, their values misguided and their education defective?

Pring (1986) writes that:

> The *educational* activities promoted by any society are intimately connected
> with what that society believes to be a valuable form of life. Furthermore, the
> particular values embodied in what is designated to be educational will be
> about the kind of *persons* that the society wishes its young people to grow up
> into – the kind of sensitivities, mental powers, basic skills and knowledge, that
> are embodied in the traditions and aspirations of that society (pp. 181–182)

My overall impression, from the stance of a teacher committed to comprehensive
education heading towards greater inclusion, was that Yugoslav society was con-
fused about what actually were 'valuable forms of life' and that its educational
system reflected this confusion. It is ironic that, as I write this about former
Yugoslavia, the UK's and Scotland's internal dissonances and tensions (Mittler,
2000) between, on one hand, the 'marketisation' of education with its attendant
imposition of attainment target-setting and, on the other hand, a 'presumption of
mainstreaming' for all children entering school, exposes this country to similar
criticisms.

The care and education of children with special educational needs

My critique of mainstream education pre-1991, above, describes it as traditional
and, to some extent, rigid. As in all such systems, wherever located, some children
were more advantaged in Yugoslav schools than others. At that time, the ideal pupil
was a high academic achiever of any background. Children with special educational
needs were, as will be discussed shortly, educated in other contexts and were then
the most obviously excluded children. However, once hostilities started after 1991,
the number of excluded, disadvantaged or undervalued pupil groups increased as
those who were not obviously identified as *'nasi'* ('ours') became less welcome.
In addition to children with SEN there were minority ethnic or mixed ethnicity
pupils, minority language or dialect users, Romany and fairground Travellers,
refugees and internally displaced children, children without families and increasing numbers of children with emotional and behavioural difficulties. Their group
identities are familiar in the UK as children who have also not been treated with
societal or educational equity.

    Children with SEN were recognised legally from the early part of the twentieth
century throughout the Republics of former Yugoslavia and now also in the new
countries. Special education provision in Yugoslavia had, until the late 1970s,
followed a pattern common in Europe and especially in Eastern and Southern
Europe (Csanyi, 2001; Ajdinski & Florian, 1997). This involved the extensive use
of semi-centralised institutions and schools, many of which were residential. Most
urban areas also had special day schools, with separate provision developed for
children with specific categories of impairments. In rural areas, there were some
mixed special classes in mainstream schools functioning as separate entities. In
general, this specialist provision was better developed in the north and east of the
country than in the south and west, and in urban, rather than rural, settings.

    Curricula were adapted to meet supposed common educational needs of the categories of impairment; differentiation was not practised. Some specialised learning aids, materials and texts were available, but not in sufficient quantity or quality. Around five to eight per cent of the total pupil population were in special schools. This was a significantly higher proportion than, for example in the UK at this time, which had up to two per cent. Children with severe cognitive or complex disabilities received medical and physical care only, since they were deemed 'ineducable,' as they were in the UK until 1974/5. The care institutions usually left much to be desired in terms of accommodation, staffing, resources and respect for human rights. Numbers of these children and others at home were unclear – as now.

The overt aims of the special education system were to minimise disabilities and to optimise young people's potential as economically productive members of society. They also relieved mainstream schools of 'non-conforming' students. The negative by-products of the special education system in former Yugoslavia included, as elsewhere, the isolation of children with learning difficulties and disabilities from their larger community and sometimes also from their families – a mutual loss. Societal attitudes to disability tended to be complex and ambivalent; human warmth and pity, rejection and fear were evident – inclusion was not.

However, in the late 1970s, Croatia and Slovenia, the most northerly republics, undertook educational reforms, followed slowly and incompletely by the southern republics. The intention was to integrate 'all children of average intelligence and above' into the mainstream, and to ensure that children with more severe disabilities were included in special schools or classes. Limited progress was made, with resistance from teachers and parents in mainstream schools.

There were, however, some encouraging signs. A review of some pilot integration projects in Croatia (Racki, 1982) showed substantial social gains in disabled and non-disabled pupils. No educational losses were recorded for non-disabled pupils, provided additional support accompanied the pupils with SEN. Pupils with SEN, in turn, experienced only minor educational losses, attributed to reduced levels of specialist support and differentiation. Children with moderate to severe learning difficulties, autism and moderate to severe multiple disabilities fell heir to vacancies in special schools. The special education teacher-therapists (*defektolog*) resented being expected to teach less able pupils and felt ill-prepared to meet the challenge.

These improvements stopped or regressed due both to public protests about other aspects of the legislation and to the collapse of the economy in the 1980s. Only Slovenia and Croatia continued to try to integrate pupils, improve the quality of special schools and extend the population included in education. In some of the less developed Republics such as rural Bosnia, southern Serbia, and Montenegro, special education remained poorly funded, and integration applied only to children with the mildest physical or sensory difficulties. Most children with severe and multiple learning difficulties were excluded completely from education – the concept of 'ineducability' for children with profound and complex learning difficulties held firm, and was sometimes applied to those with lesser disabilities.

THE YEARS OF HORROR: 1991–2001

The full educational and human rights of children with SEN were not, then, established pre-1991, despite much work by committed professionals. Families had not combined their energies into pressure groups and the Disability Movement was not prominent, although there was a small highly educated elite of sensorily and physically impaired people who were assumed to be representative when representation was, occasionally, thought necessary. Between 1991 and 2001, this marginalised position would inevitably be put at further risk. The Machel Study (UN, 1996) shows that the number of wars is increasing throughout the world, as is the involvement of civilian populations. Civilian fatalities in wartime have risen from 5% at the turn of the century, to 15% in World War I, to 65% at the end of World War II, to more than 90% during the various wars of the 1990s. The 1949 Geneva Convention (Roberts and Guelff 1989), with its codes of 'recommended' conduct, has become a risible echo from a bygone age, with non-combatants becoming targets for violence of all kinds. In wars now, disabled adults and children merely become easier targets (Hastie, 1997; Closs, 1998). Many atrocities were committed, ostensibly in the name of exclusive religious and/or ethnic identities, but in reality because of the power ambitions of politicians, generals and criminals.

I would suggest that they and their followers lacked the fundamental shared moral identity of a human being. When I visited former Yugoslavia during the wartime period, I adapted a new way of 'placing' those I met there, not according to ethnicity or religion or political orientation or even gender. I had a mental crossed axis with one axis representing the continuum from good to bad and the other from powerful to weak: the quadrant of 'good and powerful' was nearly empty; the 'bad and powerful' quadrant was full, as was the 'weak,' scattered in something probably like a normal distribution between 'bad and good' or appearing intermittently as one and then the other. The 'bad and powerful' often collaborated, even when they were ostensibly on different sides, as the Dayton negotiations and cross-frontier criminal activity throughout the ten years showed. The 'weak' were struggling for their very existence and only those with a highly developed moral human identity were able to stretch across the various divides to support others, or even to share with their own, such were the deprivations.

Between 1991 and 2001, I visited parts of former Yugoslavia, mainly Croatia, Bosnia and Serbia, at least twice a year. Visits were usually brief – one to three weeks – and usually in relation to aid or medication for children and adults with special needs. Travelling from area to area was dangerous and it was difficult to get a clear overview of what was happening to the disabled population. The next section of the chapter is, therefore, based partly on 'snapshots' of personal experience and observation and on reliable written and oral accounts of others. It also draws on data gathered through interviews during an intensive one month field visit in 2001 to these same areas, now new countries, funded by the Moray Endowment Fund of Edinburgh University.

During the field trip, I visited Croatia, Serbia, Montenegro and both entities of

Bosnia, holding 44 meetings: five of the meetings were for groups of five to twelve people, ten for small groups of two to four people and there were 29 individual interviews. The interviews were with three main groups of people:

- Policy makers and advisers at Ministerial or Assistant Ministerial levels in Education, Health and Social Services
- Service providers – heads of schools, hospitals, institutions, social care services, Non-Governmental Organisations (NGOs), international and local
- Disabled people and their representatives – disabled adults and students, parents of disabled children, officers of organisations representing the interests of disabled children and adults with all kinds of disability, congenital and acquired, including war wounded. Some of the representatives were themselves disabled.

In addition to these main groups, I also met colleagues in the fields of mainstream and specialist teacher education.

My interviews focused mainly on, first, establishing the effects of the wars on disabled adults and children and their current status in relation to human services, especially education; and second, eliciting current concepts, practices and prospects in relation to societal and educational inclusion. I had three key questions that related quite specifically to 'inclusion:'

- What do you understand by 'inclusion' and 'inclusive education'?
- Have there already been movements towards greater inclusion? Could you illustrate such moves or make a comment about inclusion?
- What are the barriers and potential ways forward to greater inclusion of disabled children and adults?

I also had an additional question that I introduced at the end of the interviews, if the interviewees had not themselves raised the issue:

- Do you see any connections between disability discrimination/exclusion/ segregation in education and other kinds of societal discrimination in your country such as those related to gender/sexual orientation, religious, linguistic and ethnic difference?

The multiple negative impacts of events during between 1991–2001 on children with special needs, their families and those who worked with them

The essence of war, in any country, is not only that lives are lost and property destroyed, but that the economy, service infrastructures and societal norms are destroyed or collapse, as they did totally in Bosnia, to a large extent in parts of Croatia and later in Kosovo in southern Serbia, and to a rather lesser extent in other parts of Croatia. In Serbia, the effects of sanctions, and of actual and moral isolation, and later of NATO bombardment, were also severe. Montenegro also experienced sanctions and isolation.

How did this impact on children with SEN? While some effects of war applied also to non-disabled children and adults, the greatest impacts were felt by vulnerable individuals and their families. This was especially true in the areas most affected by hostilities in Bosnia and Croatia and later in Kosovo. In war, even more than in peace, life favours 'those who have' – healthy, strong, smart, multi-skilled, mobile individuals, living with supportive families and with access to money and *veze* (connections).

Many schools were destroyed and others did not function during the war or curtailed their services. Most children with mild difficulties were also without schooling, but some simply registered at the nearest non-special school that was open, resulting in unplanned integration. This was particularly true of internally displaced ('ethnically cleansed') families, many of whom fled without personal records to areas where they were not known (Mesalic, 1998). Many children with more severe disabilities spent the entire wartime period with their families who had no respite:

> My wife and I and our two multiply handicapped young people lived on the ninth floor of a high-rise block of flats, with no lift, heating, light or running water throughout the entire siege [of Sarajevo]. Our building was often hit by shells and the noise was deafening even though we were on the quiet side [of the building]. One of our children is doubly incontinent and the other is terrified of loud noises. There was little food, sometimes none. We often spoke about suicide, it seemed a better end. Without good neighbours who fetched water from the standpipe and risked their lives for us we would never have survived. We are not the people we were and conditions are still terrible. (Father of two multiply disabled young people, Bosnia).

The UNHCR and aid NGOs could not supply sufficient food to children in the war-torn areas, resulting in widespread malnutrition, and some died of common infections and illnesses to which malnutrition made them vulnerable. Special dietary requirements could not be met. Some institutions received little or no aid. Others became, willingly or unwillingly, conduits through which food aid intended for their residents was passed to the various armies. Continuing unemployment and extreme poverty in many areas mean that malnutrition is a continuing peacetime problem:

> We saw the return of rickets and widespread tuberculosis, and there were specific problems in Sarajevo and Tuzla because of the sieges. Children stayed in cellars for months on end, day and night, and their eyes suffered. In the winters some died of hypothermia. Parents became ill and died because they gave any food they had to their children. There was huge weight loss, hair and teeth dropped out, almost everyone had bad skin and digestive problems and then we had terribly war-wounded children, physically and psychologically (Head of Nasa Deca, National Children's Organisation, Bosnia).

Pre-1991, primary medical care throughout the country was adequate and specialist medical care in the main cities was of western European standards. Dental care tended to be poor in rural areas. During the hostilities, and even now, health services were depleted or almost non-existent. Medical and paramedical professionals were recruited into military service, targeted for killing, or fled abroad and did not return even at the end of the fighting – a 'brain drain' that continues. Despite the heroic efforts of remaining personnel and of international NGOs, such as *Medicins* and *Pharmaciens sans Frontieres,* many children and adults died or were permanently disabled for want of routine medicine and minor surgery:

> My daughter became blind and also had her leg amputated. She could not get insulin for her diabetes regularly and of course controlling her diet was impossible. She just ate anything that was there and sometimes there was nothing (Sarajevo father).

> I started the war as a junior surgeon but now I am a senior consultant in Orthopaedic Surgery. I have done every kind of surgery, not just orthopaedic. In ten years I have had more experience, much of it soul-destroying, than any man should have in his lifetime. I hope I will never have to do another amputation on a child or young person again, but the landmines will ensure that I do (Surgeon, Bosnia).

> One little boy had hydrocephalus, he needed a valve but we could not get it in time, so he died. The sanctions were not meant to affect medical supplies but they affected transport and slowed down everything so really they affected medical care too (Children's Home Director, Serbia).

Understandably, populations are still traumatised, deeply depressed and debilitated (Smajkic, 1997; Medicins du Monde, 1999). Poor mental health is another layer of disadvantage to people disabled prior to the war or during hostilities.

Drin and Bakovici Institutes in Fojnica became battlefields during fighting between Croats and Muslims in 1993, followed by looting of their premises, leaving them without any utility services or food and with staff reduced to five people caring for over 600 severely multiply disabled children and adults. Seven patients died before UNPROFOR troops intervened. In the same year, 300 adults and children with severe learning difficulties from the Vrlika Institute in Croatia's Krajina region and their staff fled to safety in open trucks to the Juraj Bonaci Institute in Split, already full with their own clients and previous refugees and only designed to hold 70 residents and 220 day clients. The 'Children's Village' in Kamenica, Vojvodina, for children in social need, is 200 metres from the River Danube and the bridges targeted for destruction by NATO in 1999. The 150 children lived in their houses' cellars for the eleven weeks of the bombardment. With the bridges down or being bombed, most of the village's staff came to work by small boat, facing bombing and possible drowning. Many children, already orphaned, were abused or abandoned, and some staff still show signs of post-traumatic stress syndrome (Jokmanovic, 2000).

Ethnic cleansing and general migrations of populations away from war-torn areas resulted in either putting disabled children and adults 'on the road,' making them vulnerable to death from exhaustion or exposure, or of leaving them and their carers possibly to face being killed where they lived. Walking to doubtful safety in large, often insanitary, tented refugee camps often involved carrying disabled people. Some camps provided hospital tents or huts for the most vulnerable. Unsurprisingly, some families did not claim their relatives from these shelters when they themselves moved on, knowing they had a better chance of survival there.

Children in residential institutions and schools are housed and fed, something that many families found hard to ensure with no incomes. Living through war is exhausting and ageing. Parents who had coped up to and even through the wars found themselves unable to struggle on and took their children to institutions as a last resort:

> Sometimes when they bring in their children or young adults they cry, but sometimes they are too tired to cry. We know we should be providing even more for these children but in comparison with what some of them have come from, this institute seems rich (Director of an Institute for children and adults with learning difficulties, Serbia).

The long-term degradation of the country, the poorly administered welfare policy and many other reasons have led to the serious impoverishment of these institutions. The lack of essential means calls into question not only the quality of the lives of the children in institutions, but also their survival and development (Yugoslav Child Rights Centre, 2001).

Many children with SEN became separated from parents during hostilities. Some were in institutions or residential schools out of their own Republic when war started and were cut off. Others were evacuated to refugee centres, relatives, or to unknown destinations, even abroad. Some children have been 'lost' or the family-child link has been broken by parents moving away, or by the death of the parents. The ICRC and Save the Children both worked intensively on family reunification. There are also many examples of children with disabilities who became refugees abroad with their families and who have remained in the host country with a parent or older sibling when the rest of the family returned home:

> We could all have stayed (in Sweden) but it was not home. We wanted to come home together but we needed to rebuild our house, my son would not go to school, or have physiotherapy, or many things he needs. So he and my wife stayed there and the older children came back with me ... but there is no work and I have lost hope of being here together again (Father of a multiply handicapped son, Kosovo).

Death rates of children with disabilities increased but another tragedy is that numbers of children with disabilities increased directly as a result of war injuries, as the data below show.

No figures are currently available for Serbia and Montenegro although these will be far less than in Bosnia and in Croatia. Numbers of dead and wounded will continue to rise in Bosnia, parts of Croatia and in the Kosovo region of Serbia because of landmines.

Table 1: Children affected by war in former Yugoslavia

Children	Killed/Died	Wounded	Disabled	Missing
Croatia	303	1280	298	35
Bosnia (incl. Sarajevo)	16854	34351	2100	1335
Sarajevo	1600	15000	340	

[Data from Mikovic (1998) and from the Government of the Republic of Croatia (1999a)]

Why is education and especially inclusive education important in the new countries that formerly comprised Yugoslavia?

The devastation of war makes it hard to know how to start the process of rebuilding a country and its society and what to prioritise. While the regeneration of the economy is absolutely fundamental, re-establishing education is perceived as one of the essential elements in recovery: 'Our children have suffered terribly, we owe them a normal life now and attending school is part of that' (Government adviser in education, Croatia). School also allows adults and children to regain their peer activities. Family life together or apart was hugely stressful, especially where there were children with disabilities. Children attending school relieves family stress. Extended discontinuity in education can be a lasting disadvantage in development, especially for children for whom learning is more difficult: 'I often weep. I see deaf children who have had no signing, no hearing aids, no teaching for three or four year just when they needed it most. They may never make this loss up' (Teacher educator in deaf education, Bosnia)

War creates chaos but the destruction of old systems potentially clears the way for change. Wars and their aftermath bring in 'foreign influences' – good and bad – ideas and funding. Some of these changes may impact on education which may itself become a context in which new ideas can be developed and experienced. War can also sometimes indirectly emancipate previously oppressed or disenfranchised groups, for example, British women after the First World War. Could children with SEN and other marginalised groups in former Yugoslavia 'benefit' in any respect from the wars (Hastie 1997)? One important development for them would be greater societal and educational inclusion.

I would assert that, if society in the new countries that have emerged from the wars is to be a civil society, one that respects humans in all their diversity and obeys a moral and established legal system where all human life is respected, then education has to be active in the process from the beginning. But the previous education systems were not ideal models for tolerant and inclusive attitudes and practices in school or in society, as I have explained. So, what now?

Although much use of the UNESCO Salamanca Statement (UNESCO, 1994) has focused on its educational implications alone, it is its societal assertions that make it particularly meaningful in former Yugoslavia: 'Regular schools with this inclusive orientation are the most effective means of combating discriminatory attitudes, creating welcoming communities, building an inclusive society and an education for all.' The Statement also claims that, ultimately, an inclusive schooling system is also more cost-effective.

Thomas and Loxley (2001) highlight inclusion's potential to be both a model and an agent for positive changes in society: 'Taken to its logical conclusion, inclusion is about comprehensive education, equality and collective belonging' (p.118). They assert that schools have a duty, through the pursuit of inclusion, to reduce the inequalities of birth and circumstance and highlight that perceived learning difficulties result from schools' incapacity to respond to diversity (p. 118).

There are arguments too that support desirable pedagogical changes. Presence and participation of diverse pupils in inclusive schools directly imply differentiated approaches to teaching. Further, if the societal messages are to be learned, then it is suggested that they need to be learned through experiential learning within schools' democratic conditions that, it is hoped, will also become the societal norm (Crick, 2000; Beane & Apple, 1999).

Halpin (1999) makes a point salient to promoting inclusive education in the new countries:

> The relationship between inclusive schooling and the re-building of trust and social capital is then a synergetic one: each needs not only the other to exist but also their actual interaction realises an enhanced effect – a revitalisation of part of civil society through greater democratic involvement (p. 228).

'Trust,' in self and in others, is a word rarely heard now outside family circles, and social capital is seriously depleted. If inclusive education can contribute to re-establishing these, then it would indeed be a major achievement.

While there is insufficient research as yet to prove 'conclusively' either the overall educational, societal or cost-effectiveness benefits of inclusive education, it does offer hopeful action. In countries such as those that have emerged from former Yugoslavia with their social and moral image as shattered as their economy, any message of hope may be welcome. Thomas & Glenney (2002) suggest – rather unconvincingly in my view – that where there is no scientific evidence for change such as that towards inclusive education, change should proceed on the basis of common sense, experience and moral conviction about the underpinning ideals. I find myself tempted to advocate this path while at the same time being aware that I am seeking 'happy endings' and am at risk, perhaps, of grasping at straws or at inappropriate responses.

It is also not enough that colleagues and 'critical friends' such as myself, from relatively affluent, stable societies from a liberal Western educational tradition, advocate such approaches. Transferring ideas about schooling (Ainscow, 1999) or about disability (Hastie 1997, p. 79) across cultures is fraught with difficulty. Ultimately, the perspectives and actions of those who live and work there will matter much more. Is there now discussion about societal inclusion or at least inclusive educational practices in Croatia, Bosnia, Serbia and Montenegro?

Educational inclusion

Thematic analysis of the recordings of the 44 meetings in my field trip in 2001 and computer assisted analysis of their transcripts produced some insights into the situation of children with SEN and also into prevailing perspectives on inclusion in the new countries that have emerged from former Yugoslavia.

Current concepts of inclusion and practices in relation to children with special educational needs

Only a small number of respondents understood inclusion as a process bringing all children into their local elementary schools. These respondents quoted the UN Convention on the Rights of the Child (United Nations, 1989) and the Salamanca Statement (UNESCO, 1994) and were aware that there was professional debate both about the definition of inclusion and about its pros and cons in practice. Most of this minority had participated in such debates. They instanced the social model of disability and, in the case of NGO (non-governmental organisation) workers, were committed to 'empowerment' action contractually in their work with children and adults with disabilities and their families. The most active and apparently successful NGOs had employed local committed professionals and local NGOs had been spawned from their large international parent organisations. A small number of academics in Zagreb, Belgrade, Sarajevo and Tuzla were themselves running NGOs with inclusive societal and educational aims.

However, some of those who understood 'inclusive education' were opposed to its practice or believed that 'good' special schools were also inclusive, providing data on post-school employment, for example, to support their point. Among them were some Faculty lecturers responsible for training Defektalogs, the teacher-therapists most involved both in special school teaching and in clinical therapy. Defektalogs normally train as undergraduates and are not qualified to work independently as teachers in mainstream. Inclusion could therefore be seen as a threat both to their status and even their employment.

The pre-existence of significant numbers of special schools – usually in towns – may impede the development of inclusive education, as we have found in Scotland (Closs, 1996). This can mean that rural areas find it easier to implement inclusive education. In the Muslim-Croatian entity of Bosnia, education of children with SEN had almost come to a halt in rural areas during hostilities. Afterwards, UNICEF, Medicins du Monde and the Kennedy Foundation successfully established special classes attached to mainstream schools, with planned progression for pupils' inclusion and professional development in collaborative working for both special class and mainstream teachers. The independent evaluators (Rouse et al, 2001) saw such classes as a viable and pragmatic step towards greater inclusion and, significantly, noted that it was appropriate for the current situation in Bosnia.

However, in *Republica Srpska*, the Serbian entity of Bosnia, the Swiss Red Cross and an individual benefactor had provided a new purpose-built special school with residential accommodation. Some of its pupils had previously attended the special classes set up by the UNICEF, MdM and Kennedy Foundation collaboration. Some were even recruited from mainstream classes. This highlights another problem of poverty and of weak national planning – conflicting and competing developments. Countries struggling to recover from the effects of war are by definition poor. Poor countries may be obliged to dance for funding to the various pipe tunes being played by diverse and sometimes ignorant aid providers. Some of the providers have agendas that are incompatible with others or with local cultures and existing plans. Unified national and international policy and planning might help prevent fragmentation and confusion generated by aid donors. It must be asked whether some aid is in the cause of positive development or if it is, in fact, competitive neo-colonialism. Beane & Apple (1999), when writing about what they term 'democratic' schools, suggest that,

> the realisation ... does in part depend on selective intervention of the state, especially where the process and content of local decision making serve to disenfranchise and oppress selected groups of people (p. 11).

However, where national governments are weak or divided, as, for instance, have been the post war non-majority Bosnian Governments composed of the three opposing predominant nationalistic parties, or where the rights of minorities are at risk, then international bodies such as UNICEF and UN Conventions may have a mediating role between governments and aid givers.

The most frequently voiced opinion among my respondents was that special classes attached to mainstream schools, with some measure of social inclusion, was the best way to 'integrate' children with SEN. The idea that mainstream schools would themselves plan to be inclusive was considered doubtful at best, and laughable by many. Many mainstream school buildings in former Yugoslavia are in poor material condition, and have two or even three daily 'shifts' of pupil populations and school staff. Pupil populations and staff numbers are still fluctuating with the ebb and flow of those returning to, or leaving, catchment areas in the post-war chaos. This hardly seems fertile ground for inclusion.

A few other respondents considered that inclusion meant bringing 'all' children, including those in institutional care, into education of some kind, even if some children attended special schools. However, the concept of 'ineducability' remained firmly rooted in the minds of most in relation to children with profound and complex difficulties and institutions have growing, rather than lessening, numbers of children.

In Croatia, government planning (Government of the Republic of Croatia, 1999b) affirmed integration and a reduction in institutionalisation, but practice lags behind policy. There is recognition there that successful pre-school inclusion is more likely to lead to positive inclusion outcomes in the later stages of education. More recently, in June 2001 and 2002 respectively, the Ministries of Education in Montenegro and Serbia have also held national conferences on the theme of educational inclusion, partnered by UNICEF and the local Save the Children teams, active in inclusive pre-school developments and parental partnership. The summary of decisions issued by the Assistant Minister of Education of Serbia after the Conference in Belgrade (Deljanin, 2002), concludes that:

> This means opening of schools for all, that is an inclusive type of education wherever it is possible to be carried out with variations and sub-variations like particular classes at regular schools, partial inclusion into some forms of regular teaching process and complete inclusion into regular classes. Where inclusion is not possible as it is not in the case of the most serious forms of disability, a special system of education should be worked out.

The statement, however, makes it plain that a gradualist approach is envisaged, starting with pilot programmes in pre-school provision and that subsequent developments will depend on the outcomes from early programmes.

Serbia is far from Scotland in so many ways, yet the chosen route seems deeply familiar in its caution. Should we cheer this progress or be dismayed that the statement sounds less than convinced and convincing? Are we ourselves really convinced about the more total forms of inclusion?

Inclusion, yes or no? And when?

Substantial barriers lie in the way of progress towards educational inclusion of children with SEN. They include exhaustion of the populations as a whole, exacerbated by the unbearable slowness of economic recovery. This leaves all the areas concerned, particularly Bosnia, with so much physical destruction, population disruption and political uncertainty, dependent on international aid. Larger international organisations are ponderously slow in action and distracted by competing crises throughout the world. Smaller aid organisations tend to come, promise much, and leave without accomplishing all they promised. Policy has been fragmented between different levels of successive national and local government and international organisations that have sometimes alienated local populations and professionals (Hastie 1997). Reliable statistical data on the populations involved are unavailable, rendering planning problematic. Special school and residential institutional staff are key players in any potential change but have both personal and professional interests in maintaining the 'status quo' of segregation. Mainstream schools are under huge pressure currently and their staffs have not engaged in the inclusion debate at all. Sadly too, the 'market' influences of the West are already making themselves felt with the opening of a few private and religion-based schools where there were none before.

On the side of inclusion is international pressure at governmental level, with UN and future EC funding dependent on evidence of inclusive intent. The long-term international and local NGOs with funding to see their pro-inclusion projects through are also influential. One high level Minister indicated his response to these pressures:

> If nothing else, we all need to recover our humanitarian credibility in the rest of the world and be seen to be doing our best for those who have greatest needs. We signed the Conventions. Laws and statements help to persuade our people and attract international funding ... So, we will follow the trend even if it is slower and harder for us (Minister for Health, Sarajevo Kanton).

Children, too, appear to want greater inclusion, with a Youth Conference held in Bosnia in 2001 calling for, among other things, the integration of children with special needs into regular education systems and prevention of sexual, ethnic and racial discrimination in education (UNICEF, 2001).

However, the most significant voices yet may be the voices of disabled people themselves and of parents of children with SEN. Both have been empowered by NGOs and have learned to lobby, work with the media and advertising and to use ICT and the Internet. While media and advertising may have a potential downside that is pity-evoking rather than rights-evoking, they are forces that can be harnessed in constructive ways, as some very provocative posters throughout former Yugoslavia show. ICT has enabled organisations and individuals to network with a much wider world that demonstrates that greater inclusion is possible.

On the sensitive but important question of whether there are links between exclusion of children with SEN and other forms of exclusion in this troubled area (and elsewhere nearer home), few respondents agreed in relation to themselves or their co-nationals. Perhaps the question was too hard, too soon, and put by 'an outsider.' One respondent, however, replied:

> You are asking really if we are bad people, do we exclude and harm the weaker amongst us? Well, perhaps I must say yes, we did – we do. But I must also say that this potential lies in everyone in all countries, just as the potential for great good does. We need to find forms of government and education everywhere that develop the good and not the bad. Perhaps inclusive education is one way forward (Child psychologist).

Perhaps this psychologist, like me, wanted a happy ending and would have jumped at any hopeful suggestion, although she at least 'belongs' in ways that I cannot.

Michael Ignatieff (2002), in the *New York Times*, took issue with the underlying motivation of those that push for 'their' changes at 'their' selected pace in the countries of others:

> Our need for noble victims and happy endings suggests that we are more interested in ourselves than we are in the places like Bosnia that Americans have taken up as causes. This may be the imperial kernel at the heart of our interest in reconstruction and nation building. For what is empire but the desire to imprint our values on another people?

On balance, I believe there are some prospects for greater educational and societal inclusion for children with SEN and other excluded groups throughout the areas most affected by the last ten terrible years in former Yugoslavia. I have indeed witnessed 'great good,' huge efforts to survive and to show humanity towards others, in the families of children with special needs, in the children themselves and in many of the professionals who worked on throughout the most difficult of circumstances. Many of those acts of goodness were across what might have been, for others, unbridgeable ethno-religious divides. But it will be a very long, hard and challenging journey towards inclusion, as other countries in much easier situations are still finding.

CONCLUSION

The Colloquium at which an earlier version of this paper was given asked the contributors to address four questions relating to inclusion. While I hope that some of my responses to the questions are implicit in what I have already written, the most persistent questions in my own mind have actually been: 'Is inclusion, and specifically inclusive education, a significant positive development in countries devastated by civil and invasive wars?' and 'Do I, or any other foreigner, have any right to suggest to another country devastated by war the ways in which they might proceed?' I shall now try to answer the Colloquium's questions posed more directly.

What are the goals/ambitions for inclusion and what forms of participation are necessary to achieve these? What changes in culture and politics are implied?

In former Yugoslavia, most forms of exclusion and aggression have been practised during the last ten years. A basic but enormous aim therefore has to be living at peace without rejecting or abusing others and the second aim is for those now living in the new countries 'to want this coexistence.' The first has to do with desisting from negative actions, supported or, if necessary, enforced by the rule of law but the second has to do with a change of heart and mind in those that exclude, hate and harm others because they are perceived as different, as 'not ours,' as threatening.

The first aim has been achieved to a significant extent, albeit with difficulty and certainly not completely. Some political changes have been effected by the people themselves in Croatia and Serbia voting for politicians who are certainly not liberal but who are not inhumane and who have some respect for national and international law, especially when this brings economic benefit. In Bosnia, law is imposed on a still divided country and government by the international High Officer, by remaining UN troops and by a European trained and led police force.

The second aim, I fear, will probably never be fully achieved, but must still be attempted in any way that offers hope. The generations for whom the wars served to confirm their worst stereotypes of 'the other' will not forgive or forget and will probably indoctrinate their children to some extent. Educational inclusion at elementary school age, in the hands of teachers trained to model and develop inclusion across all the various divides, offers a chance for stereotypes to fade and for individually positive school experiences of 'the other' to be substituted for them.

The development of a culture of self-criticism may be fundamental to inclusion-orientated change in former Yugoslavia and is an aspect of thinking and learning that could reasonably be developed in schools. It not only allows people to reject tried past ways but allows them to go out to seek alternatives. This is surely preferable to alternative ways being offered or imposed by those who have little deep understanding or long-term commitment in the various countries. The issue of criticism, of any kind, is a particularly sensitive one when a country is under threat or has been damaged by others, as we have also seen recently in the US. It is also evident in the Balkans. Silber and Little (1995) refer to Serbia's 'rich seam of national grievance' (p. 34) – a phrase that could also be applied to any of the former Yugoslav counties both towards each other and individually and collectively towards Western Europe. Blaming 'the other' and adopting the identity of victim, often in the teeth of evidence, were, and are still, more common responses than critical self-reflection.

Apple (2002) suggests that criticism of state is actually the 'duty' of citizens, when he reflects on the impact on pedagogy of the events of 11 September 2001 in the USA:

> In my mind, however, social criticism is the ultimate act of patriotism ... rigorous criticism of a nation's policies demonstrates a commitment to the nation itself ... It signifies that *I/we live here* and that this is indeed our country and our flag as well (p. 7).

However, such reflective voices require courage as they often become objects of abuse from compatriots. Not surprisingly perhaps, the most evident sources of national self-criticism in former Yugoslavia are women, just as they were also the key members of the anti-war movements in former Yugoslavia, such as the Women in Black (Susak 1996). Are women perhaps in a better position to understand and practice the concept of 'tough love'- love and commitment that is most critical of those whom it holds dearest?

The Indian writer, Arundhati Roy (2001), in urging America's self-evaluation of past actions, points out that absence or weakness of such internal criticism opens the doors to external criticism which may also not be welcome: 'Because then it falls to the rest of us to ask the hard questions and say the harsh things. And for our pains, for our bad timing, we will be disliked, ignored and perhaps eventually silenced,' This is at least equally true for former Yugoslavia.

What is the nature of the interaction between inclusion and identity (both individual and collective)?

Drakulic (1992) described how, following the Yugoslav Army's invasion of Croatia in 1991, it became impossible to voice any criticism of any aspect of Croatia or its government, 'So right now, in the new state of Croatia, no one is allowed not to be a Croat' (p. 52). In other words, an exclusive identity had been imposed. This was also true in other areas or within other groups where identities had been imposed by leaders and agitators with their own egotistical agendas or had been taken on defensively as a perceived means to survival. Drakulic also recognised that such banning of personal views, understandable but not excusable in a time of immediate danger, had negative implications and could not continue, 'all the human victims will have been in vain if the newly born independent countries do not restore to us a sense that we are before all else individuals as well as citizens' (ibid).

My personal stance is rather that the governments of the new countries have a duty, not merely to return to their citizens and to any other people within their boundaries the sense of individuality, but also to foster a 'common moral identity of human being' with all others, whatever their multiple other identities. It is only with a sense of such a shared identity that people with diverse 'sub-identities' can live together in peace and security. One contribution to this end – and no more than that should be claimed – could be the introduction of overtly inclusive education that brings together children and staff across all the multiple divides. However, while people still struggle against acute poverty to survive and are still coming to terms with huge personal loss, progress may be desperately slow and a return to human security will be the work of several generations to come. As we have seen not only in former Yugoslavia, but also in the US, following the 11 September devastation in New York, defensive nationalistic and other identities, such as more extreme gendered identities (Ugresic, 1995; Richter-Malabotta, 2002), may be adopted very swiftly and let go very slowly where people feel threatened.

Is it possible to specify an ethical framework for inclusion?

This seems a worthy, but extremely ambitious, aim and one about which I have substantial uncertainty. It seems to me that the UN Convention on the Rights of the Child (United Nations, 1989) does provide a broad outline within which greater inclusion can be developed without imposing a single model or one that derives from other cultures, socio-economic contexts and times or that reflects current 'accepted' practices. The right of those most affected – all children, including those who may be identified by themselves or others as potentially at disadvantage individually or collectively with others – to be informed, and then to make informed plans and choices, has to be defended within any framework. My assertion of this right must logically allow 'opting out' of inclusion in society and in education, but this may weaken the overall process.

Ensuring that potentially disadvantaged children and adults have a powerful voice in social and educational planning is undoubtedly important. This is not unproblematic, not least in who may represent whom. In former Yugoslavia there was little evidence of unity or collaboration between groups of disabled people, indeed there were clear signs of rivalry, hierarchies and direct animosity, not least between disabled adults and parents of disabled children, and between war wounded and other groups of disabled people. One young war-wounded veteran summed up his dichotomous view neatly to me: 'There are heroes and then there are accidents in life or of nature. We (war veterans) deserve more.'

Whichever avenue I explore, I am brought back again and again to the need for national economic recovery and emotional recovery, money and time, time and money. We delude ourselves if we imagine that a framework for inclusion can proceed successfully without these. But there is also a need for models that prove that inclusion 'can' work and perhaps that is where international support can be helpful, both in inviting visitors to their own models and in offering funding and advice – when asked for – for pilot programmes to be set up in former Yugoslavia by those who live and work there.

What kinds of consequences can be specified in relation to inclusion?

Consequences may be hoped for, but surely not specified – specification seems un-realistic, especially in countries that have experienced such destruction and despair as those of former Yugoslavia. Let us hope that greater societal and educational inclusion will bring greater respect and collaboration across previous divides but let us also remember that although 'being together' is a necessary condition for learning about each other, it is an insufficient condition for ensuring real understanding and respect, far less liking. Shared participation in meaningful activities will help, as will ensuring that positive but honest images are nurtured of all. This is not just an issue for individuals and social and educational planners; it is an issue for media and for local and national politicians, two bodies that have in the past betrayed the populations they were supposed to represent. Perhaps fostering opportunities for inclusion is an opportunity for some kind of earthly human redemption.

REFERENCES

Ainscow, M. (1999). Reaching out to all learners: some lessons from international experience. *School Effectiveness and School Improvement,* 11(1), 1–19.
Ajdinski, L. & Florian, L. (1997). Special Education in Macedonia. *European Journal of Special Needs Education,* 12(2), 116–126.
Allcock, J. (2000). *Explaining Yugoslavia.* London: Hurst.
Apple, M. (2002) Patriotism, Pedagogy and Freedom: On the Educational Meanings of September 11. *Teachers College Record,* 104(8), Retrieved June 18, 2002 from http://www.tcrecord.org.
Beane, J. & Apple, M. (1999). The case for democratic schools, in M. Apple & J. Beane (Eds.), *Democratic Schools: Lessons from the Chalk Face.* Buckingham: Open University, 1–29.
Closs, A. (1996). Education for tolerance and other aspects of adulthood : Could school-age education in ex-Yugoslavia improve its contribution? in S. Bianchini & M. Faber (Eds.), *The Balkans: Religious Backyard of Europe.* Ravenna: Editore Longo, 197–212.
Closs, A. (1998). Disabled people, in J. Allcock, M. Milivojevic, & J. Horton, (Eds.), *Conflict in the Former Yugoslavia: An Encyclopedia.* Santa Barbara, Ca.: ABC-CLIO, 75–77.
Crick, B. (2000). *Essays on Citizenship.* London: Continuum.
Csanyi, Y. (2001). Steps towards inclusion. *European Journal of Special Needs Education,* 16(3), 301–308.
Deljanin, L. (2002). Conclusions from the Conference on Current Status in Education of Children and Youth with Special Needs (7 June, 2002) and Reform Directions. (Informal

Document issued in September 2002 to Conference particpants and interested parties. Belgrade: Ministarstvo Prosvete I Sporta Republike Srbije.

Djilas, M. (1974) *The New Class: An Analysis of the Communist System*. New York: Praeger Publishers.

Djordjevic, J., Jogan, S., Ribicic, M. & Vratusa, A. (1982). *Samoupravljanje: Jugoslovenski Put u Socijalizam (Self-management: The Yugoslav Way to Socialism)*. Belgrade: Jugoslovenski Pregled.

Donia, R. & Fine, V. (1994). *Bosnia and Hercegovina: A Tradition Betrayed*. London: Hurst.

Drakulic, S. (1992, 20 January). Overcome by nationhood. *Time*, p52.

Government of the Republic of Croatia (1999a). *National Program of Action for Children in the Republic of Croatia*. Zagreb:Government Publications.

Government of the Republic of Croatia (1999b). *National Program for the Improvement of the Quality of Life of the Disabled*. Zagreb:Government Publications.

Hall, S. & Du Gay, P. (1996). *Questions of Cultural Identity*. London: Sage Publications.

Halpin, D. (1999). Democracy, inclusive schooling and the politics of education. *International Journal of Inclusive Education*, 3(3), 225–238.

Hastie, R. (1997). *Disabled Children in a Society at War: A Casebook from Bosnia*. Oxford: Oxfam.

Ignatieff, M. (2002, 27 October). When a bridge is not a bridge. New York Times Magazine. Retrieved on October 27, 2002, from http://www.nytimes.com/2002/10/27/magazine/27MOSTAR.html.

Jokmanovic, S. (2000). *Projekat potpore celokupnog razvojnog procesa dece i adolescenata u ustanovi decje selo. (Project to support the holistic development of children and adolescents in the Children's Village)*. Novi Sad: SOS Kinderdorf, Dr Milorad Pavlovic.

Medicins du Monde (1999). *Duga Centre: Psychosocial Aid for the Adolescents of Sarajevo*. Sarajevo: ECHO/Medecins du Monde.

Mesalic, L. (1998). Rehabilitacija i uticaj ratnih zbivanja na sustav skolovanja hendikepirane djece na Tuzlansko-podrinjskom kantonu. (Rehabilitation and the influence of war circumstances on the system of schooling of handicapped children in the Tuzla-Drin region.) Unpublished paper given at the 5th Scientific Conference of the Faculty of Special Education and Rehabilitation, University of Zagreb, Zagreb, September.

Mikovic, M. (1998). Assessment of children at risk – a holistic approach, in M, Dervisbegovic and S. Hessle (Eds.), *Social Work with Children under Post-War Conditions*. Sarajevo: Department of Social Work, Sarajevo University.

Mittler, P. (2000) *Working Towards Inclusive Education: Social Contexts*. London: David Fulton Publishers.

Pavlowitch, S. (1992). *Tito: Yugoslavia's Great Dictator: A Reassessment*. London: Hurst.

Pring, R. (1986). Aims, contexts and curriculum contents, in P.Tomlinson & M. Quinton (Eds.), *Values Across the Curriculum*. London: Hodder and Stoughton, 181–194.

Popov, N. (Ed.), (1996). *Srpska Strana Rata: Trauma i Katarza u Istorijskom Pamcenju (The Road to War in Serbia: Trauma and Catharsis)*. Beograd: Republika.

Racki, J. (1982). Resultati i problemi u ostvarivanju preobrazaja odgoja i obrazavanja djeci i omladini s teskocama u rajvoju. (Results and problems in the implementation of reforms in the education and schooling of children and young people with developmental difficulties.) *Proceedings of the Conference on Rehabilitation and Protection of the Disabled*. Faculty of Defektology, Zagreb, July 1982. Zagreb: University of Zagreb,78–96.

Richter-Malabotta, M. (2002). A new marginalisation of women as a result of war and ethnic conflict, in *Systems in Transition: Collected Papers*. Berlin: Systems in Transition e.V.

Roberts, A. & Guelff, R. (Eds.), (1989). *Documents on the Laws of War*. Oxford: Clarendon Press.

Rouse, M., Florian, L. & Connolly, J (2001). External Evaluation of the Project, Special Classrooms for Children with Disabilities in Bosnia and Herzegovina. Retrieved October 1, 2002, from www.unicef.org/bosnia/Download/title1.pdf.

Roy, A. (2001). The algebra of infinite justice. *The Guardian*. September 29, 2001.

Salom, N. (Ed.), (1999). *Sto Dvadeset Godina Prve Gimnazije u Sarajevu 1879–1999 (One Hundred and Twenty Years of the First High School in Sarajevo 1879–1999)*. Sarajevo: Federal Ministry of Education Ref 03-15-5421/99.

Silber, L. & Little, A. (1995). *The Death of Yugoslavia*. London: Penguin Books/BBC Books.

Singleton, F. (1985). *A Short History of the Yugoslav Peoples*. Cambridge: Cambridge University Press.

Smajkic, A. (1997). *Zdravsteno-Socialne Posljedice Rata u Bosni I Hercegovini: Prijedlog Sanacija, (Health and Social Consequences of the War in Bosnia and Hercegovina: Rehabilitation Proposal)*. Sarajevo: IP Svejtlost.

Susak, B. (1996) Alternativa ratu (Alternatives to war), in N. Popov (Ed.), *Srpska Strana Rata: Trauma i Katarza u Istorijskom Pamcenju*. Beograd: Republika.

Thomas, G. & Loxley, A. (2001). *Deconstructing Special Education and Constructing Inclusion*. Buckingham: Open University Press.

Thomas, G. & Glenny, G. (2002). Thinking about inclusion. Whose reason? What evidence? *International Journal of Inclusive Education*. 6(4), pp 345–370,

Thompson, M. (1994). *Forging War: the media in Serbia, Croatia and Bosnia: Hercegovina*. London: Article 19, International Centre against Censorship.

Ugresic, D. (1995) *The Culture of Lies*. London: Phoenix/Orion Books.

UNESCO/Government of Spain (1994). *World Conference on Special Needs Education (Salamanca Statement)*. Madrid: Spanish Ministry of Education.

UNICEF (2001, April). Youth conference defines priorities for children and youth. Retrieved October 1, 2002, from www,unicef.org.bosnia/English/whats_new.html

United Nations (1996). *Study on the Impact of Armed Conflict on Children (The Machel Study)*. New York: UN.

United Nations (1989). *The Convention on the Rights of the Child*. Geneva: United Nations Children's Fund.

Woodward, S. (1995). *Balkan Tragedy: Chaos and Dissolution after the Cold War*. Washington DC: The Brookings Institution.

Yugoslav Child Rights Centre (2001). *The Situation of Children in Institutions of Social Care in Serbia*. Belgrade: YCRC.

Zukin, S. (1975). *Beyond Marx and Tito: Theory and Practice in Yugoslav Socialism*. London: Cambridge University Press.

PART THREE

PRESSING FOR CHANGE

MEL AINSCOW AND DAVE TWEDDLE

10 UNDERSTANDING THE CHANGING ROLE OF ENGLISH LOCAL EDUCATION AUTHORITIES IN PROMOTING INCLUSION

Local Education Authorities (LEAs) in England are accountable to their electorates and to the Secretary of State for maintained schools in their areas. In this sense they can be seen as part of the democratic process by which educational provision is made available for all children and young people within a local area. However, since 1988, a series of national reforms have gradually eroded the power of LEAs. In essence, the stated aim has been to delegate greater responsibility to the level of schools in the belief that this will help to foster improvements in standards.

In this chapter, we consider the implications of these changes for efforts to develop more inclusive forms of education. In particular, we reflect upon our recent experience of working with colleagues in a number of English LEAs as they have attempted to move policy and practice forward. This begins the process of mapping out the issues in order to guide further research and development activities. It also leads us to be concerned about the way in which the erosion of local control of education may make it more difficult to foster inclusive arrangements.

Inclusion is arguably the major issue facing the English education system. Although the Government boasts of apparent improvements in national test and examination results, many pupils still feel marginalised, others are excluded because of their behaviour, and, of course, a significant minority are separated into special education provision. Meanwhile, following the publication of national examination results in the summer of 2002, it was widely reported that some 30,000 youngsters had left school without any qualifications at all.

It is hardly surprising, therefore, that the two most consistently recurring national policy themes in English education over the last few years have been concerned with 'raising standards' and 'promoting inclusion.'. The challenge for Local Education Authorities (LEAs) has been, and continues to be, the pursuit of these twin aims during a period of fundamental reform of the education service.

CONTEXT

The significance of the changes that have occurred, and are continuing to occur, in respect of the role of LEAs can only be understood if they are viewed within the context of the wider developments in the English education service over the last twenty years or so. In particular, there has been an intensification of political interest

J. Allan (ed.), Inclusion, Participation and Democracy: What is the Purpose?, 165-177.

in education, especially regarding standards and the management and governance of the state system. This led to a variety of legislative efforts to improve schools during the 1980s, culminating in a series of Acts of Parliament, of which the 1988 Education Reform Act was the most significant. These Acts were consolidated by further legislation in the early 1990s and continued by the Labour Government that came into office in 1997.

Broadly speaking, there are four key elements of government policy that, taken together, provide the context within which LEAs are now required to operate (Ainscow et al, 1999). First of all, they are required to have Educational Development Plans (EDPs) in which they must describe their proposals for approval by the Secretary of State, setting out performance targets, a school improvement programme, and a range of supporting information. Then, the *Code of Practice on LEA-School Relations* makes explicit the principles, expectations, powers and responsibilities that must guide the work of LEAs in relation to schools. In particular, it lays down the principle that LEA intervention in schools must be 'in inverse proportion to success,' and places clear responsibilities on LEAs to intervene in schools found to have serious weaknesses, or placed in special measures, following an inspection. So, as the EDP prescribes what LEAs are required to do, the Code focuses on how it should be done. *Fair Funding* sets out to clear the 'funding fog' surrounding education budgets by requiring resources to be allocated transparently and in line with a clear definition of the respective roles of schools and the LEA. Finally, the *Framework for the Inspection of Local Education Authorities* defines the basis of the inspection framework that, it is argued, will identify the strengths and weaknesses of each LEA inspected. Together, then, these four strands of government policy determine what LEAs address, how they operate, how all of it is funded, and how the whole process is monitored and evaluated.

Over a period of less than twenty years, therefore, the governance of the education service in England has been fundamentally changed. These changes have, perhaps, been reflected most significantly in the evolving relationships between schools, and between schools and their LEA. In particular, schools have become much less dependent on their LEAs. This movement from 'dependency' towards greater 'independence' has been consistently orchestrated through legislation and associated guidance from the Department for Education and Skills (DfES). This shift was summarised in the Government's 1997 consultation document, *Excellence in Schools*, which stated that the role of LEAs was not to control schools, but to challenge all schools to improve and support those which need help to raise standards.

The relationship between schools has also changed. Competition between schools is now seen to be one of the keys to 'driving up standards' and further reducing the control of the local authority over provision. This was encouraged through the introduction of grant-maintained status for schools (now referred to as 'foundation schools') and open enrolment, supported by the publication of league tables of school results. All of this was intended to 'liberate' schools from the bureaucracy of local government and establish what has been described as school quasi-markets, in which effective schools would have an 'arms-length' relationship with the LEA and, indeed, with each other (Thrupp, 2001).

So fundamental has been the reform of the education service, and so significant have been the reductions in the powers of the LEA, that the question may now be asked: 'Do LEAs any longer have the capacity to make a difference?' Our own research indicates that, in terms of the promotion of inclusive policies and practices, significant differences exist between 'similar' LEAs, and that these differences, at least in part, are due to strategic planning and policy decisions taken at the LEA level (Ainscow et al, 2000). Moreover, there is abundant statistical evidence to indicate that some groups of children and young people are most 'at risk' of marginalisation, underachievement or exclusion – particularly in a climate in which schools and LEAs are under such severe pressure to improve test results. What follows, therefore, is based on two assumptions. First of all, we presume that LEAs can and do 'make a difference' to the development of inclusive education; and secondly, we believe that LEAs have a fundamental responsibility to promote inclusion, whilst simultaneously seeking to 'raise standards.'

COLLABORATIVE INQUIRY

The work that we have been doing involves the use of an approach to research that we refer to as 'collaborative inquiry.' This approach advocates practitioner research, carried out in partnership with academics, as a means of developing better understanding of educational processes (Ainscow, 1999). Kurt Lewin's dictum that you cannot understand an organisation until you try to change it is, perhaps, the clearest justification for this approach (Schein, 2001). In practical terms, we believe that such understanding is best developed as a result of 'outsiders,' such as ourselves, working alongside headteachers, local authority staff and other stakeholders as they attempt to move policy and practice forward by seeking practical solutions to complex problems.

We argue that this approach can be used to overcome the traditional gap between research and practice. What is proposed here is an alternative view, in line with Robinson (1998) suggestion that research findings may well be ignored, regardless of how well they are communicated, if they bypass the ways in which practitioners formulate the problems they face and the constraints within which they work. The potential benefits of collaborative inquiry, in which an open dialogue can develop, are considerable. The ideal we aspire to is a process through which critical reflection leads to understandings that can have an immediate and direct impact on the development of thinking and practice in the field. However, it has to be recognised that participatory research of this kind is fraught with difficulties, not least in terms of developing ways of ensuring that the findings have relevance to a wider audience.

A programme of collaborative research that we have undertaken during the last four years forms the basis of this Chapter. This started with a small-scale study, commissioned by the DfES, that led to the publication in 1999 of a report called

Effective Practice in Inclusion and in Special and Mainstream Schools Working Together (Ainscow et al, 1999). This work analysed policy and practice in twelve LEAs, and explored factors that seem to facilitate or inhibit the development of inclusive practices. Then, in April 2000, we were commissioned by DfES to evaluate the work of the *Special Educational Needs Regional Partnerships* (Ainscow et al, in press). One of the core activities of these Partnerships is to promote inclusive policies and practices, and our observations during the past two years have undoubtedly further developed our understanding. In addition, we have worked as external consultants to several individual and, more recently, groups of LEAs engaged in reviewing and developing their strategies in this area (Ainscow & Tweddle, 2001). All of this work, and the people with whom we have collaborated, have contributed to the ideas presented here.

A new paradigm

We recently listened to the Chief Education Officer in a large LEA addressing a conference of headteachers. In his speech, he dealt with the changes that have occurred in education during the last twenty years, referring to many of the events summarised earlier in this chapter. He then went on to present his view of 'where we are now' and 'what we need to do in the future in order to move forward.'

The Chief Officer was talking in particular about the evolving relationship between schools and the LEA. However, we believe that his argument applies to a much wider range of stakeholders involved in providing services to children and young people. He began by describing the work of LEAs twenty years ago. The relationship of schools to the LEA was, at that time, essentially characterised by 'dependency.' Indeed, schools depended on the LEA for just about everything – curriculum policies, the replacement of staff, repairs, 'capitation,' support services, and so on. However, much of the legislation of the last twenty years, as we have described, has been geared towards giving schools much greater 'independence.' That is, independence from the LEA, and indeed independence from one other. Both approaches, he argued, were deeply flawed and should, therefore, be abandoned. In particular, an emphasis on school autonomy within an environment that is preoccupied with competition and choice is unlikely to foster progress in respect of equity. Rather, it creates a policy context within which the success of one school, or, indeed, one group of pupils, is achieved at the expense of the failure of others. What is needed, therefore, is a paradigm shift towards the notion of 'inter-dependency.'

This analysis crystallises much of what we are trying to do in our own work. Whilst there is strong research support for the idea of individual schools having the space and resources to plan their own improvement strategies (Hopkins et al, 1994), it is increasingly being recognised that they are likely to be better placed to make progress if they have access to 'effective' forms of support and challenge, both from the LEA and from neighbouring schools. There is, for example, an increasing body of evidence pointing to the benefits of peer support and challenge at the level of individual schools (Ainscow et al, in press). This approach, in which colleagues from one school become involved with colleagues in another school, seems to have the potential to foster learning for each party. The school being visited benefits from the new perspectives and reflections brought by a 'fresh pair of eyes,' and the visitor takes away insights and ideas derived from looking at how another school carries out its tasks. This leads us to argue that the approach may have considerable potential for developing policy and practice at LEA level, although this is as yet largely untested. In other words, we propose that LEAs should similarly benefit from such an inter-dependent, symbiotic relationship both with their schools and with other LEAs.

Currently, we are working with a consortium of six LEAs in the North West of England. At the heart of the methodology being used in this initiative is the notion of 'peer supported self-review.' This involves each individual LEA in planning and managing a self-review process that is focused on some aspect of policy and practice relating to inclusion. In this way, each LEA is responsible for making judgements about its own practice, and any decisions taken about future developments are made solely by the LEA concerned. However, the process of self-review is supported and challenged by a team of appropriately experienced colleagues from neighbouring LEAs, in addition to 'outsiders' from the University.

Introducing such approaches in the current context is far from straightforward. We recall, for example, a meeting we attended some time ago in one particular LEA. It had been called to discuss the logistics of, and the possible benefits and problems associated with, a proposal to establish clusters or families of schools. In other words, we were planning to put the idea of inter-dependency into action. Eventually, one secondary headteacher, whilst acknowledging that he had enjoyed the debate, said: 'OK, but, what's in this for me and my school?' He went on to argue that the idea would only 'take off' if key stakeholders could see that there would be significant, practical benefits for their own schools or organisations. In other words, he wanted to be convinced that the proposed arrangement would enable his school to move forward. Rather similar questions were asked when our current work with the six LEAs was being planned, and this initiative will, no doubt, only continue to gain momentum for as long as key people in the participating LEAs perceive that benefits are accruing for their own organisations. All of this seems to suggest that self-interest is, in fact, an important component of inter-dependency. A group of individuals are only likely to develop a sense of inter-dependence when they recognise that an event that affects one member affects them all. In practice, participants need first to understand and then to experience the potential benefits of inter-dependent working arrangements.

The notion of inter-dependency has, of course, a currency beyond the relationship between LEAs and schools. Both also have to work with a wide range of other stakeholders. Schools, for example, need to work closely with parents, the local community, and with other statutory and voluntary agencies. They cannot function effectively in isolation. Similarly, LEAs need to nurture inter-dependent working relationships with the plethora of other stakeholder groups involved in providing services to children, young people and their families, such as: Central Government, local politicians, the health department, other local authority services, including Social Care and Housing, the independent sector, and a wide range of community and other voluntary organisations.

Management implications

In providing this account of the emergence of what we see as a new paradigm based on the development of inter-dependent relationships, we are not laying claim to a major breakthrough in thinking. In fact, many of the Government's own policy initiatives in recent years have imposed a requirement on different agencies and stakeholder groups to work together. It is also true that throughout the country, in all regions and localities, there are people from different organisations working together in order to solve problems relating to the education of children and young people.

Nevertheless, the paradigm shift does present major new challenges for senior managers in LEAs. It is clear that local schools are much less dependent on their LEA than they once were; at the same time, local schools cannot function effectively in isolation from their LEA. As our Chief Education Officer colleague was arguing, schools and LEAs are inter-dependent; they need each other. Moreover, we believe that LEAs also need to develop similar, inter-dependent relationships with other LEAs and with other voluntary and statutory agencies providing services to children and their families. All of this points to the need for the development of new cultures, relationships and ways of working.

In our work, we have been trying to understand the nature of effective inter-dependent relationships. Here we have found Michael Fielding's (1999) distinction between collaboration and collegiality helpful to our thinking. He characterises collaboration as being a means to a clearly defined end. Consequently, it is driven by a set of common concerns, is narrowly functional and is focused strongly on intended gains. The partners in the activity are regarded as a resource, or a source of information. Fielding goes on to suggests that collaboration is, in a sense, a plural form of individualism in which participants are typically unwilling to devote time to anything other than the task in hand or the core purposes of the business. Fielding goes on to point out that once the driving force behind collaboration is weakened, the task has been completed or priorities have changed, such collaborative working arrangements may dissipate, disappear or become more tenuous. Collegiality, on the other hand, is characterised as being much more robust and as rooted in shared ideals, aspirations and valued social goals. It is, by definition, less reliant upon narrowly defined and predictable gains.

In practice, instances of LEAs working together, or working with other agencies, often do not fall neatly into either definition. Moreover, it may be that for some, combinations of stakeholders, collaboration has to be a forerunner to the growth of collegiality. In other words, stakeholders experience the practical benefits to their organisation of collaborating when the outcomes are clearly defined, whilst seeking to develop a common language and shared aspirations that might, in the longer term, provide a basis for the development of a more collegial relationship.

In our current work, we are trying to nurture collegiates of LEAs working together. Our starting point has been to plan collaborative activity in which the outcomes and benefits are articulated. In the longer term, however, our collective aim is to develop a shared understanding of the nature of inclusion that will provide the basis for self-sustaining collegial relationships.

Our central argument here is that, as the context has changed, so the challenges of strategic management at the LEA level also have to change. Furthermore, we believe that the development and management of inter-dependent working relationships holds the key to effective policy development. Such relationships are the means by which LEAs can work effectively with their schools and with other relevant agencies within the locality, particularly in respect of the issue of inclusion.

TOWARDS A REVIEW FRAMEWORK

Through our work, then, we have tried to 'map' the factors that have the potential to either facilitate or inhibit the promotion of inclusive practice. These are all 'variables' which LEAs either control directly, or over which they can at least exert considerable influence. We intend that this work will eventually lead to the development of a framework that will provide a basis for self-review processes. With this in mind, there follows our working list of twelve factors, each with a small number of associated questions.

Definition
Is there clarity about what is meant by 'inclusion?' Is this definition short, clear, and widely understood? Is it widely supported by key stakeholders within and beyond the LEA?

Leadership
Is there effective management from senior management in the LEA and elected members on inclusion issues? Does this include articulating a clear and consistent vision for the LEA to the wider educational community? Does it include recognising and celebrating good practice, and challenging unacceptable practice?

Attitudes
Is the LEA a positive, solution-focused organisation that is fully committed to identifying and removing barriers to promoting inclusion in schools?

Policies, planning and processes
Does the LEA's definition of, and commitment to, inclusion 'permeate' all of its self-review and strategic planning processes?

Structures, roles and responsibilities
Does the structure of the LEA facilitate effective support and challenge to schools on inclusion issues? Do all units and services within the LEA understand their contribution to this aim and work effectively together to provide a coherent and co-ordinated service to schools?

Funding
Are the funding levels to support the LEA's policy on inclusion comparable to those of the LEA's statistical neighbours? Are the mechanisms used for distributing available resources designed to empower individual schools, and groups of schools, to identify and overcome barriers to promoting inclusion?

Support and challenge to schools
Do schools understand the LEA's policy aspirations for the development of inclusive education? Does the LEA facilitate systems of school-to-school support and challenge?

Responding to diversity
Does the LEA encourage and facilitate the development of additional programmes, curriculum initiatives and other provision in 'all' schools that are designed to reduce the risk of underachievement, marginalisation and exclusion?

Specialist provision
Is there is a clear role for other specialist provision, including special schools, that supports the LEA's commitment to promoting inclusion? Is the pattern of additional specialist provision within the LEA (i.e. non-mainstream provision) matched to the known and anticipated pattern of need?

Partnerships
Is there a strong partnership between the LEA and its schools that is characterised by a shared commitment to, and effective communication about, the LEA's policy on inclusion? Is there effective co-operation between the LEA, and Health and other Council Departments, on inclusion? Does the LEA work effectively with other LEAs to provide mutual support and challenge on inclusion issues?

Use of evidence
Does the LEA have clear success criteria that are linked directly to its definition of inclusion? Is evidence collected by the LEA, and by individual schools, that can be used to evaluate progress towards more inclusive practice? Does this evidence include the views of pupils and their families about the services they receive?

Staff development and training
Does the LEA have a properly funded Staff Development and Training Strategy that

recognises the importance of continued professional development and ensures that all of its members of staff are provided with awareness raising and role-specific training opportunities on inclusion issues?

Some of these twelve factors seem to be potentially more potent than others. Within the current English system, for example, it is evident that the use of evidence acts as an important lever for change. Similarly, the ways in which resources are allocated are extremely important in respect to the development of practice in the field. However, our work suggests that one factor seems to be superordinate to all others, namely clarity of definition.

DEFINING INCLUSION

There is still considerable confusion in the field about what inclusion actually means (Ainscow et al, 2000). To some extent, this lack of clarity might be tracked back to central Government policy statements. For example, the use of the term 'social inclusion' has been associated mainly with improving attendance and reducing the incidence of exclusions from schools. At the same time, the idea of 'inclusive education' has appeared in most DfES guidance in connection with the rights of individual children and young people categorised as having special educational needs to be educated in mainstream schools, whenever possible. Most recently, Ofsted, the inspection agency, has introduced the term 'educational inclusion,' noting that effective schools are also inclusive schools. The subtle differences between these concepts adds to the sense of uncertainty as to what is intended and, of course, it is now well established that educational reform is particularly difficult in contexts where there is a lack of common understanding amongst stakeholders (Fullan, 1991).

This being the case, in our own work we have supported LEAs as they have attempted to develop a definition of 'inclusion' that can be used to guide policy development. Predictably, the exact detail of each LEA's definition is unique, because of the need to take account of local circumstances, culture and history. Nevertheless, four key elements have tended to feature strongly, and these are commended to any LEA intending to review its own working definition. These are as follows:

Inclusion is a process

That is to say, it is not simply a matter of setting and achieving a few targets and then the job is complete. In practice, the job will never be completed. Rather inclusion has to be seen as a never-ending search to find better ways of responding to diversity. It is about learning how to live with difference and, learning how to learn from difference. In this way, differences come to be seen more positively as a stimulus for fostering learning, amongst children and adults.

Inclusion is concerned with the identification and removal of barriers

Consequently, it involves collecting, collating and evaluating information from a wide variety of sources in order to plan for improvements in policy and practice. It is about using evidence of various kinds to stimulate creativity and problem-solving.

Inclusion is about the presence, participation and achievement of all pupils

Here 'presence' is concerned with where children are educated, and how reliably and punctually they attend; 'participation' relates to the quality of their experiences whilst they are there and inevitably therefore incorporates the views of the learners themselves; and 'achievement' is about the outcomes of learning across the curriculum, not merely test or examination results.

Inclusion involves a particular emphasis on those groups of learners who may be at risk of marginalisation, exclusion or underachievement

This indicates the moral responsibility of the LEA to ensure that those groups that are statistically most 'at risk' are carefully monitored and that, where necessary, steps are taken to ensure their presence, participation and achievement in the education system.

In the twelve LEAs that took part in one of the research projects cited earlier (Ainscow et al, 1999), despite the lack of consensus about the meaning of inclusion, we did find evidence of widespread agreement about the kind of definition, or position statement, that would be most useful within a LEA context. Specifically, delegates from the participating LEAs argued for the development of a statement that was 'short, clear, stable, capable of being internalised, transportable, widely supported and led by the LEA.' The phrases 'capable of being internalised' and 'transportable' are significant here, in that they indicate that a common understanding of what is meant by the term inclusion is necessary in order to move policy and practice forward. This, they argued, would increase the likelihood of the principles underpinning the development of inclusive practices permeating other review and planning processes within the LEA. All of this, of course, accords with Fielding's view of the development of a collegiate.

Throughout our work, we have been mindful of the notion of 'levers' (Senge, 1989), actions that can be taken that have the effect of moving practice forward by changing the behaviour of the organisation and those individuals within it. Our experience is that some initiatives launched at the LEA level can appear high profile whilst having little impact on practice, that is they have low leverage. However, achieving clarity about the meaning of inclusion amongst stakeholders, whilst difficult to achieve, is usually a high leverage activity. Simple though the point may be, we cannot overstate its importance. Without a clarity of definition across an LEA, strategic planning becomes deeply problematic and, as we will argue, effective evaluation is, therefore, almost impossible.

Evidence

Our search for 'levers' has also led us to acknowledge the importance of evidence. In essence, it leads us to conclude that within the English education system, 'what gets measured gets done.'

Nowadays, LEAs in England are required to collect far more statistical data than ever before. This is widely recognised as a double-edged sword precisely because it is such a potent lever for change. On the one hand, data are required in order to monitor the progress of children, evaluate the impact of interventions, review the effectiveness of policies and processes, plan new initiatives, and so on. In these senses, data can, justifiably, be seen as the life-blood of continuous improvement. On the other hand, if effectiveness is evaluated on the basis of narrow, even inappropriate, performance indicators, then the impact can be deeply damaging. Whilst appearing to promote the causes of accountability and transparency, the use of data can, in practice, conceal more than they reveal, invite misinterpretation and, worst of all, have a perverse effect on the behaviour of professionals. This has led the current 'audit culture' (Strathearn, 1999, p. 309) to be described as a 'tyranny of transparency' (ibid).

All of this suggests that great care needs to be exercised in deciding what evidence is collected and, indeed, how it is used. LEAs are, of course, required by Government to collect particular data. Given national policies, they cannot opt out of collecting such data on the grounds that their publication might be misinterpreted, or that they may influence practice in an unhelpful way. On the other hand, LEAs are free to collect additional evidence that can then be used to evaluate the effectiveness of their own policy and practice in respect of progress towards greater inclusion. The challenge for LEAs is, therefore, to harness the potential of evidence as a lever for change, whilst avoiding the problems described earlier.

Our own work suggests that the starting point for making decisions about the evidence to collect should be with an agreed definition of inclusion. In line with the suggestions made earlier, then, we argue that the evidence collected by an LEA needs to relate to the 'presence, participation and achievement' of all pupils, with an emphasis placed on those groups of learners regarded to be 'at risk of marginalisation, exclusion or underachievement.'

LOOKING TO THE FUTURE

We began by acknowledging that the development of inclusive policies and practices at the LEA level is a complex process occurring in a rapidly changing context. This chapter is, therefore, an attempt to make a contribution to a better understanding of these complex issues in the field. As such, it is intended that the ideas discussed here will stimulate thinking and debate in ways that will enable further progress to be made in taking forward the inclusion agenda.

As we continue working with the LEAs in which we are currently involved, we have two inter-linked aspirations, both of which are inherent in our approach to collaborative research. First, we hope that they will derive direct and practical benefits from their involvement and that, as a result, children, young people and their families will receive more inclusive educational services. Then, in the longer term, we hope that the 'collaborative' working arrangements established between participating LEAs will develop 'collegiate' relationships, based on a shared understanding of the nature of inclusion.

Secondly, we hope to make further progress in understanding and articulating some of the complex issues involved in this work. In general terms, we intend that the analysis that has been developed will eventually provide the basis of a LEA review framework for the development of inclusive policies and practices.

With these aspirations in mind, our current research involves LEAs working in partnership to explore the use of peer supported self-review. In this way, the notion of inter-dependence is being extended to incorporate an LEA-to-LEA dimension. The LEAs involved in this study have agreed to cooperate in a programme of visits, during which they set out to challenge and support one another as they review those policy dimensions that seem to have the potential for high leverage.

It is important to remember that much of what goes on within organisations such as LEAs is largely taken-for-granted and, therefore, rarely discussed. In other words, practices are manifestations of organisational culture (Schein, 1985). Our assumption is that some of the barriers experienced by learners arise from these existing arrangements and circumstances. Consequently, the peer supported self-review strategy sets out to use the involvement of 'outsiders' to interrupt existing thinking, in order to encourage 'insiders' to explore overlooked possibilities for moving practice forward. Our research so far suggests that a focus on the issues of definition and the related use of evidence has the potential to create such inter-ruptions.

REFERENCES

Ainscow, M. (1999). *Understanding the Development of Inclusive Schools*. Falmer.

Ainscow, M., Farrell, P. and Tweddle, D. (1999). *Effective Practice in Inclusion and in Special and Mainstream Schools Working Together*. London: Department for Education and Employment.

Ainscow, M., Farrell, P. And Tweddle, D. (2000). Developing policies for inclusive education: A study of the role of local education authorities. *International Journal of Inclusive Education*, 4(3), 211–229.

Ainscow, M., Farrell, P. And Tweddle, D. (in press). *An Evaluation of the SEN Regional Partnerships*. London: Department for Education and Skills.

Ainscow, M., Howes, A., Farrell, P. and Frankham, J. (in press). Making sense of the development of inclusive practices. *European Journal of Special Needs Education*.

Ainscow, M. and Tweddle, D. (2001). *Developing the roles of local education authorities in relation to achievement and inclusion: barriers and opportunities*. Paper presented the Senior Education Officer's National Conference, Cambridge, 13th July 2001.

Department for Education (1997). *Excellence in schools*. Consultation document. London: DfEE.

Fielding, M. (1999). Radical collegiality: affirming teaching as an inclusive professional practice. *Australian Educational Researcher,* 26(2), 1–34.

Fullan, M. (1991). *The New Meaning of Educational Change.* London: Cassell.

Hopkins, D., Ainscow, M. and West, M. (1994). *School Improvement in an Era of Change.* London: Cassell.

Robinson, V.M.J. (1998). Methodology and the research-practice gap. *Educational Researcher,* 27, 17–26.

Schein, E. (1985). *Organisational Culture and Leadership.* San Francisco: Jossey-Bass.

Schein, E.H. (2001). Clinical inquiry/research. In P.Reason and H. Bradbury (Eds.) *Handbook of Action Research.* London: Sage

Senge, P.M. (1989). *The Fifth Discipline: The Art and Practice of the Learning Organisation.* London: Century.

Strathearn, M. (2000) The tyranny of transparency. *British Journal of Educational Researc h, 26(3), 309–321.*

Thrupp, M. (2001). *School quasi-markets in England and Wales: Best understood as a class strategy?* Paper presented at the conference of the British Education Research Association. Leeds, September 2001.

JULIE ALLAN

11 DARING TO THINK OTHERWISE?
EDUCATIONAL POLICYMAKING
IN THE NEW SCOTTISH PARLIAMENT

INTRODUCTION

The opening of the Scottish Parliament on 1 July 1999 signalled great hope for a form of democratic renewal which would remoralise politics (Cohen, 1996) and, in Putnam's (2000) terms, recreate civil society as a moral realm that can 'counter the political amorality of excessive individualism of a dominant state' (Paterson, 2000a, p. 49). One of the Parliament's main activities, within its eighteen Committees, has been to conduct Inquiries into a range of aspects of public life and as adviser to the Education, Culture and Sport Committee on one of these Inquiries, I have gained a unique insight into this form of policymaking within Parliament. Written policies appear coherent and rational, but as Foucault (1984) argues, they consist of 'the accidents, the minute deviations ... the errors, the false appraisals and the faulty calculations that gave birth to those things that continue to exist and have value for us' (p. 81). My experience as adviser suggests that the Inquiry genre has provided a new productive space for policymaking which disrupts the usual forms of closure. This 'new policymaking culture' (Hassan, 1999, p. 13) is, I will argue, transforming 'conservatism and caution' into 'innovation and forward thinking' (ibid). Sniping about the escalating costs of the new Parliament building and the struggles with 'regulating cronyism in Scottish life' (Schlesinger et al, 2001, p. 267) continue with a depressing predictability. Yet, within its Committee rooms, the MSPs appear to have succeeded in 'thinking otherwise' (Ball, 1998, p. 81) about educational policy.

The Scottish educational policymaking scene

Prior to the establishment of the Scottish Parliament, educational policymaking in Scotland was directed by the Scottish Education Department and, according to Bryce and Humes (1999), has been centralised, consensual and orthodox. Dissenting voices are marginalised and strategies of containment limit the flow of information and create a conformist ideology in which discussion is restricted to procedural matters (ibid). The Scottish Education Department, whilst having a tight hold on the structures of policymaking, has not, however, always been able to control some of the processes (McPherson & Raab, 1989; Paterson 2000b). Government

179

J. Allan (ed.), Inclusion, Participation and Democracy: What is the Purpose?, 179-193.
© 2003 *Kluwer Academic Publishers. Printed in the Netherlands.*

quangos, set up to oversee matters such as curriculum and assessment, involved some educationists who stood in opposition to the Department. McPherson and Raab conclude that the authority base of educational policymaking has resided 'with the policy community of educationists that linked government with society and from which Ministers and politicians were for the most part excluded' (ibid, p. 173).

More generally, educational policy has been characterised by what Stronach and Morris (1994) have termed 'policy hysteria' (p. 4), with frequent cycles of recurrent reform, the erosion of professional discretion by centralisation of control and an endemic crisis of legitimation. Furthermore, the 'tyranny of targets' (Fielding, 1999, p. 279) speaks against visions of pluralism, inclusiveness and co-operation, by introducing further fragmentation and exclusionary mechanisms into the education system and policies which contradict and undermine each other. The promotion of raising achievement and social inclusion is one example of such oppositional policy-making, in which raising achievement has been presented within policy documents in terms of more narrowly defined attainment, accompanied by standards and targets for pupils and schools; at the same time, social inclusion strategies have targeted disenfranchised groups or individuals identified as being 'at risk.' Implicit within this normalising discourse is the categorising of individual pupils, whose lower attainment is attributed to factors such as ethnicity, gender or special educational needs and inclusion of these pupils is discouraged by the pressures of performativity. Gillborn and Youdell (2000) note the causal relationship between raising standards and deepening inequality, contending that 'reforms seem relentlessly to embody an increasingly divisive and exclusionary notion of education' (p. 41). They also highlight the contradictory messages from Central government, contrasting Blair's pronouncement that 'education *is* social justice' (p. 17) with Morris's assertion that 'performance tables help focus debate on standards' (ibid) and Blunkett's claim that 'standards not structures are now the prime concern' (ibid).

Paterson (2000b) suggests that in the years leading up to the establishment of the Scottish Parliament there existed in Scotland a strong vision of social democracy which had resisted the intrusions by the New Right, but which was, however, frustrated by the lack of fulfilment of social rights. The education system was seen as insufficiently radical and the Scottish Parliament was charged with challenging this and finding a means of satisfying the Scottish 'predilections for social justice' (ibid, p. 52).

Opening parliament: Opening politics?

The ceremony which opened Parliament provided the ritual for a renewal of civic virue – in the sense that Durkheim (1976) has observed is necessary for any society – in order to uphold and re-affirm 'the collective sentiments and the collective ideas which make its unity and its personality' (p. 427). For Scotland, this amounts to a strong tradition of social networks which have their bases in the civic insitutions of the philanthropists, public boards and in its abundance of intellectuals (Paterson, 2000a). The legacy of this social capital (Putnam, 2000) is a romanticised version of in the mythical alter-ego of the Gael (McDonald, 1996); a commodification of its heritage – Scotland the Brand (McCrone et al, 1995); a garish collation of tartan, shortbread and 'kailyard' values of 'bucolic intrigue and ... shrewd insight into human nature' (Nairn, 1977, p. 158) – the canny man; and much mythologising of its education system as outstanding. The Scottish Parliament was the chance to revive Scotland's distinctive social capital and to assert some new values in the shape of greater accountability and openness. Setting out the requirements for education, Bryce and Humes (1999) asserted that Scottish politicians must confront the major substantive issues and urged them to 'interrogate senior officials and hold the Executive to account in ways that have not been possible before'.

The three functions of any Parliament are to introduce legislation which improves the lives of the electorate, to scrutinise the Executive and ensure it is acting responsibly on behalf of the electorate, and to provide a forum for the discussion of public issues (Watson, 2001). The Scottish Parliament undertakes these activities through its Committee structures, which combine the functions carried out at Westminster by the separate Standing and Select Committees and have significantly greater power. Legislation can only be shaped by Westminster's Standing Committees; all of the Scottish Parliamentary Committees can do this. A major aspect of the work of the Scottish Parliamentary Committees is its Inquiries and it is one of these that I will now examine.

The 'special needs' inquiry

The Education, Culture and Sport Committee decided in November 1999 that one of its first Inquiries should focus on special needs. Specifically, it set out:

- To examine the diversity of provision across Scotland in special needs education
- To investigate the effectiveness of current integration strategies at all levels of pre-school and school education
- To investigate the effectiveness of transition arrangements for special needs pupils at each stage in the school education system
- To consider how effectively the requirements of special needs families are understood and fulfilled by education services.

The language used here – for example 'integration' and 'special needs families' – indicated that a major aspect of the Inquiry would have to be the education of MSPs out of their 'benevolent humanitarianism' (Tomlinson, 1982, p. 5) and into an awareness of the distinction between integration and inclusion. Indeed the politicians expressed their intention to find out what it would take to achieve an inclusive education system and to try to make this a reality. The Inquiry began in May 2000 and the report was published in February 2001 (Scottish Parliament, 2001a). A request was made for written evidence and 150 submissions were received from local authorities, professional associations, voluntary organisations, parents and disabled individuals. On the basis of these, selected individuals and groups were invited to give oral evidence to the Committee and MSPs undertook visits to a range of provisions. The Committee was diverted from its deliberations onto a more public investigation into the 'exam fiasco' in the summer of 2000, in which the Scottish Qualifications Authority botched the exam results of thousands of teenagers. This understandably demanded all of the MSP's concentration and they returned to the special needs Inquiry in January 2001 and agreed on the final version. The Scottish Executive had to respond within six weeks and a full debate, lasting three hours, was held on 17 May 2001 (Scottish Parliament, 2001b).

The report set out the 'changes that would be necessary to achieve an inclusive education system for all children' (Scottish Parliament, 2001b, Col 770) and its most significant aspects were:

- An indication that parents were disadvantaged by a 'geographical lottery,' a lack of information and support, and a disregarding of their views by professionals
- A clear definition of inclusion, as increasing participation and removing the structural, environmental and attitudinal barriers within schools
- A requirement that the system of assessing and recording children with special needs be reviewed and possibly discontinued because of its iniquity, inefficiency and failure to meet the needs of children and their parents
- A requirement to involve disabled children and their parents more fully in decision-making and in the training of staff in mainstream schools
- An affirmation of the 'presumption of mainstreaming,' contained in the new legislation
- An indication that special schools would need to demonstrate their contribution to inclusion or clarify their role as national providers.

The MSPs expressed pride in the report, reading it, and the Inquiry process, as allowing them to engage with the major issues affecting their electorate:

> The report is another example of Scotland becoming a much better place to live in because of the existence of the Scottish Parliament, which is able to address subjects that would not have been given any kind of political airing under the old political system with which we are all too familiar (McAllion, Labour, Scottish Parliament, 2001b, Col 801).

My role, as adviser to the Committee on this Inquiry, was to read the evidence and identify the significant issues; select the witnesses to provide oral evidence and establishments to be visited; prepare briefing notes and questions for the MSPs; and draft the report for approval by the MSPs. My positioning as an insider/outsider who could encourage the politicians' towards more robust forms of questioning raised significant methodological and ethical and dilemmas, both in relation to the conduct of the Inquiry and the reporting of that process. A high degree of reflexivity was required in order to manage the considerable uncertainty experienced by being an absent presence throughout the Inquiry. The insider/outsider account provided here represents merely one more interpretation of the early work of the Parliament, to be placed alongside those speaking from the inside (Ritchie, 2000; Watson, 2001) and those offering a more distanced observation (Hassan and Warhurst, 2000).

Productive space? Rereading the inquiry genre

The deconstructive rereading of the Inquiry process that follows appears to suggest its function as a productive space in which the politicians have dared themselves to 'think otherwise' (Ball, 1998, p. 81). These seem to be reflected in their preparedness to learn about what it takes to be inclusive and to understand what barriers stood in the way of inclusion; the displacing of party politics; the pursuit of a politics of undecidability and a reframing of accountability in ways which enabled them to hold the Scottish Executive to account.

Learning and unlearning

One of the biggest barriers to inclusion is the tendency among professionals to mythologise progress towards it, pronouncing that it is 'not yet there.' This discourages the radical rethinking of structures and practices that are necessary to achieve full inclusion (Allan, 1999). It also presupposes that we have a clear idea of what full inclusion actually looks like in practice. Certainly, standards and indicators identify the kinds of norms which schools and local authorities should aspire to, but these only relate to the geographical location of pupils and not to any consequences which the pupils and their families might consider to be meaningful (Slee and Allan, 2001). When the MSPs first began talking about the Inquiry, they pronounced themselves ignorant of the issues, but were aware from their constituents that this was a highly stressful area. They did, however, wish to learn all they could and appeared to have succeeded in this respect:

> I will make something of a confession. When I began my part in the Committee's Inquiry process, back in November 1999, I was sceptical of mainstreaming, probably because of my own experiences as a child. I never encountered any children with special educational needs in my classroom – they went away in a bus to a school somewhere else, because they were different, and could not be educated with me. Looking back on that, I realise that that is exactly the kind of impression that we must challenge among young people who are growing up now. Children with special educational needs, despite those needs, are not different from other children in Scotland and should not be treated differently. They should be able to expect the same high standard of education that every other child does (Gillon, Labour, Scottish Parliament, 2001b, Col 819–820).

> I knew very little about this subject when the Inquiry started. I approached the subject and my first visit to some schools involved with trepidation, but I have scarcely seen more caring, loving and enjoyable places in which to spend time (Russell, SNP, ibid: Col 781).

Clearly there is still some residue of 'benevolent humanitariansim' (Tomlinson, 1982, p. 5), further evidenced in the Conservative MSP Mundell's comment that 'the tremendous dedication of the staff and parents and the courage of the children gives tremendous insight and a greater confidence in humanity' (ibid, Col 794). Nevertheless, the majority of MSPs seemed to grasp the point that inclusion was about both maximising participation 'and' removing the barriers to that participation (Barton, 1997). Furthermore, they reached the understanding that much of the existing knowledge and practice of special education constituted one of the major barriers to inclusion. This is a fundamental point which remains beyond the grasp of many practitioners, teacher educators and advocates of inclusion (Brantlinger, 1997; Slee and Allan, 2001), but it was not lost on the Committee, one of whose members argued that its recommendations represented a departure from the 'We know best orthodoxy' (Peattie, Labour, Scottish Parliament, 2001a, Col 785) that had dominated special education for some time. Gorrie (Liberal Democrat) was among several MSPs who pronounced themselves well pleased with the 'serious advance in our efforts to deal with the issues' (ibid, Col 799), contending that 'We are on our way to producing a more civilised society' (ibid, Col 801).

Displacing party politics

For most of the Inquiry, there was an absence of party politics, consensus over the main issues arising from the evidence, and a shared desire to make improvements. This contrasted with the relatively aggressive stance adopted by the Conservative and Scottish Nationalist MSPs, intent on calling for ministerial resignations over the 'exam fiasco' or the raised tempers witnessed in the Social Justice Committee, when the Convenor was accused of introducing amendments to a report which were less negative about the Scottish Executive (Watson, 2001). In the special needs Inquiry, a comment by one MSP, specifying the goal of establishing an inclusive education system for all pupils and making recommendations which would ensure that this was realised, received endorsement from the whole Committee. It was only when the report was being finalised, that the Conservative MSP, Monteith, began to be concerned about the implications for special schools, many of which he had defended in the past, and called for further debate. Concerned about the impact of further delay, the MSPs moved to publish the report, with some agreed amendments and recorded the Conservative MSP's dissent on eight points, all of which concerned the future of special schools.

The debate in Parliament was marked largely by cross-party consensus and this was signalled at the outset by a change in protocol. Normally a motion would be moved by the convenor or vice convenor of the Committee, but in this case an MSP from a different party introduced the motion. Politicians from all parties indicated their support for the report's recommendations and, when the dissenting Monteith tried to generate discussion about the nature of his objections, which he had already voiced in a private session of the Committee, this was refused on a point of order. In a series of farcical exchanges, the extent to which Russell's (SNP) cough, which occurs 'when a member is saying something that Mr Russell does not like hearing' (Monteith, Conservative, ibid, Col 812), 'constitutes a Parliamentary activity' (Gorrie, Liberal Democrat, ibid, Col 812) was considered. The Deputy Presiding Officer agreed to investigate and report back the 'quality of Mr Russell's cough' (ibid, Col 812), but closure of this particular aspect of the debate was provided by McIntosh's (Labour) marginalisation of Monteith as someone who 'spreads discontent where there is harmony' (ibid,Col, 809) and who ought to know better:

> In some ways, I resent having to spend so much time discussing an issue on which there is broad agreement. Mr Monteith should know that the strength of Committees lies in their ability to deliver unanimous and cross-party analyses and recommendations. I believe that this could have been achieved in this case. The argument is not between mainstream and grant-aided schools, but about how we can improve facilities, resources and standards throughout the sector (ibid, Col 809).

The notion that Monteith might have been voicing legitimate concerns was not entertained by the Committee, whose members viewed his resistance as an unsavoury form of party politics. Monteith's contention that the Committee had, in not providing a funding framework to determine the future of the grant-aided schools, 'passed the buck' (ibid, Col 811) was thrown out in favour of projecting the 'broad support across the party-political spectrum for the policy objective of maximising participation of all children in mainstream schools' (ibid, Col 805–806). This 'triumph of consensus over combat' (Irvine, cited in Watson, 2001, p. 167) sent a significant message that responding to the needs of children and families was of greater concern than party politics.

Entering the politics of undecidability

The MSPs were presented in the oral evidence sessions with a series of opposing views which left them, at times, bewildered. A former special school pupil described having 'escaped' (Scottish Parliament, 2001a, p. 5), while a pupil now attending a special school for deaf pupils used the same term in relation to a mainstream school. Parents reported highly negative encounters with the education system and a lack of information and support, whereas local authorities and the Scottish Executive claimed that communication with, and support for, parents was increasingly effective. Teachers in mainstream schools were said to lack the confidence to meet the diversity of pupils needs, but the Executive indicated that: 'There is no shortage of advice about what teachers ought to be doing' (Scottish Parliament 2000a, Col 1104). The most contentious issue facing the MSPs related to the process of formally assessing children with special educational needs within a system of Records of Needs, which the Committee concluded was 'cumbersome and time consuming ... adversarial ... and inaccessible to parents' (Scottish Parliament, 2001a, p. 10).

The MSPs expressed their frustration that they could not produce solutions to all of the problems that had been reported to them, but their growing awareness of the complexity of this area of educational policy led them to realise that easy answers would not be possible. Rather than seeking to reconcile the various oppositions they encountered, the MSPs framed these in what might be termed a serious of aporias or contradictory pressures (Derrida, 1992a) which were by their very nature unresolvable, but which opened the door to possibilities:

> I will even venture to say that ethics, politics, and responsibility, *if there are any,* will only never have begun with the experience and experiement of the aporia. When the path is clear and given, when a certain knowledge opens up the way in advance, the decision is already made, it might as well be said that there is none to make; irresponsibly, and in good conscience, one simply applies or implements a program ... It makes of action the applied consequence, the simple application of a knowledge or know how. It makes of ethics and politics a technology. No longer of the order of practical reason or decision, it begins to be irresponsible (pp. 41–45).

The first of the contradictory pressures faced by the MSPs related to the need to provide recommendations which were just, yet which did not create closure by their certainty and clarity. Derrida (1997) suggests that injustice is a product of a pressure to reach a just decision, and the instant when this occurs is a 'madness' (Derrida, 1992b, p. 26). Furthermore, he argues, the certainty with which recommendations need to be made allows for the evasion of responsibility (Derrida, 1992b). The cross-party debate on inclusion was presented by the MSPs as an ethical one which 'takes the impasse of the dilemma seriously and offers educators better understanding of the dilemma itself' (Edgoose, 2001, p. 125).

The MSPs sought to foreground a number of aspects which would create openings for change rather than closure. The most significant of these were:

* *Parents and children's views guide practice*: 'Parents and children are the key to the solution of special educational needs – not the vested interests of one profession or another, or one party-political interest or another' (Gillon, Labour, Scottish Parliament, 2001b, Col 822).
* *The approach to meeting needs is pragmatic and child centred*: 'We are not asking for a philosophical or high-level commitment to the involvement of parents: we want a response to the blood, sweat and tears – too often and too many – of parents who are battling with the system' (Stephen, Deputy Minister for Education, Europe and External Affairs, ibid, Col 772).
* *Inequalities created by conflicting policies, eg inspection and target setting, are addressed:* 'It is important that the framework of inspection is revised to take due account of the differences in working practices' (Peattie, Labour, ibid, Col 786); 'Targets need to reflect the nature of the school population. They should not be a deterrent to the development of inclusive practices' (ibid, Col 787).
* *Professionals' need for support is recognised:* 'Teacher training should ensure understanding ... Teachers need time to share and prepare, to network and exchange information and to develop appropriate methods and materials for lessons' (ibid, Col 787).

Rather than seeking to provide a firm resolution to the problem of formal assessment, in its 'recommendations,' the Committee advised the National Advisory Forum, charged with the task of reviewing the Records of Needs procedures, to 'consider the options of either replacing the system or revising it substantially' (Scottish Parliament, 2001a, p. 3). It also set out a number of characteristics which a new system of assessment should have, but beyond that, did not specify a model or mechanism. Monteith (Conservative) endorsed the Committee's action in this case: 'as there was so much to do on that area, we were right to draw a line' (Scottish Parliament 2001b, Col 784). The MSPs' acknowledgement that certain issues require further investigation or cannot easily be resolved and their resistance of closure certainly represents a different approach to policymaking from the fudge and compromise model that has been the norm.

A second dilemma for the MSPs related to the positioning of special schools within the education system. The more dogmatic inclusionists have asked how we can ever become inclusive as long as special schools exist (Dessent, 1987; Jenkinson, 1997), but the MSPs' understanding of this issue was far more sophisticated, and was based on the evidence they had taken from a range of sources. Their difficulty was how to insist that special schools justify their existence as part of an inclusive education system whilst also ensuring that the experiences of the young people, their parents and the staff within the special schools were valued. The MSPs' discussion centred on the purposes of inclusion beyond school and their acute observation that the school is often perceived as the main end point for inclusion led them to contend that a wider debate about inclusion, and the role school plays in this process, was needed.

A third contradictory pressure concerned an impasse over expertise in special educational needs. The evidence had highlighted the problems of the 'special needs empire' which had often led to exclusionary practices, but the MSPs also understood that teachers were crying out for skills, knowledge and expertise in order to meet children's needs effectively. Furthermore, it had become clear to the MSPs that many of the people with the greatest expertise about how to include – young disabled people and their parents – were disregarded as part of the privileging of professionally based discourses within education. The MSPs' dilemma here concerned how to mobilise the existing expertise and to ensure that it is available to those who need it most. The difficulty in this regard is how to break down the wall erected by an Executive which claims that teachers are well supported.

The final issue which the Committee confronted was how to ensure effective accountability within the education system without disadvantaging children with special educational needs. They acknowledged that league tables and inspections of schools, which fulfilled some important scrutiny of standards and quality, also made it difficult for schools to pursue inclusive policies and practice. The incompatibility of the standards and social justice agendas was a source of much agonising among the MSPs, and while they saw no way out of this impasse, they considered it feasible to at least draw their Ministers' attention to the oppositional nature of the two agendas. This they did as part of their more general efforts to reframe the way in which accountability has operated and this is discussed below.

Reframing accountability

The Inquiry enabled the MSPs to hold the Executive to account in ways which were playful and disruptive, and which Watson (2001) described as having been accomplished 'with vigour and some success' (p. 162). Officials appearing before the MSPs were required to accept the responsibilies of their office and to make public promises to take action. This made fabrication difficult, if not impossible. The MSPs took evidence from three Executive officials and the Depute Minister for Education and here they engaged in some robust questioning:

> How do you intend to ensure that local authorities will be given the resources? (McLeod, Lab, Scottish Parliament 2000a, Col 1293)

> Would you accept that the experts are thin on the ground? (Jenkins, Lib Dem, Scottish Parliament, 2000b, Col 1104).

The politicians made tenacious efforts to ensure the officials did not get away with avoiding difficult questions or providing obscure answers:

> I did not think that the answer to [Jenkins, Lib Dem] question was clear. He asked whether having a special unit in a mainstream school would count as mainstreaming of youngsters with special needs. Could you give me a shorter answer to that question? (Monteith, Cons, Scottish Parliament, 2000b, Col 1101).

The MSPs also confronted the Executive officials with some of the contradictory pressures:

> The future of grant-aided schools has been raised, alongside the presumption on mainstreaming. If money is being given back to local authorities and mainstreaming is presumed, how can the future of very specialised schools be ensured? Will that become a difficult debate, in which people cannot always find the answer? We visited a school in my constitutency that is for children with cerebral palsy who have very specialised needs. How will those children be mainstreamed when the school moves away from grant-aided funding? Has there been any discussion of those issues? How do you or the team think that we can square the circle? (Gillon, Lab, Scottish Parliament, 2000a, Col 1290–1291).

The Deputy Minister for Education who fielded this question was, like the MSPs, apparently resistant to closure, but in his case this was only until the correct answer was arrived at:

> The debate about the seven grant-aided schools is extremely important ... and we will not make any rushed decisions that would jeopardise the future of those schools. We must be absolutely satisfied that we have got the balance right. [The Education Minister] and I have received advice from officials on this matter and we have asked for further advice. I must make it clear that

we will not rush any decisions. For example, we are deliberately waiting to hear what the Committee has to say on the matter before coming to any conclusions (Ibid, Col 1292).

The tension between accountability and inclusion was also rehearsed with the Deputy Minister:

> One of the things that came across from educational practitioners to whom we spoke … is that the requirements of the target-setting system can and do operate as disincentives to inclusion of children with special needs because, to put it brutally, they can depress schools' efforts to achieve their targets. It has come across strongly that there is tension between setting targets and encouraging parents to use the results to choose schools, and the social inclusion agenda. Are you aware of that? What are your thoughts on how to get round the problem to ensure that we genuinely encourage inclusion? (Sturgeon, SNP, Ibid, Col 1297).

The Deputy Minister indicated that he understood the argument about setting targets, but his response, in which he indicated that schools could 'adjust its targets down … in light of the number of children with special educational needs and records of needs' (Col 1297), suggested otherwise. In some cases, the MSPs secured undertakings from the Deputy Minister:

> Do you intend to monitor the application of section 12A(2) to see how many times it is applied to exclude ? (McLeod, Lab, ibid, Col 1294)

> I am happy to give that assurance (Deputy Minister, ibid).

> Concern has been raised recently about the fact that the auxiliary who is supporting those children has not been trained in special needs … will you comment on that? (Convenor, Lab, ibid, Col 1289)

> Your point is well made … I will take that point away and ensure that we address it (Deputy Minister, ibid).

The Parliamentary debate was a further opportunity to hold the Scottish Executive to account, in this example, over their refusal to accept the definition of inclusion provided by the Committee as 'maximising the participation of all children in mainstream schools and removing environmental, structural and attitudinal barriers to their participation' (Scottish Parliament, 2001a, p. 2). The Scottish Executive (2001), in its response to the report, had said that the definition provided in the Parliamentary report:

> makes a welcome contribution to the debate about inclusive education. However, there is a wide spectrum of views about approaches to inclusive education and a commonly agreed definition, which might also refer to the removal of educational barriers, would be difficult to secure (p. 2).

The MSP who opened the debate took a swipe at the Executive on this point, indicating that she was 'disappointed that ministers felt unable to endorse our definition of inclusive education or to accept the need for a clear and agreed definition' (McGugan, SNP, Scottish Parliament, 2001b, Col 772). She made the high expectations of MSPs clear, saying: 'I hope that the minister will inform us of the actions that he will pursue in the light of our recommendations' (ibid).

The kind of accountability witnessed in the Inquiry and in the Debating Chamber seems to have had a number of features. First, it took place in public, with the discussions part of the formal record of Parliament. Second, it privileged responsibility over transparency, with the MSPs enjoining the Executive to take action rather than provide a retrospective account of their inactivity. This required the Executive to publicly acknowledge the existence of problems, which they did, following much cajoling from the MSPs. Third, the MSPs used somewhat emotive language, referring to 'concern' among teachers and parents, their response to the 'blood sweat and tears' of parents and their 'disappointment' at the Executive's failure to accept their definition of inclusion. All of this appeared to take accountability into the realm of ethics and social justice.

DARING TO THINK OTHERWISE?
PRODUCTIVE SPACES FOR POLICYMAKING

> I am very glad to welcome some young people from Stanmore [grant-aided special] School who have just arrived in the public gallery, because today's debate is not about statistics, money or the minutiae that Brian Monteith has tried to suck us into. Instead it is about supporting, helping, caring for and involving the children who are in the chamber today and many others. If we see the debate in such a way, the Parliament is not some dry and arid place, but part of the living development of the Scottish community ... The debate is not about figures, politics or – as Mr Monteith said in his opening remarks – dogma; it is about belief, faith, caring and the creation of community ... it is about human rights and human beings (Russell, SNP, ibid, Col 816).

The Parliamentary Inquiry process appears to have created a space for politicians to engage in a more sophisticated form of policymaking than has hitherto been the case and to demand greater responsibility from government ministers and officials. The level of understanding about inclusion achieved by the MSPs who served on the Education, Sport and Culture Committee, and by those who spoke at the Parliamentary debate was impressive. Not only did they grasp the point that inclusion required significant change to the culture, ethos and practices of mainstream schools, but they also refused to reduce the debate to simplistic binarisms in the way that so many aspects of educational policy are handled. In addition, some of the groups who provided evidence subsequently expressed their satisfaction that their views had been represented and taken account of. Speaking on behalf of the Minority Ethnic Learning Disability Initiative, for example, Almeida Diniz and Usmani (2001) indicated that the 'open manner in which the Committee conducted itself in seeking to deal with a deeply contested field of social policy is a significant change from previous encounters' (p. 27) and described themselves as 'heartened by its willingness to listen' (ibid).

The politicians took the view that the special needs Inquiry has generated 'a better-informed debate from now on' (Jenkins, Lib Dem, Scottish Parliament, 2001a, Col 792) and has allowed the politicians to dare themselves and others to think imaginatively about how to be inclusive. The reframing of inclusion within an ethical context should be helpful to professionals and academics attempting to disrupt the 'production of inequalities' (Gillborn and Youdell 2000, p. 1) within education, but who have been frustrated by the inertia which has characterised the system to date.

The positioning of academics in an insider/outsider space is not unique to the Scottish Parliamentary Inquiry system. More and more individuals have found themselves in the role of policy adviser, consultant or expert witness and as Universities expand their research activities to include commercialisation, academics are increasingly expected to 'brand' their particular areas of expertise. It will be important to generate debate about how academics should conduct themselves in such roles, in ways which ensure that new open and productive spaces for policymaking can be forged. This also requires some discussion about reflexivity and how the positioning of academics within insider/outsider spaces should be reported. More generally, as Gewirtz (forthcoming) contends, there is a need to bring politics back into the educational policy debate. This implies that academics have to 'foreground the struggles between competing interest groups over key concepts such as accountability, performance indicators and quality' (Vidovitch and Slee, 2001, pp. 450–451).

It is too early to say whether the Scottish Parliament has provided Scotland with the much needed renewal of social capital or the remoralising of politics that Putnam (2000) has called for. At the very least, it has produced a productive space for openings rather than closure, which Derrida (2001) views as absolutely necessary to avoid the irresponsibility generated by certainty:

> Any presumption of guarantee and of non-contradiction in so paroxystic a situation ... is an optimistic gesticulation, an act of good conscience and irresponsibility, and therefore indecision and profound inactivity under the guise of activism or resolution (p. 71).

That the MSPs have behaved 'responsibly' is very much to their credit. How far they can go in this respect, will depend on their own confidence, the support of the electorate and the responsiveness within the education system to this invitation to think otherwise.

REFERENCES

Allan, J. (1999). *Actively seeing inclusion: pupils with special needs in mainstream schools* London: Falmer.

Almeida Diniz, F. and Usmani, K. (2001). Changing the discourse on race and special educational needs. *Multicultural teaching, 20*(1), 25–28.

Ball, S. (1998). Educational studies, policy entrepreneurship and social theory in R. Slee, G. Weiner, S. Tomlinson (Eds.), *School effectiveness for whom?* London: Falmer.

Ball, S. (2000). Performativities and fabrication in the education economy: towards the performative society? *The Australian Educational Researcher*, 27(2), 1–23.

Barton, L. (1997). Inclusive education: romantic, subversive or realistic? *International Journal of Inclusive Education*, 1(3), 231–242.

Brantlinger, E. (1997). Using ideology: cases of non-recognition of the politics of research and practice in special education, *Review of Educational Research*, 67(4), 425–459.

Bryce, T. and Humes, W. (1999). Policy development in Scottish education. Synergy for the Scottish Parliament: perspectives on policy. Retrieved on March 7, 2002, from http://www.strath.gla.ac.uk/synergy/policy/index.html.

Cohen, A. (1996). Personal nationalism: a Scottish view of some rites, rights and wrongs, *American Ethnologist*, 23, 802–815.

Derrida, J (1992a). *The other heading: reflections on today's Europe* (P. Brault and M. Naas, Trans.). Bloomington and Indianapolis: Indiana University Press.

Derrida, J. (1992b). Force of law: the mystical foundation of authority. In D. Cornell, M. Rosenfield and D Carlson (Eds.), (M. Quaintance, Trans.). *Deconstruction and the possibility of justice* New York and London: Routledge.

Derrida, J. (1997). The Villanova roundtable: a conversation with Jacques Derrida in J. Caputo (Ed.), *Deconstruction in a nutshell: a conversation with Jacques Derrida* New York: Fordham University Press.

Derrida, J. (2001). A certain 'madness' must watch over thinking: interview with François Ewald, in G. Biesta and D Egéa-Kuehne (Eds.), *Derrida & education* London: Routledge.

Dessent, T. (1987). *Making the ordinary school special* London: Falmer.

Durkheim, E. (1976). *The elementary forms of religious life*, trans. J. Ward London: Allen & Unwin.

Edgoose, J. (2001). Just decide: Derrida and the ethical aporias of education in G. Biesta and D Egéa-Kuehne (eds.) *Derrida & education* London: Routledge.

Fielding, M. (1999). Target setting, policy pathology and student perspectives: learning to labour in new times, *Cambridge Journal of Education*, 29(2), 277–287.

Foucault, M. (1984). Nietzsche, Genealogy, History in P. Rabinow (Ed). *The Foucault reader* Harmondsworth: Penguin.

Geewirtz, S. (forthcoming). *Bringing the politcs back in: a critical analysis of quality discourses in education*

Gillborn, D. and Youdell, D. (2000). *Rationing education: policy, practice, reform and equity* Buckingham: Open University Press.

Hassan, G. (1999). The new Scottish politics: the establishment of a Scottish Parliament in G. Hassan (Ed.) *A guide to the Scottish Parliament*. Edinburgh: The Stationary Office.

Hassan, G. and Warhurst, C (Eds.), (2000) *The new Scottish politics: the first year of the Scottish Parliament and beyond.* Edinburgh: The Stationary Office.

Jenkinson, J. (1997). *Mainstream or special? Educating students with disabilities.* London: Routledge.

McCrone, D., Morris., A. and Kiely, R. (1995). *Scotland the brand: the making of Scottish heritage.* Edinburgh: Edinburgh University Press.

McDonald, S. (1996). *Reimagining culture: histories, identities and the Gaelic renaissance.* Oxford: Berg.

McPherson, A. and Raab, C. (1989). *Governing education.* Edinburgh: Edinburgh University Press.

Nairn, T. (1977). *The break up of Britain.* London: Verso.

Paterson, L. (2000a). Civil society and democratic renewal in S. Baron, J. Field and T. Schuller (Eds.), *Social capital: critical perspectives.* Oxford: Oxford University Press.

Paterson, L. (2000b). *Education and the Scottish Parliament.* Edinburgh: Dunedin Academic Press.

Putnam, R. (2000). *Bowling alone: the collapse and revival of American community.* New York: Simon and Schuster.

Ritchie, M (2000). *Scotland reclaimed: the inside story of Scotland's first democratic Parliamentary election.* Edinburgh: The Saltire Society.

Salter, B and Tapper, T. (2000). The politics of governance in higher education: the case of quality assurance, *Political Studies,* 48, 66–87.

Schlesinger, P., Miller, D. and Dinan, W. (2001). *Open Scotland? Journalists, spin doctors and lobbyists.* Edinburgh: Polygon.

Scottish Executive (2001). Scottish ministers' response to the Education Committee's report on its enquiry into special educational needs.

Scottish Parliament (2000a). Official report, 4/7/00.

Scottish Parliament (2000b). Official report, 30/5/00

Scottish Parliament (2001a) Official report of special needs Inquiry. Retrieved on February 18, 2002, from http://www.scottish.Parliament.uk/official_report/session-01/sor0517-02.htm.

Scottish Parliament (2001b) Official report of debate on motion S1M-1931: special educational needs. Retrieved on February 18, 2002, from http://www.scottish.Parliament.uk/official_report/session-01/sor0517-02.htm.

Slee, R. and Allan, J. (2001). Excluding the included: a reconsideration of inclusive education, *International Studies in the Sociology of Education,* 11(2), 173–191.

Stronach, I. and Morris, B. (1994) Polemical notes on educational evaluation in the age of 'policy hysteria.' *Evaluation and Research in Education,* 8(1 & 2), 5–20.

Tomlinson, S. (1982). *A sociology of special education. London: Routledge and Kegan Paul.*

Vidovitch, L. and Slee, R. (2001) Bringing universities to account? Exploring some global and local policy tensions. *Journal of Educational Policy,* 16(5), 431–453.

Watson, M. (2001). *Year Zero: an inside view of the Scottish Parliament.* Edinburgh: Polygon.

FERNANDO ALMEIDA DINIZ

12 'RACE' AND THE DISCOURSE ON 'INCLUSION'

In this chapter, I will offer a reflexive account of my involvement in the struggle of black people against racial oppression in contemporary Scotland. Drawing on autobiography, my recent experience of working in the Scottish academy and the socio-political context and ethos of the time and place, I provide a snapshot of the climate of systemic racism that is endemic in Scottish society. I will attempt to explain how I have learned to understand my creeping sense of 'rage' at the level of racial injustice and have connected with the black voluntary sector to develop various forms of resistance through community activism in the light of the establishment of the Scottish Parliament. I conclude by attempting to address the broader issues of the Colloquium.

Before responding to the remit that I have set myself, I believe that it is important to make explicit the ethical position that I have adopted for assuming the role of a self-appointed 'voice,' the key influences that have shaped my analysis and acknowledgment of my limitations and frailty in this human problematic. I write from a black anti-racist perspective, that is, from an acknowledgement of 'colour consciousness,' as opposed to 'colour blindness,' and see my contribution as part of an ethical project, in the spirit of resistance against racial oppression, a quest for social justice, an endeavour to counter the institutionally racist practices that prevent the participation of oppressed minority ethnic communities in the political process. It is a personal testimony of someone who is vividly conscious of the 'racialised spaces' that black academics are assigned to in white institutions which require us to be experts in 'race' matters, as well as in the academic disciplines of study that brought us into university careers (Carter et al, 1997)

A racialised identity?

My involvement in the 'struggle' against racism in Scotland started after I had moved from London to take up my university post in Edinburgh, in 1990. Rather naively, perhaps, I had assumed that I was moving from one part of the UK to another and anticipated that the attempts to confront the social problems of racism, that had been on the agenda for the 25 years that I had lived in England, would be part of life in Scotland. I was soon to discover that, 450 miles from the Westminster Parliament, lay another nation, steeped in its history, tradition and social norms. I witnessed the deep sense of alienation that Thatcherism had engendered and the undercurrent of anti-English sentiment that was present, and still surfaces here. The latter issue is not one that is too readily acknowledged. Not long after I

195

J. Allan (ed.), Inclusion, Participation and Democracy: What is the Purpose?, 195-206.
© 2003 *Kluwer Academic Publishers. Printed in the Netherlands.*

arrived, I was beginning to realise that my appointment as the first black person to hold a senior post in a Scottish university faculty of education had brought me an unsolicited 'visibility.' I found myself being told that I am 'English:' alternatively, I have recently been endowed with an assimilationist Scots identity 'because you are now here,' whereas I have always described myself as a British citizen and 'Black-British' in terms of a racial identity. Apart from the need for much more theorising about what constitutes being a 'Scot' or 'English'- let alone a 'Black-Scot' or 'Black-English' – I soon realised that I was, and still am, immersed in a national political discourse about identity, citizenship and immigration status in which 'race' continues to be a determining factor in shaping the interests of black communities. Some things have not changed much since then and my racial, ethnic and cultural origin has continued to be as much an area of interest as my professional background. I was then, and frequently am now, expected to be the expert on 'race,' something that has since been reported by minority ethnic academics in other British universities (Carter et al, 1997)

So how do I see myself and how has this influenced my perspective and professional action? In an invited response to the interim report on *The Future of Multi-ethnic Britain*, this is the position that I adopted, and still hold today (Almeida Diniz, 2001). I see myself as a black man – a naturalised-British citizen, born in Africa of Indo-Portuguese heritage, married to a Brazilian woman of Japanese ethnic origin, the father of a daughter born in London and we now live in Scotland. This disclosure of my family origin and context was not meant to suggest an exotic identity but was indicative of the forces that have shaped my thinking about who I am and am becoming, as an individual and member of a family unit – a hybrid of hyphenated diasporas – living in a multi-racialised Scotland, United Kingdom and Europe.

Engaging in 'race' talk

Talking about 'race' is dirty talk, unpleasant, painful, and is even considered irrelevant by some. Talking about 'white supremacy' is even more risky. So why do it and why 'me?' I would rather be talking about other matters, but this is where autobiography comes in. On one of my regular visits to meet with black scholars in the USA, two of us got to talk about our families and about being Dads: 'My kids do that too! Always complain about my apparent preoccupations – Here he goes again, talking about racism,' said my African-American contact. The reality is that racism, or more precisely white supremacy, touches all aspects of our daily lives as black people. Witnessing the re-emergence of white supremacist groups and seeing their rhetoric and beliefs gain acceptance in wider discourses is startling, frightening and designed to silence. By acceptance, I include the collusion by large chunks of white society and institutions that don't or won't see it. Even more important is the fact that such denial allows race and racism to remain depoliticised in social policy and service provision, as is the case in Scotland. For decades, we have witnessed mainly African-Caribbean males expressing their resistance to the oppression they experience and, in the summer of 2001, it was the turn of the 'model' Asian young people to take to the streets in violent protest in English cities. Here is another generation of young British citizens expressing their frustration, unwilling to remain in denial and prepared to engage in organised resistance. The hope, that all those 'cultural habits' that were present in their forebears would be cured through a good British education, has been precisely that: hope. Racism has persisted, and they are unwilling and unlikely to put up with it as their parents had done before. The solution for some politicians in the rich world is to pull down the shutters and not let anymore of them in, as in the case in the Australian and European governments' responses to the waves of refugees moving across boundaries. In a recent address to commemorate 40 years of the Immigration Act 1962, Sivanandan offered this assessment of the current situation:

> The fight against that institutional racism, which maims and kills and blights the lives of young African-Caribbean and Asian peoples and other minority groups, continues. But there is a new racism abroad in the land, even more virulent and devastating than the ones we have seen before. And this is the racism that is meted out to refugees and asylum seekers irrespective of their colour. This is the racism that is meted out to Romas and Sintis and poor whites from Eastern Europe. This is the racism that pretends to be based on the fear of strangers and gives it the respectable name of xenophobia. It may be xeno, in that it is directed at aliens, strangers, but it is racism in the way it operates against them. It is xeno in form but racism in content. It is XENO-RACISM ... To fight this racism successfully, however, we have got to understand how it is imbricated, layered, in the processes of globalisation and the anti-terrorist ideology that western powers are instituting through legislation, government and the media (IRR, 2002).

A nation in denial?

'Race' thus has a troubled history, both within the public imagination and in academic discourses across Britain. Over two decades after the introduction of legislation to outlaw racial discrimination, controversy remains about how 'race' is conceptualised and whether it is or should be represented in social policy and practice. While dominant thinking about 'difference' in multicultural Britain continues to assign visible minorities to static 'ethnic' categories, defined in terms of heritage cultures and languages, there is less evidence of an explicit recognition of the existence of 'race' as an integral part of a colour-coded classificatory system through which a racialised social order is reproduced and maintained by institutional racism in British society. Central to my argument is the belief that the British state's obsession, over the past decades, with 'multiculturalism,' 'ethnicity' and 'ethnic minorities' has been a distraction from the core issue of 'racial oppression,'which the Stephen Lawrence Inquiry (REF) so graphically documented.

Scotland has had a particularly poor record on race issues, as I discovered when I arrived here from London in1990. The absence of a Scottish-based research literature on equality issues, particularly 'race,' was evident, though the scale of neglect did surprise me. In academic life and outside, it was not uncommon to hear strongly held views that 'there is no problem here,' 'there are few ethnic minorities,' 'we don't have them,' and 'the Scots are friendly and egalitarian society,' a perspective that would not have gained much credence among minority ethnic communities, were they given a voice in public and political discourse. In an audit of research on minority ethnic issues, commissioned by the Scottish Executive, Netto et al (2001) have documented the invisibility of 'race' in mainstream academic social research, the under-representation of black perspectives in all sectors of public policy, failures of the Scottish criminal justice system to guarantee race equality and the discriminatory impact that this race-blind approach has had on a wide range of public and voluntary services for minority ethnic communities.

With colleagues, I have given particular attention to the issue of inclusion in education policy and practice (Almeida Diniz, 1999; Almeida Diniz & Usmani, 2001), arguing that the discourses on special educational needs and inclusive education are themselves exclusive. They have failed to recognise issues of race and racism. I have highlighted the proliferation of books about 'inclusive educa-tion,' authored by leading academics in the USA, UK and Australia, noting that most of the writers are white, speakers of English as a first language and from within the field of special education. What I have questioned is not something to do with national language, per se, or colour or professional territories; rather, it is the claim that current discourses on 'inclusion' are themselves representative of the legitimate concerns and perspectives of diverse groups in society. There is little evidence to assure all schools that the serious social inequalities, including the 'new racisms' experienced by other vulnerable children as a consequence of global ethnic conflict, xenophobia and mass migration are reflected in the above discussions on inclusion. A key question that this has raised for all who are com-mitted to an anti-racist Scotland is whether such failures to address the problematic of 'racism' are mere oversights or, as hooks (1995) contends, a deliberate strategy to maintain power and privilege:

> Denial is in fact a cornerstone of white European culture, and it has been called out by the major critical voices who speak to, for, and from the location of whiteness (Marx, Freud, Foucault). After all, if we all pretend that racism does not exist, that we do not know what it is or how to change it – it never has to go away (p. 4).

Only recently has there been an acceptance in British legislation of the racialised power dynamics operating within institutions rather than assumptions about gaps in tolerance of individual cultural, linguistic and other lifestyle factors. Suddenly, 'Race Matters' in Scotland and it is now an official part of the national political discourse (Scottish Executive, 2000). Welcome though this is, the legacy of decades of neglect cannot be underestimated and continues to be most in evidence in politics, academic research, social policy and the professions.

How does this new optimism square with the increasing global tensions that

Sivanandan has warned of and what, if any, recognition does the Scottish academy pay to the current situation in its institutional life?

Racial exclusion in the Academy

Most of my professional life has been of the 'only one' type in universities in England and Scotland, during which I can think of no studies that have attempted to research issues of 'ethnicity and employment' in British higher education. My earlier life and career as a teacher and academic had been spent in the 'the world city' of London. I had not haboured any desire to be seen as a 'model' or 'exception' and had attempted to go about my professional life as a private individual. Where difficulties had surfaced I thought of these as 'private troubles' rather than 'public issues' (Wright Mills, 1959). When Carter et al (1997) published their findings, the internal university system appeared to react with scepticism. Black academics like myself observed, with little surprise, the absence of any mention of 'race,' let alone 'racism,' in the language of the current critical discourse. In my view, we were once again witnessing what amounts to a racialised analysis premised on problematic categories of 'ethnic minorities' and 'multiculturalism.' Nevertheless, it was the first time that funds had been dedicated to commission such research and that powerful institutions of the state – Parliament, funding councils, university chancellors, trade unions – appeared to be willing to acknowledge what black academics had known and experienced as the reality of academic life in Britain. For the first time too, university managers were faced with compelling documented evidence that minority ethnic academics:

- Are disproportionately under-represented at all levels in teaching, research and management
- Are more likely to be in short-term contract posts, particularly in research
- Are paid considerably less than their white peers, even when a few 'stars' attain the 'pinnacle' positions of academic achievement and privilege – professorial rank
- Have reported high levels of racial harassment and discrimination, while white colleagues consider that it is not a problem.

The immediate action by the government was signalled by the UK Education Secretary's call for reform, hinting that progress might be linked to future institutional funding; there was no equivalent response from the Scottish minister. Two years on, the university community's main reaction has been to do what it does best – organise conferences and establish Equal Opportunities committees to address inequality in the areas of gender, race and disability. Two decades of discredited generic equality policies form the backcloth to the failure by Britain's universities to the combat systemic racial discrimination that continues to exclude black qualified people from participation as vice-chancellors, professors, deans and senior researchers. This is the ethical challenge waiting to be grasped by higher education in Scotland, including the leadership of the teacher education faculties who have failed in their responsibility to reverse the racialised divide in our schools, where the pupils are multiracial, multicultural and multilingual while the education profession and its leadership remains resolutely white and monolingual. It will be interesting to see how universities respond to the recent changes brought about by the introduction of the Race Relations Amendment Act 2000.

Had I spent the past three decades in British academia in denial, believing that I was working in institutions where my activities were going to improve matters and generally contribute to progress? Or did this give some meaning to the sense of frustration and creeping rage that I often felt, particularly as I dared to enter the upper echelons of academia?

Understanding 'rage' as a catalyst for resistance and resilience in professional life?

In common with other black academics who are reported to experience institutional racism in daily life in British universities, I continue to journey across the Atlantic to have the rare opportunity to be with other black scholars; getting 'a fix of blackness' is part of the sub-text of achieving critical understanding, sustenance and resistance. From these encounters, I have been inspired by the works of two black American scholars and have drawn on their thinking in developing my critique and guiding efforts in community action.

Killing rage, Ending racism, (hooks, 1995) spoke to me at a time when I was seriously questioning my institutional experience and public exposure as the only black senior academic in a Scottish university faculty of education, and gave me the conceptual tools to explain my growing feelings of political 'rage' at the widespread denial of racism in Scotland. hooks offers a conceptualisation of 'rage' that is the very reverse of the common pathologising of black people, in which racism is represented as an issue of, and for, black people – a mere figment of our perverse paranoid imaginations and something that we have caused because we are here. She sees using 'rage' as a catalyst to gain critical consciousness, as something other than sickness, and as a potentially healthy and healing response to racial oppression and exploitation. This is much in line with Malcolm X whose commitment to social justice was a very public demonstration of 'rage.' Like hooks, I find this no easy task. It demands a lot of unlearning of institutionalised norms and practices that have governed my education and life and goes back to the days of Vasco da Gama. I have learned that this is a journey of struggle for racial justice and inner peace that can, and often does, leave me with feelings of isolation, under attack and in pain, particularly in institutional life. I have since realised that it was after coming to Scotland that I have been most active in 'race talk' and in some ways think that I had been plunged into it when I entered the senior managerial sector of education. Through solidarity with other black academics, I have become critically conscious of what my life has been like in the racialised spaces in which I have worked. It reminds me of a term 'space invaders' that Puwar (2001, p. 1) coined to characterise the situation of black senior civil administrators employed in The British Civil

Service, 'an institution that is deemed to be at the absolute apex of disembodied, neutral professionalism' (ibid) She argued that 'an engagement with the interview accounts of these *space invaders* allows us to grasp some idea of what it is like for them to coexist in a place that is built on a *racial contract* which has demarcated spaces in accordance with racialised corporealities' (ibid). It came as such a relief to read hook's analysis of being 'the black professor' in the white department. (p. 185). This resembles my own experiences, but I certainly have not wished to see myself as 'victim,' even though pain was evident and expressed at times. To do so would be to give away the power of self-determination. And self.

One of the important lessons I have learned is that it is not possible for those like myself, who have a 'high profile' in the system, to remain invisible or expect to be neutral in the light of the level of racial discrimination experienced by fellow members of Britain's minority ethnic communities. Indeed, I would be prepared to pay the price in accepting bell hook's (1995) challenge that:

> the time to speak a counter hegemonic race talk that is filled with the passion of remembrance and resistance is now. All our words are needed. To move past the pain, to feel the power of change, transformation, revolution we have to speak now – acknowledge our pain now, claim each other and our voices now (p. 6).

What I have done is to make a conscious decision to re-connect with other black people, including black academics; at a grass-roots level, this has meant learning to think, plan, engage with, and account to, black communities. At the same time, I have had to think about engaging (remaining healthy) in professional life in a resolutely white supremacist university system. But, most important, I have learned to re-affirm 'who' I am and 'why' I wish to do what I do.

SHAPING THE RESEARCH AGENDA

Mainstream British social research, largely conducted by white academics, has either remained resolutely raceless or has pathologised minority ethnic groups and ignored the racial discrimination and oppression operating throughout society. Why is this topic not one that is included in standard textbooks on research methodology? Why are black researchers under-represented in Scottish universities and what impact does this have on the social production of research? These are questions that SABRE, a small network of black researchers in Scotland, have been attempting to address, by drawing on the work of Charles W Mills (1997). In his book, *The Racial Contract*, Mills exposes the racial exclusion that exists in his professional field of political theory. Rather than use the language of ethnicity and culture, Mills tackles the thorny issue of the role of global white supremacy, arguing that racism is itself a political system, a racial social contract between those categorised as white over the nonwhites, that is designed maintain white power and privilege. From his perspective, the problem of the invisibility of race in social research or political theory is consistent with the terms of the Racial Contract, which prescribes an epistemology of ignorance that has the outcome that white and colonised minority ethnic researchers will in general be unable to recognise the world that they themselves have made. 'Race' is in no way an 'afterthought,' a 'deviation' from ostensibly raceless Western ideals, but rather a central shaping constituent of those ideals.

The struggle for racial equality within research goes well beyond the tweeking of textbooks. It goes to the heart of global political discourse which sees the current crises in Iraq from the prism of Western rich interests to the exclusion of the aspirations and human rights of the majority poor world. This challenge posed by Mills is a tall order for SABRE to combat, but he has nevertheless offered inspiration and sustenance to oppressed groups and their white allies in this small nation. British educational research must recognise this level of subtlety if social inclusion is to be more than a tokenistic project.

Scotland has for a long period had a small but committed counter-force of black anti-racist activists who have mobilise their efforts in challenging racism and discriminatory behaviour in schools and other public services. What is now different is the way in which these diverse professionals have formed a coalition to work strategically for change. Some examples of such community activism are described below and illustrate how the dearth of research and literature, referred to above, and the changes signalled at the time of the establishment of the Scottish Parliament have created spaces not merely to 'plug gaps' but to ensure that alternative voices are heard in policy.

SABRE: Developing anti-racist research methodologies

Nine months into the life of the Parliament, the Scottish Executive Central Research Unit held a consultation workshop entitled: *Researching Ethnic Minorities in Scotland,* The expressed purpose was to take forward the Executive's decision to commission research in this area and to consider the strategic direction that this would take. The event was attended by policymakers, researchers and members of minority ethnic communities and organizations and led to a healthy debate. Black researchers present (the paucity was evident) questioned the underlying ideological framework for the exercise and whether it was examining 'deficit and needs' or 'institutional racism' We drew attention to the absence of an ethical code for researching 'race' in Scotland, that is, an explicit acknowledgement of the impact of racism in mainstream conceptual frameworks and research methodologies, and asked how this might be addressed in future. While we acknowledged that there are serious gaps in Scottish research that merit attention, we maintained that it was equally necessary to address fundamental questions relating to the purpose and process of research to combat racism in Scotland. For example:

• What is the purpose of research in this area and how is it to be conceptualised?
• Who should be involved in deciding the research agenda?

- What would be the nature of their involvement?
- What would be the most appropriate methods of enquiry?
- Which analytical tools would best serve the purpose of the research?
- How will the outputs of the research be disseminated, and to whom?

These questions, in turn, raised issues concerning the ideological framework underpinning anti-racist research and the associated methodological implications, both of which remain deeply problematic in the current discourse in Scotland. Shortly after the above workshop, a symposium of black researchers was held, which led to the establishment of SABRE and development of the *Ethical Code for Researching 'Race,' Racism & Anti-racism in Scotland* (SABRE, 2001). The Code has benefited from the thinking of Charles Mills' (1997) *The Racial Contract* and is intended to contribute to the developing discourse on anti-racist research and to promote good practice in the light of the implementation of the Race Relations Amendment Act (2000).

The first question the Code addresses concerns the ideological framework under-pinning research. Much of existing research on 'ethnicity' draws on two theoretical discourses: 'multi-culturalism' and 'anti-racism.' The former is largely concerned with acknowledging and adapting practice to differences in language, religion, cultural norms and expectations, which can prevent effective communication and create misunderstanding between the majority and minority ethnic communities. In contrast, the latter takes the view that the current political, social and economic position of minority ethnic communities must be understood within the context of the historical legacies of colonialism and post-colonial relationships. Accordingly, anti-racist approaches have tended to concentrate on highlighting structural disad-vantages and experiences of racism faced by minority ethnic communities; more recently, some scholars have acknowledged that while an anti-racist approach is valuable in taking account of structural disadvantages, those who are subject to the experience of racial discrimination draw on their cultural and religious resources in coping with and resisting this experience. In the light of these competing discourses, the Code locates itself within events following on from the murder of Stephen Lawrence, arguing for the acknowledgement of institutional racism in research. It advocates an anti-racist approach to research that:

- Is embedded in social justice and human rights concerns and legal obligations
- Is explicit in its commitment to anti-racism and to promoting social inclusion
- Is empowering and actively inclu les black and minority ethnic peoples' perspectives.
- Addresses the complex and problematic nature of concepts of 'race,' racism and ethnicity
- Ensures that it does not pathologise, stereotype or is exploitative, particularly of black and minority ethnic people
- Values and addresses the diversity within the black and minority ethnic

population and recognises the inter-connections with colour, age, gender, disability, sexuality, culture, class, language, belief, context and other socially defined characteristics
• Acknowledges the 'power-relations' inherent in social research processes, for example between 'white' and 'black,' 'researchers' and 'researched' and families and communities
• Ensures that the whole research exercise is underpinned by a commitment to confidentiality.

The second problematic question concerns the conduct of research, in particular the roles of researcher and researched. Whereas, in practice these questions are often resolved through a continual process of negotiation and re-negotiation that occurs with individuals and organisations at various levels, failure to do so risks the increased marginalisation of those communities that such research seeks to alleviate. A key aspect of paying due attention to process is the scrutiny of whether the aims and objectives of the research are potentially beneficial to the groups or communities involved. In particular, the involvement of black people that is restricted to their participation in research as 'subjects' or interviewees of research, or as black research-assistants operating research frameworks designed by white researchers, severely constrains their power to influence and drive change, as it leaves the power to interpret and communicate the results of research in this area to others. The Code advocates an explicit anti-racist approach in which the researcher:

• Challenges theoretical assumptions that are rooted in a historical legacy of racism by adopting frameworks that address institutional racism in research
• Gives due regard, without discrimination, to the diversity within black minority ethnic communities, in terms of colour, age, gender, disability, sexuality, culture, class, language, belief, context and other socially defined characteristics
• Recognises the limitations in the use of current categories of 'race' and 'ethnicity' and employs multiple methodologies to secure full representation and inclusion
• Does not undervalue or exploit the contribution of black & minority ethnic researchers at all levels of the research
• Respects the rights of individuals and groups to withhold or withdraw confidential information
• Makes explicit their respective racial and ethnic origins, principles, ethics and authority and acknowledges the potential impact that this has had
• Provides a full description of the scope, constraints and procedures for gaining access to black minority ethnic communities, the ethnic categories used and their effects on the results in terms of plausibility, validity, reliability and generalisabilty.

To date, the Code has been well received as a tool to promote focused discussion on methodological issues by researchers and students and by policymakers commissioning research. What long term impact it will have has yet to be evaluated.

The Audit of research on the needs of ethnic minorities from a 'race' perspective (Netto et al, 2001) was commissioned by the Scottish Executive's Central Research Unit and conducted by a team of mainly black researchers and was headed by Gina Netto. It was the first of its kind and covered a comprehensive range of social policy and public service provision. The conceptual framework that the team chose to use is worth noting; that is, we were clear that our analysis would be premised on issues concerning race, racism and anti-racism, as advocated in the SABRE Code.

The contributors to the special issue of *Multicultural Teaching: 'Race' in the New Scotland* were a group of academics, community activists and practitioners. As the guest editor, my aim was to offer 'voices from north of the Border,' to generate wider interest in recent developments since the setting up of the Scottish Parliament and to begin to plug the gap in the literature. The publication also represented part of a strategy for combating the institutional barriers that black professionals experience in influencing policy and research and in publishing their work, though it is important to note that this was not a 'blacks-only' group. All the writers are active in Scottish initiatives, groups and organisations and have a critical grasp of surface and deep changes that are taking place in anti-racist thinking in their fields of activity. All were asked to reflect on the issue of 'race' in Scottish public policy within the 'new Scotland.' The emphasis of the articles is on promoting institutional change. On the whole, the articles convey a glimpse of the challenges that are present in research, policy and practice and are intended to contribute to positive change in Scotland.

The Minority Ethnic Learning Disability Initiative (MELDI) is Black Voluntary Sector Advocacy Group (www.meldi.org.uk) which supports minority ethnic families and carers of disabled persons through case work and development work It places an emphasis on providing practical strategies to support minority ethnic families who experience racial discrimination in accessing education and welfare services for their disabled children. MELDI has worked in partnership with the University of Edinburgh, statutory and voluntary sector agencies and with communities themselves to develop more inclusive services across Scotland.

REFRAMING THE DISCOURSE ON INCLUSION

I have pointed to the narrowness in the conceptualisation of inclusion and the neglect of serious social inequalities, including the 'new racisms' experienced through global conflict, xenophobia and mass migration. A reframing of the discourse on inclusion, therefore, needs to embrace a much wider interpretation of social exclusion that recognises global political contexts. 'Race,' it follows, has to be explicit, and since, as Mills (1997) reminds us, the Racial Contract is constantly being rewritten, then we need constantly to subject the 'epistemology of ignorance' and misrecognition generated by the the Contract to critique. In practical terms, this means that 'race' has to occupy a central place in policy, practice and research, rather than exist as an afterthought, an addendum or another specialism. Clearly, for this to be achieved, strenuous efforts need to be made to reconnect with communities in setting the agenda for policy, practice and research. Finally, there needs to be explicit action to address the paucity of minority ethnic role models – in our universities, in our schools and elsewhere.

REFERENCES

Almeida Diniz, F. (1999). Race and special educational needs in the 1990s. *British Journal of Special Education,* 26(4), 213–217.

Almeida Diniz, F. (2001) Invited response to *The future of multi-ethnic Britain.* Unpublished paper.

Almeida Diniz, F. and Usmani, K. (2001). Changing the discourse on race and special educational needs. *Multicultural teaching,* 20(1), 25–28.

Carter, J., Fenton, S. and Modood, T. (1997). *Ethnicity and employment in higher education.* London: Policy Studies Institute.

hooks, B. (1995) Killing rage, ending racism. New York: H. Holt & Co.

Institute of Race Relations (2002). The Contours of Global Racism. Address by A Sivanandan. IRR News. Retrieved on January 16, 2003, from http://www.irr.org.uk.

Mills, C.W. (1997). *The racial contract.* Ithica: Cornell University Press.

Netto, G., Arshad, R., de Lima, P., Almeida Diniz, F., MacEwen, M., Patel, V., & Syed, R. (2001). *Audit of research on minority ethnic issues in Scotland from a 'race' perspective.* Edinburgh: Scottish Office.

Puwar, N. (2001). The racialised somatic norm: institutionalised racism in the senior civil service. *Sociology,* 35(2), 651–670.

Scottish Association of Black Researchers (2001). An Ethical Code for Researching 'Race', Racism and Anti-racism in Scotland. SABRE: www.sabre.ukgo.com.

Scottish Executive (2000) *Researching Ethnic Minorities in Scotland.* Edinburgh: Scottish Executive.

Wright Mills, C. (1959). *The sociological imagination.* New York: Oxford University Press.

ROGER SLEE

13 TEACHER EDUCATION, GOVERNMENT AND INCLUSIVE SCHOOLING: THE POLITICS OF THE FAUSTIAN WALTZ

A REMARK THAT YOU MADE

Education Queensland, together with the Department for Innovation and Information Economy, recently convened the *Science Works for the Smart State Conference* in Brisbane, Australia. Following concerns raised by the Ministerial Council for Educational Renewal, the conference was one event in a series of initiatives designed to bring science educators and researchers from across the schooling, training and higher education sectors and practising scientists from government and industry together to consider the state of science education.

One of the keynote speakers at the conference was Professor Ian Lowe from Griffiths University. His address was a *tour de force* that interrogated the epistemology and political economy of science and science education. At the heart of his paper was a call for the trans-disciplinary orientation necessary for establishing a new ethics for an education for sustainable futures. I was moved by a remark that he made, almost as an aside: 'working with government is always something of a Faustian Waltz.'

For this conference delegate, Lowe invited sustained and critical reflexivity. For the past two years I have been seconded by the Queensland Government from the Higher Education sector to the role of Deputy Director-General of the Department of Education (Education Queensland). For an academic who has been researching education politics and policymaking, this has been a unique opportunity to become an ethnographer of bureaucracy and government. This however, suggests a detachment and political cleanliness that denies the salience of Lowe's observation about working for government. I hasten to add that civil servants are not alone in having to deal with the politics of pragmatism and compromise. Halpin and Troyna's (1994) collection of reflections on the ethics and politics of researching education policy in the UK and Walford's (1994) work on researching the powerful are representative of numerous accounts of the complex politics of education research. Notwithstanding these (self-serving) caveats, I am simultaneously exhilarated and oppressed by the possibilities and limitations of this dance with government.

The education of disabled students is an area of my responsibility that weighs heavily upon my mind. Previously, I have been a vociferous critic of departments of education as they struggle with the politics of disablement (Slee, 2001; 2002).

J. Allan (ed.), Inclusion, Participation and Democracy: What is the Purpose?, 207-223.

Now that I find myself at the centre of this intensely contested site, this political maelstrom, I am no less committed to the necessity of critique, but I am very much more sensitive to the fact that critique is a more straightforward and a much easier task than is policy reconstruction. Writing another paper on policy shortfalls holds its own difficulties as we struggle to push the genre further. Developing ameliorative policy is a far more difficult orchestration of competing multi-variants.

In this chapter, although I will provide some general comments on inclusive education, I do not intend to rehearse a conceptual analysis of the field. Instead, I will outline the reform agenda for public education in Queensland as outlined in Queensland State Education – 2010 (Education Queensland, 1999) and situate the struggle for more inclusive schooling within that reform narrative. It is also my intention to describe the complex politics surrounding inclusive education for students with disabilities in Queensland. The chapter will also offer some reflections on the implications of inclusive education for teacher education in Australia. To be sure, the themes that arise in this discussion are seasoned travellers, holding trans-continental resonance. Incidentally, let me demonstrate the lessons of my civil service apprenticeship by suggesting that the argument offered in this chapter is not the view of Education Queensland. For this I must take sole responsibility.

Queensland: Tourist capital or smart state?

The state of Queensland has traditionally presented itself as a sub-tropical farm, tourist playground and retirement haven – an Australian Miami. The present government has relinquished that tradition to adopt a mobilising slogan of 'Queensland, The Smart State.' The political imperative is to reposition the Queensland economy from the volatile primary production and tourist industries to more high-tech industries within the information economy, bio-technology and medical research and development. There is a desire to re-affirm support for the importance of the former economic drivers of primary production and tourism, but these are not recognised as the levers for a sustainable future. This policy discussion even manifests itself in a debate over which slogan should be used on the registration plates for motor vehicles: 'Queensland – The Sunshine State,' or 'Queensland – The Smart State.'

What possible relevance does this hold for the politics of inclusive education and teacher education, I hear you ask? I will attempt to secure the connection. After suffering a cerebro-vascular accident, Jean-Dominique Bauby dictated his book, *The Diving-Bell And The Butterfly*, by blinking his eye-lid as an assistant pointed to letters on an alphabet board. Much of the book is dedicated to observation of those whom he calls the 'inmates' of the Naval Hospital at Berck-sur-Mer on the French Channel coast. His prose is economical and deeply poignant. In a chapter entitled *Tourists*, Bauby describes the 'denizens' of the hospital. He notes a reconstituted social order where comatose patients, 'plunged into endless night,' never emerge from their rooms: 'Yet everyone knows they are there, and they weigh strangely on our collective awareness, almost like a guilty conscience' (Bauby, 1997, p. 39).

Then there are those 'who have made their nest in a dead-end corridor of the neurology department' (Bauby, 1997, p.40). The survivors of accidents who pass through the hospital are called 'tourists' and they are fearful of engagement with the long-term 'inmates.' Bauby describes the politics of the social relations as they are played out in the physiotherapy room where the groups are brought into contact with each other:

> I would like to be part of all this hilarity, but as soon as I direct my one eye towards them, the young man, the grandmother and the homeless man turn away, feeling the sudden need to study the ceiling smoke-detector. The *tourists* must be very worried about fire (Bauby, 1997, p. 41)

I would concede that inclusive education in Queensland, like elsewhere, is slow and falters on challenges to traditional forms of knowledge about disability and difference, established power relations, institutional rigidities, and fiscal restraints. The progression from a tourist state to a smart state in public education is slow work in the area of students with disabilities. The task we are engaged in is shifting people's gaze from the smoke detectors so that we can engage in more authentic reform processes pursuant to inclusive schooling. Drawing from Bauby, there remains a present danger that we have moved the 'dead-end corridors' from segregated sites outside the school perimeter to integrated sites inside the school fence.

Inclusive education as a travelling theory

Inclusive education is at conceptual, as well as political, risk. A vehement protest against the segregation of disabled students from the rights of participation in the neighbourhood school, inclusive education may reasonably be accommodated (excuse the play on words) within a neo-liberal ensemble of policies, procedures and physical arrangements to absorb or assimilate, as Bernstein (1996) puts it, rather than include or represent a difficult and different group of people into regular educational provision.

Recently, Edward Said (2001) reconsidered an essay he had previously written about what he calls 'travelling theory.' His proposition was that when theories travel to other times and situations they are prone 'to lose some of their original power and rebelliousness' (Said, 2001, p. 436). Put simply his argument is summarized as follows:

> the first time a human experience is recorded and then given a theoretical formulation, its force comes from being directly connected to and organically provoked by real historical circumstances. Later versions of the theory cannot replicate its original power (ibid).

To illustrate his point, he draws on Lukacs' theory of reification that charts 'the radical separation of object and subject, the atomisation of human life under bourgeois capitalism' (2001, p. 437). Said argues that by the time Lucien Goldman in Paris and Raymond Williams in Cambridge took up reification as an analytic tool, the idea had shed its insurrectionary force and had been tamed and domesticated. Simultaneously, travelling theory acquires a prestige and authority that solidifies to dogmatic orthodoxy. In short, a social theory itself becomes a distraction from the social project.

Looking at the emergence of a theory of inclusive education, there is a fusion between the then 'new sociology of education' (Bernstein, 1971; Young, 1971; Bowles and Gintis, 1976; Bourdieu and Passeron, 1977; Willis, 1977; Apple, 1982; Connell et al, 1982; Whitty, 1985), which itself had been silent on matters of disability and education, and an emerging social model in disability studies (Finkelstein, 1980; Oliver, 1996). A number of important educational sociology texts emerged in the 1980s that invited critique of traditional special educational formulations of defectiveness and remediation. They argued that issues of unequal social relationships had been mis-attributed for professional and social expedience. Social issues were reduced to personal troubles (Wright Mills, 1959). Amongst the texts to which I refer are Sally Tomlinson's (1982) *A Sociology of Special Education*, Len Barton and Sally Tomlinson's (1981) *Special Education: Policies, Practices and Social Issues*, and Len Barton's (1988) *The Politics of Special Educational Needs*.

Tomlinson enlisted sociological tools to chart cultural bias in the politics of IQ and to demonstrate a growing professional interest in segregated provision for so-called special students. This built upon her earlier work on the politics of sub-normality, in which she identified the continuing disproportionate referral of Caribbean children to special educational trajectories as a political, rather than a medical, condition (Tomlinson, 1981). Drawing on the work of his colleague Mike Oliver, Len Barton (1988) positioned special educational needs as an invention to maintain institutional equilibrium, a euphemism for the failure of schools to meet the needs of all students and a necessary technique of the politics of disablement.

This work generated a lively new literature that confronted the dominant medical model embraced by traditional special education. Predictably, it ushered in the literature of qualification. Here I refer to that work which deployed the language of inclusion to argue for a repositioning of special education (Jenkinson, 1997; Ashman & Elkins, 1990, Mittler, 2000). This restorative work failed to interrogate its epistemic core and served to domesticate and tame the more strident calls of the educational sociologists. Still others were far less surreptitious and simply called for a return to segregation (Kauffman & Hallahan, 1995) on the basis that inclusion was an ideological imperative and therefore devoid of scientific validity. Utilizing Dunkin's (1996) methodological benchmarks as set out by Kauffman and Hallahan (1995), Ellen Brantlinger (1997) systematically unpicks the fabric of their argument. An earlier rendition on the debate over partisan research had been waged between Foster and his colleagues (1996) and Troyna (1994).

My point is that inclusive education has, in some quarters, become generalised and diffused, domesticated and tamed. In this way Said's forewarning about travelling theory is apposite. Here I must be very careful not to generate confusion around my argument. In the case of the education of disabled students, however it is not that the conditions have changed for disabled people and the call for political change is unwarranted. The issue is that as the language of inclusive schooling has

been generalised as an organising theory across a number of different constituen-
cies, its conceptual clarity and political intent has lost acuity and force. How do
we respond to this?

At one level it places greater urgency on the work of theory builders. Indeed,
over recent years we have seen that debates within the disability research community
have led to a necessarily variegated dispersal of narratives that challenge the power
of single-theory explanations to account for the multiplicity of experiences of disability and disablement (Allan, 1999; Thomas, 1999; Corker and French, 1999).
Moreover there has been a healthy outpouring of insider perspectives (Moore,
2000) that have made difficult the task of the researcher and thereby increased the
potential for more sophisticated research outcomes as a basis for more informed
policymaking. This is important epistemological work, but the project needs more.
I believe that it was Halsey who reflected on the poverty of attempting to achieve
reform through exhortation.

For this reason I am, at one level, disinclined to spend time arguing for a princi-
pled clarity to enforce dogma and purity. When mounted in isolation from the policy
arenas, this form of theorising may become distractive, removed from the reach of
disabled people and inconsequential to the sites of educational decision-making.
In this context, I am persuaded by the urgings of Tony Booth (1995) to keep our
eye trained towards exposing exclusion and systematically working towards its
deconstruction as a means for building a theory and practice of inclusion. In this
way, his work with colleagues Mark Vaughan and Mel Ainscow in developing the
Index of Inclusion (Booth et al, 1999) is instructive. The harder edge of Richard
Reiser's project of conscientisation with young people maintains an insurrectionary
presence in schools and policymaking circles and is lacking in this country.

INCLUSION AND AN EDUCATION REFORM AGENDA

The reform agenda for Queensland public education proceeds from a blueprint
entitled Queensland State Education – 2010 (Education Queensland, 1999). The
document was written to answer the question: 'what kind of schooling is necessary
to equip commencing students with the requirements to successfully deal with the
world in their year of graduation in 2010?' The document provides a comprehensive mandate for changes to curriculum and pedagogy, workforce recruitment and
development, school organisation and inter-agency relationships and work practices.
Like other Third Way charters (Giddens, 1998; 1999; 2000; Hutton & Giddens,
2000), QSE – 2010 engages with New Times (Hall & Jacques, 1989) dilemmas:

- Globalisation, with its attendant absorption of local identities and cultures through
  the press of global economic networks (Held et al, 1999), pressing against what
  Appadurai (1998) refers to as the counter assertions of globalisation
- Transformed information and knowledge production, technology and
  dissemination where the world wide web has contracted time and space (Castells,
  1996) and introduced multiple carriers of knowledge to the classroom

- Institutional structures that privilege individualism, yet exhort new communitarianism in the face of social atomisation, atrophy and anomie (Beck, 1992; Fukuyama, 1995; 1999). The struggle to build inclusion and social capital (Putnam, 2000; Touraine, 2000) in a context of competitive markets and new world disorders
- Education and skill development for jobs that do not yet exist
- International press for high stakes minimum standards paper and pencil testing in an age of multi-literacies as a yard-stick of individual and systemic educational performance
- Rhetorical acknowledgement of importance and representation of diversity and pedagogic applications of homogeneity.
- Demand for deeper knowledge and problem-solving ability in the face of continuing extensions to or 'stretching and thinning' of the curriculum.

In summary, QSE – 2010 promises a high quality educational experience for all comers, the raising of participation in and completion of twelve years of schooling from 68% of the commencing student cohort to 88% by the year 2010, and a new deal on equity. In order to challenge the hegemony of the traditional subjects structure of the curriculum, Luke and colleagues (1999) produced a technical paper as a basis for establishing a trial of New Basics curriculum organisers. The New Basics seeks to secure the links between Bernstein's school message systems: curriculum, instruction and evaluation, and to ensure that they engage with the worlds of the children and their optimal futures. In other words, the New Basics is organised around the triad of:

- New Basics: what is taught
- Productive Pedagogies: how it is taught
- Rich tasks: how it is assessed.

The knowledge organisers for what is taught comprise:

- Life pathways and social futures
- Multi-literacies and communications media
- Active citizenship
- Environment and technologies.

Put simply, this experiment across 59 schools represents a revolt against disconnected atomised knowledge as presented through the traditional curriculum; uni-dimensional pedagogy pitched at the imagined middle level student; and simplistic forms of assessment and evaluation that produce narrow data sets for teacher judgments.

The importance of this trial is critical as it represents the necessary next step in school reform that moves beyond DIY tracts about self-management and organisational restructuring. In other words, it takes up that which a number of the effectiveness and improvement writers avoid: curriculum, instruction and assessment. My argument is that moving beyond reform through exhortation in inclusive education requires deep engagement with matters of curriculum, pedagogy, assessment and school organisation. This point is not lost on researchers such as Ainscow (1999).

The QSE – 2010 participation targets adhere to OECD (1997) data and conform to that organisation's projection that life chances for employment and continuing education are enhanced through participation in twelve years of formal schooling. For Queensland policy, this has resulted first, in the movement towards a preparatory year of schooling to enhance infants' readiness for formal schooling; second, in the greater integration of information technology into teaching and learning (The State of Queensland, 2002a); and third, in a commitment to reconstruct schooling to engage the 'at least 10000 young Queenslanders aged 15 to17 (who) are not in school, not in training and not in any kind of substantial work' (The State of Queensland, 2002b, p. 6). This last point is critical, as it has generated a cross-agency commitment between the schooling and training sectors and the Department of Families, to collaborate to reinvent vocational and educational pathways through schooling for 'all' students. In effect, we have an admission that schooling, as an industrial age artefact (Schlechty, 1990; Tyack & Cuban, 1995; Sizer, 1996; Hartley, 1997), is inadequate for the task of educating increasing numbers of young people not considered to have special needs. This is a particularly important point as there is a tacit admission of what many commentators have been charting as the net widening process of special education to compensate for the closing down of the unskilled labour market (Slee, 1995).

Inclusive schooling, within this reform agenda, may be separated from narrow debates across unhelpful special and regular education binaries to a post special needs era of reconstructing schooling for all. Shortly after I came to Education Queensland, the Association of Special Education Administrators asked if my agenda centred on the closure of special schools. The real politic renders my answer obvious (After all, I am only a very civil servant.) Any Australian Education Minister would not move from a platform of 'an array of settings' in one step and risk the inevitable political backlash. So in reality, even if it were an aim, presently it is not an option. My response has been to point out that I believe that it is the wrong question to ask. The question is restorationist, a rear-view mirror take on educational policy. I suggested to people that it is the wrong question and that we ought to ask what kind of schooling young people need to take their place in viable future options. The subsidiary questions become those that address the skills we have and need, and what kind of institutional arrangements will equip us to shape the world we want. This is a question for all educationists, special and not so special. The recent White Paper, Queensland the Smart State: Education and Training Reforms for the Future (The State of Queensland, 2002b) is a discursive tactic to move government agencies, schooling and training beyond old cultures that emanate from bureaucratic turf and territory.

Equity – What's the deal?

For the purpose of this discussion, I want to reconsider the last QSE – 2010 proposal, a new deal on equity. Throughout the 1990s, equity had steadily been diluted to, or conflated with, a preoccupation with the basic reading and number skills (Lingard, 1998). Conservative thinking suggested that if poor kids could read, write and add, osmosis would lend them the agency equal to the task of liberating them from the deep structures of poverty. As a result, governments could shift their gaze from the more complex intersections of identities and poverty (Connell, 1994) to establish high stakes national minimum standards tests at year levels 3, 5 and 7. This strategy is flawed in many ways. Principally, it separates disadvantage from the policy agenda and seeks to suggest that phonics will eliminate poverty. Second, it threatens to secure its aim and promote schooling for minimum standards by reordering the priorities of the teaching force.

As a civil servant sharing responsibility for implementing the 2010 blueprint, I have used the discourse of the 2010 document to argue for a new equity deal that invites a reconsideration of the education of students with disabilities, Aboriginal and Torres Strait Islander students and students living in disadvantaged areas (pain zones) within an overarching discussion of democratic schooling, citizenship and educational access, participation and achievement (Slee, 2002). Specifically, I have insisted on inclusive education as our organising language and closed the special needs chapter. This was done as part of the necessary cultural foundations that needed to be laid. Education Queensland had hitherto pursued its work with students with disabilities from an organisational unit called the Low Incidence Unit. People inside Education Queensland did not recognise the offensiveness of the name. Moreover, a Senior Officer in the organisation responsible for developing the special education action plan urged me not to use inclusive education as the official nomenclature as it had had an unsuccessful history in Queensland. My response was that other principles such as democracy and equity have had troubled histories and that we needed to redouble our efforts rather than abandon them, modernist though they may be (although I am confident that his was not the objection of a disgruntled postmodernist.) Before outlining the strategy for inclusive education it is necessary to introduce an additional piece in the reform jigsaw.

Prior to the election of the Beattie Labor government, its conservative predecessors had commissioned a major research project ($1.3 million) to examine the links between school-based management and enhanced student outcomes. The findings of the research have been published under the title of The *Queensland School Reform Longitudinal Study* (QSRLS, Education Queensland, 2001). The research enlisted researchers from the University of Queensland and the University of Newcastle (not upon Tyne).

They quickly established that there was no hypodermic link between school-based management and improved student achievement. One could lead to the other, but the evidence seemed to suggest that because school-based management seemed to establish a field of gravity that led school principals towards myopic preoccupation with budget, protocols, structures and management theory, there had been a corresponding decline in productive educational leadership.

A core issue for the researchers was the establishment of the constituents of enhanced student achievement. It needed to comprise cognitive and affective elements. In determining the research plan, the researchers referred to the work of Fred Newmann and Associates (1996) on authentic student achievement, Michael Fullan (1993) on educational reform and Andy Hargreaves (1994) on teachers' work to suggest the elements of enhanced student achievement and the impact of education policy and teacher performance on student achievement.

Newman and Associates' research, through the Centre for Organisational Restructuring and Schools (CORS), identified a series of standards for authentic instruction. Building on their work, the QSRLS researchers developed a classroom observation manual that addressed two questions:

1. What forms of classroom practice contribute to more equitable student outcomes?
2. What forms of classroom practice contribute to increased student outcomes for all students?

The research comprised large-scale teacher and principal interviews together with statistical analyses and observations of over 975 classroom lessons in Key Learning Areas of English, mathematics, science and social studies across twenty-four schools, representing a range of schools and geographic regions. On the basis of the coded observations, the QSRLS study developed a more elaborate multi-dimensional model for the observation and assessment of classroom instruction that was named productive pedagogy. It comprised four dimensions:

- Intellectual quality
- Relevance
- Supportive classroom environment
- Recognition of difference.

The conclusion of the research was that observed performance was relatively low on all four domains of productive pedagogy. The best rating was achieved in the area of a supportive classroom environment. Intellectual demand rated lower as did relevance and recognition of diversity. While teachers demonstrated an ability to extend the intellectual demand on students in their lessons, this tended to be diminished through inappropriate or lower-level assessment tasks. It was also evident in interviews that teachers had taken up the global back to basics discourse and placed academic excellence at the bottom of a list of priorities presented to them by the researchers. Add to this questions surrounding teacher threshold knowledge and there exists cause for concern about the quality of teaching. I hasten to say that it would be extremely unproductive to slide into a tract of teacher vilification. As Education Minister, Anna Bligh, observed when presented with the draft report, it provided a more precise platform for targeted professional development. Conversely, the Queensland Teachers' Union which has a membership of approximately 98% of the Queensland public education teaching force initially wanted to dismiss the findings of the report.

The Queensland School Reform Longitudinal Study (Education Queensland, 2001) also found an absence of connection between students and what they were being taught. Connections between the curriculum, pedagogy and the world of the students were at best tenuous. The researchers also concluded that although teachers were generally able to enter into informed and engaging discussions about student diversity, there was little evidence of teaching for diversity in the classrooms they observed. Methodologically, this remains the weakest link in the research design itself.

Though the results of the research are indeed disappointing, they do provide a platform for teacher development consistent with the larger '2010' reform agenda. In this way, we have been able to link the inclusive schooling agenda to a more general reform of curriculum and pedagogy. A new deal on equity warrants a reconsideration of how we achieve Bernstein's requirement for connection between productive knowledge, connected and demanding instruction and multi-dimensional evaluative approaches for all children.

A new deal on equity also suggests a targeted funding mechanism that re-affirms Rawls' (1971) call for distributive justice. The QSRLS findings on diversity press us to elaborate Rawls' work consistent with Fraser's (1997) reminder that redistribution of itself does not guarantee a politics of recognition. It is the politics of recognition that has been absent from discussions of the so-called special needs policy agenda. This has to be the point of embarkation for a new deal for disabled students, their families and advocates in Queensland.

SCHOOL REFORM AS CULTURAL POLITICS

As a precondition for 'a school that democratises,' Alain Touraine (2000, p. 283) announces that 'in a world of intense cultural exchanges, there can be no democracy unless we recognise the diversity of cultures and the relations of domination that exist between them' (ibid, p. 185). Given the QSRLS conclusion of the absence of evidence of the recognition of diversity in their classroom observations, there remains intense cultural work to be undertaken in Queensland public schooling. The challeng is to ensure that this objective does not stumble into a neo-liberal fog of 'developing students' and teachers' 'tolerance of difference.' I still find myself taking the red pen to policy texts that continue to exhort Queenslanders to 'tolerance of difference. Tolerance is the language of oppression. A disabled colleague once told me that if anyone else inferentially told him that they would tolerate him and those like him, he would 'kick their fucking head in!' My reportage of the vernacular is not gratuitous, it serves to emphasise our obliviousness of the impact of our careless language.

Peter McLaren takes up the issue for us:

Diversity that somehow constitutes itself as a harmonious ensemble of benign cultural spheres is a conservative and liberal model of multi-culturalism that, in my mind, deserves to be jettisoned because, when we try to make culture an undisturbed space of harmony and agreement where social relations exist within cultural forms of uninterrupted accords we subscribe to a form of social amnesia in which we forget that all knowledge forged in histories that are played out in the field of social antagonisms (McLaren, quoted in bell hooks, 1994, p. 31)

An immediate area of policy work in Education Queensland, therefore, has been the reconstruction of educational disablement as cultural politics. Hitherto, special education has been delivered and defended as technical work where expertise and an array of physical and student support resources is deployed to minimise the disabling effects of individual student defectiveness. To suggest that what we once called special education is a default vocabulary for the domination of cultural groups we have rendered 'strangers' (Bauman, 1997) is not an easy, but a necessary, task. A key element in a new deal has to be a firm reassurance to people with disabilities, their families and allies that there is a new culture and that they themselves will play a key part in shaping inclusive education.

The politics surrounding the schooling of disabled students in Queensland have been savage. The teachers union, parent advocacy organisations and Education Queensland have vacillated from outright hostility to uncomfortable stand-offs. There has been vexatious litigation, disputes waged through the local press and bureaucratic belligerence. The language used in letters from central office is often unnecessarily officious and unhelpful to the users of the education service. Though the teachers' union has a strong track record when working on issues of race, it adopts a simple calculus of equity (Slee, 1996) that renders them less capable of more lateral thinking about equity when it comes to disability.

One of my initial goals was to bring the various parties, including Education Queensland, out of the trenches and bunkers, by setting up an important forum where all parties were represented and were charged with responsibility for advising the Minister on issues of inclusive education. This has meant that people have had to learn to treat each other with respect and dignity and to listen to each other in ways that were not previously countenanced. This body is the Ministerial Taskforce on Inclusive Education and is chaired by Professor John Elkins. Minister Bligh having previously been Minister for Disability Services in Queensland has been a powerful positive influence in reshaping the pitch and timbre of a new dialogue.

It is worth mentioning that shortly after commencing in my position I invited members of Queensland Parents of People with Disabilities into my office for a lunchtime meeting. They observed that this was the first time that they had been invited into the central office. We now have monthly meetings at each other's offices in order that we can discuss and monitor issues.

As a matter of course, members of the teachers' union, the principals' and headmasters' associations, the special schools administrators' organisations and parent groups attend meetings where policy is being developed. I repeatedly declare a commitment to the practice, rather than the rhetoric, of collaboration. Learning to talk with each other has been a key element of the new deal for cultural change and is a hallmark of the present Education Minister's approach.

I believe it was Barry MacDonald who declared: 'you can't dismantle the master's house with the master's tools.' To that end, an immediate task was to abolish the Low Incidence Unit and establish a Students with Disability Policy Unit within the newly formed Inclusive Education Branch. This unit sits alongside the Partners for Success (Aboriginal and Torres Strait Islander Unit) and the Inclusive Learning Unit. To lead this area, I recruited Michael Walsh from Disability Services Queensland, a person who carries a new set of bags and is an extremely competent and personable administrator and policy worker. A Staff College – Inclusive Education, to lead professional development, was also established and Dr Suzanne Carrington, a respected teacher and academic who has been involved with international Index for Inclusion projects (Booth et al, 2000), was appointed as the Principal. Not surprisingly, some of our colleagues have evacuated the building as they feel dissonance with new times: some believe that we have gone too far with inclusive education; others say we have not gone far enough.

In my first year I invited Mark Vaughan from the Centre for Studies in Inclusive Education to spend time with teachers across the state discussing the Index for Inclusion (CSIE, 2000). At this time, the Inclusive Education Branch commenced a major round of consultations in preparation for a Inclusive Schooling Summit to be facilitated by Mel Ainscow later in the year. Bringing together principals, teachers, parents, community organisation leaders, administrators and students, the summit delivered a statement of principle that calls for presence, access, participation and achievement for disabled students in Queensland schools and an action plan which is being considered by the Minister. Julie Allan, Sally Tomlinson and Keith Ballard have also responded to calls to work with Education Queensland to explore the cultural, community, pedagogic and policy implications of inclusive schooling.

As I write, there are other ongoing projects that sit across the harder dilemmas for reformers. Resources, or more precisely funding, has always been held up as central to the reconciliation of the problem of including students with disabilities in regular schools. Certainly, many students have differing support requirements in order to be able to access the curriculum. This is not disputed. Often, however, the resources card is dealt to trump inclusion, a distraction from the real desire to exclude. In Queensland, an algorithm called ascertainment is used to distribute additional resources to students with disability seeking inclusion in regular schools. It is a six-tiered schedule where resources are given when a student is ascertained at levels four, five or six. Not surprisingly most arrive quickly at levels five and six. The absurdity is that all level six students attract exactly the same amount of resource allocation to their schools despite differing levels of educational support needs. A student with a level six speech language impairment is treated the same as a student with profound multiple disabilities. Neither is there any recognition in the calculations that schools with larger numbers of students may utilise economies of scale.

The ascertainment process is itself flawed in its varied administration, relying as it does on volunteers. Add to this the fact that it manufactures disability as a resource driver and pressures people towards emphasising deficits rather than abilities and you have a negatively geared labeller. Underlying this is a more fundamental issue for government surrounding competing budget priorities across agencies. From a government perspective, students with disabilities may represent an annual cost blow out. More categories of disability are added to the ascertainment schedule (for example, implementation of the Disability Discrimination Legislation will result in the addition of psychiatric illness and acquired brain injuries), and more students, those who were traditionally jettisoned from school prematurely to the unskilled labour market, are seeking entitlement to additional funds on the basis of behaviour disorders. I recently heard a speaker from UNESCO correct the record to describe school dropouts as school shove-outs. While students with disabilities represent 3.1% of the total student cohort and this is modest in comparison to some other Australian states, it will continue to escalate and impress itself on the cabinet and treasury mind as a problem.

We have engaged economic modellers who have worked on a range of human services projects to reconsider the allocation mechanism within the broader context of social accounting and school funding. There is also an attempt to introduce profiling that will assess educational need for students rather than calibrate disability. Of course, these projects are incomplete. Once again there has been the involvement of a range of constituents in these developments.

Major changes have been made in relation to enrollments procedures. Formerly, there was a 'placement policy' for disabled students. All other students are enrolled, but disabled students are placed! This has changed and has also ushered in proposals for changes to transport assistance to increase accessibility to schools of choice. Other work to be done lies around the establishment of an independent complaints forum.

Finally, and here I return to earlier remarks, is the project around pedagogy, curriculum and assessment. Through the work of the Staff College – Inclusive Education, a series of projects is being co-ordinated where schools are trialing the Index for Inclusion and others are developing local cluster resource management. A consortium of special schools has taken up New Basics as a force for developing inclusive schooling for special schools. Certainly, I have witnessed progress from traditional remediation and training patterns, but it remains to be seen that this is not a tactic of subversion and restoration.

Educating teachers

It is beyond the scope of this paper to develop a treatise for a 'new deal' for teacher education. Elsewhere I have considered the dilemmas for teacher education (Slee, 1999). At that time I expressed my continuing concern that teacher educators are subject to traditional special educational hegemony, where units in special education are mandated by state education authorities to transform teachers into experts on student defectiveness. If our teachers are to become, to use Said's term, the public intellectuals to lead us into new inclusive times, a traditional curriculum of defectology and the technology culturally laden diagnostic testing will not suffice.

Familiarity with difference across the broad spectrum of identities and cultures and implications for classroom practice is required. Also required is an education in reading cultural politics, so that teachers can recognise the benefits to be gained from a range of differences incorporated into curriculum and pedagogy. The baseline for development of teacher education programmes in Queensland comprises both QSRLS and the New Basics.

In summary, I would argue that teacher education for inclusion requires a trans-disciplinary team to consider new times requirements for an education for the future for all comers. Questions surrounding curriculum and pedagogy for different identities, be they associated with English as an additional language, deaf education, visual impairment, refugee issues, Indigenous identities, and so the list goes on, stand at the centre of what in effect must be a teacher education to establish schooling as an apprenticeship in democracy.

How civil should a servant be?

Retrospectively, I do sense progress with markers of substantive achievements. Ahead, I sense further obstacles to the securing of the inclusive education I speak of. Civil servants do dance around the politics of pragmatism while attempting to retain ethical integrity. Compromise is, I contend, an element of the politics of progress. A well-known Chinese agrarian revolutionary used to talk to his comrades about living to fight another day. Though his biographers credit his background as a teacher, I sense something of a civil servant in his training. A Year 10 Asian history student of mine, Sylvie, when asked to define guerrilla warfare declared that: 'Guerrilla warfare is where you trick the enemy by winning.' I remain grateful to Sylvie and hope that I will be able to sum up my work for inclusive education in the Queensland bureaucracy in similar fashion.

REFERENCES

Ainscow, M. (1999). *Understanding the development of inclusive schools*. London: Falmer Press.
Allan, J. (1999). *Actively seeking inclusion*. London: Falmer Press.
Appadurai, A. (1998). *Modernity at large: cultural dimensions of globalization*. Minneapolis: University of Minnesota Press.
Apple, M. (1982). *Education and power*. London: Routledge and Kegan Paul.
Ashman, A. and Elkins, J. (Eds.) (1990). *Educating children with special needs*. Sydney, Prentice-Hall.
Barton, L. (Ed.), (1988). *The politics of special educational needs*. Lewes: Falmer Press.
Barton, L. and Tomlinson, S. (Eds.), (1981). *Special education: Policies, practices and social Issues*, London, Croom Helm.
Bauby, J. D. (1997). *The diving-Bell and the butterfly*. London: Fourth Estate.

Bauman, Z. (1997). *Postmodernity and its discontents*. Cambridge: Polity Press.

Beck, U. (1992). *Risk society: Towards a new modernity*. London: Sage.

Bernstein, B. (1971). *Class, codes and control, Vol. 1*. London: Taylor & Francis.

Bernstein, B. (1996) *Pedagogy symbolic control and identity*. London: Taylor & Francis.

Booth, T. (1985) Mapping inclusion and exclusion: Concepts for all. In C. Clark, A. Dyson, & A. Millward (Eds.), *Towards inclusive schools*. London: David Fulton.

Booth, T., Ainscow, M., Black-Hawkins, K., Vaughan, M., & Shaw. L. (2000). *Index for Inclusion*. Bristol: Centre for Studies on Inclusive Education.

Bourdieu, P. & Passeron, J. (1977) *Reproduction in education, society and culture*. London: Sage.

Bowles, S. & Gintis, H. (1976) *Schooling in capitalist America*. London: Routledge and Kegan Paul.

Brantlinger, E. (1997) Using Ideology: cases of nonrecognition of the politics of research and practice in special education. *Review of Educational Research, 67*, 425–459.

Castells, M. (1996) *The Rise of the networked society*. Massachusetts: Blackwell Publishers.

Connell, R.W., Ashenden, D., Kessler, S. and Dowsett, G. (1982). *Making the difference*. Sydney: George Allen &Unwin.

Connell, R.W. (1994). Poverty and education. *Harvard Educational Review, 64*(2),125–149.

Corker, M. and French, S. (Eds.), (1999). *Disability discourse*. Buckingham: Open University Press.

Dunkin, M.J. (1996). Types of errors in synthesising research in education. *Review of Educational Research, 66*, 87–97.

Education Queensland (1999). *Queensland State Education – 2010*. Brisbane: Queensland Government.

Education Queensland (2001). *The Queensland school reform longitudinal study (QSRLS)*. Brisbane: Department of Education.

Finkelstein, V. (1980). *Attitudes and disabled people: Issues for discussion*. New York: World Rehabilitation Fund.

Foster, P., Gomm, R. & Hammersley, M. (1996). *Constructing educational inequality*. London: Falmer Press.

Fraser, N. (1997). *Justice interruptus: Critical reflections on the postsocialist condition*. New York: Routledge.

Fukuyama, F. (1995). *Trust*. New York: The Free Press.

Fukuyama, F. (1999). *The great disruption*. London: Profile Books.

Fullan, M. (1993). *Change forces*. London: Falmer Press.

Giddens, A. (1998). *The third way*. Cambridge: Polity Press.

Giddens, A. (1999). *Runaway world: How globalisation is reshaping our lives*. Cambridge: Polity Press.

Giddens, A. (2000). *The third way and its critics*. Cambridge: Polity Press.

Hall, S. and Jacques, M. (Eds.), (1989). *New times: The changing face of politics in the 1990s*. London: Lawrence and Wishart with Marxism Today.

Halpin, D. and Troyna, B. (Eds.), (1994). *Researching education policy: Ethical and methodological Issues*. London: Falmer Press.

Hargreaves, A. (1994). *Changing teachers, changing times*. London: Cassell.

Hartley, D. (1997). *Re-schooling society*. London: Falmer Press.

Held, D., McGrew, A., Goldblatt, D. and Perraton, J. (1999). *Global transformations: politics, economics and culture*. Cambridge: Polity Press.

hooks, B. (1994). *Teaching to transgress*. New York: Routledge.

Hutton, W. and Giddens, A. (Eds.), (2000). *On the Edge: living with global capitalism.* London: Jonathan Cape.

Jenkinson, J. (1997). *Mainstream or special?* London: Routledge.

Kauffman, J.M. and Hallahan, D.P. (Eds.) (1995). *The illusion of full inclusion.* Austin: Pro-Ed.

Lingard, B. (1998). The disadvantaged schools programme: caught between literacy and local management. *International Journal of Inclusive Education,* 2(1), 1–14.

Luke, A., Matters, G., Herschell, P., Grace, N., Barrett, R. and Land, R. (1999). *New basics: Technical paper.* Brisbane: Education Queensland.

Mittler, P. (2000). *Working towards inclusive education: social contexts.* London: David Fulton.

Moore, M. (Ed.), (2000). *Insider perspectives on inclusion: Raising voices, raising issues* Sheffield: Philip Armstrong Publications.

Newmann, F.M. and Associates (1996). *Authentic achievement: Restructuring schools for intellectual quality.* San Francisco: Jossey-Bass.

OECD (1997). *Education Policy Analysis.* 1997 Edition. Paris: OECD.

Oliver, M. (1996). *Understanding disability: From theory to practice.* Basingstoke: Macmillan Press.

Putnam, R. D. (2000) *Bowling alone: The collapse and revival of american community.* New York: Touchstone Books.

Rawls, J. (1971). *A theory of justice.* Oxford: Oxford University Press.

Said, E. (2001). *Reflections on exile and other literary and cultural essays.* London: Granta Publications.

Schlechty, P.C. (1990). *Schools for the 21st century.* San Francisco: Jossey Bass.

Sizer, T.R. (1996). *Horace's hope. What works for the American high school,* New York: Mariner Books.

Slee, R. (1995). *Changing theories and practices of discipline.* London: Falmer Press.

Slee, R. (1996). Clauses of conditionality. In L. Barton (Ed.), *Disability and society: emerging issues and insights.* London: Longman.

Slee, R. (2001). Social justice and the changing directions in educational research: the case of inclusive education. *International Journal of Inclusive Education,* 5(2/3), 167–177.

Slee, R. (2002). Inclusive education: The heart of the reform agenda, *Education Views,* 11(21), 16.

The State of Queensland (2000a). ICTs for learning: School information kit 2002–2003. Brisbane: Department of Education.

The State of Queensland (2002b). *Queensland the smart state: Education and training reforms for the future.* White Paper. Brisbane: Department of Education.

Thomas, C. (1999). *Female forms: Experiencing and understanding disability.* Buckingham: Open University Press.

Tomlinson, S. (1981). *Educational subnormality: A study in decision-making.* London: Routledge & Kegan Paul.

Tomlinson, S. (1982). *A sociology of special education.* London: Routledge & Kegan Paul.

Touraine, A. (2000). *Can we live together? Equality and difference.* Cambridge: Polity Press.

Troyna, B. (1994). Critical social research and education policy. *British Journal of Educational Studies,* 42(1), 70–84.

Tyack, D. and Cuban, L. (1995). *Tinkering toward utopia.* Cambridge, MA: Harvard University Press.

Walford, G. (1994). *Researching the powerful in education.* London: UCL Press.

Whitty, G. (1985). *Sociology and school knowledge: curriculum theory, research and politics.* London: Methuen.

Willis, P. (1977). *Learning to labour.* Westmead: Saxon House.

Wright Mills, C. (1959). *The sociological imagination.* New York: Oxford University Press.

Young, M. F. D. (Ed.) (1971). *Knowledge and control: New directions for the sociology of education.* London: Macmillan.

JULIE ALLAN

14 CONCLUDING REMARKS

These concluding remarks are provided, not in an attempt to either summarise or synthesise the various contributions; rather, they are offered in the hope of highlighting some of the key insights which the authors have generated into the 'bigger picture' of inclusion, participation and democracy, and ensuring that the debates they have provoked can continue elsewhere.

Let us return to the questions posed to the Colloquium participants:

- What are the goals/ambitions for inclusion and what forms of participation are necessary to achieve these? What changes in culture and politics are implied?
- What is the nature of the interaction between inclusion and identity (both individual and collective)?
- Is it possible to specify an ethical framework for inclusion?
- What kinds of consequences can be specified in relation to inclusion?

These are difficult questions and it is to the contributors' credit that they have attempted to address these, either explicitly or implicitly, in their chapters. Many of the authors pointed to the tautological nature of discourses on inclusion, particpation and democracy, echoing Hobsbawm's (1994) and Bauman's (2001) contentions, regarding community and democracy respectively, that these are most keenly talked about when they are perceived to be undergoing some form of crisis. Hobsbawm, for example suggests that 'never was the word community used more indiscriminately and emptily than in the decades when communities in the sociological sense became hard to find in real life' (p. 428). Bauman makes a similar point regarding democracy, with his suggestion that 'you can tell a democratic society by its never fully quelled suspicion that its job is unfinished: that it is not democratic enough' (p. 202). Bauman also points to the 'spectacular rise of the identity discourse,' (ibid, p. 141) in which the problem is:

> not so much how to obtain the identities of their choice and how to have them recognised by people around – but which identity to choose and how to keep alert and vigilant so that another choice can be made in case the previously chosen identity is withdrawn from the market or stripped of its seductive powers (ibid, p. 147).

The contributors to this volume have refused to dodge the confusion, contradictions and ambiguities – and indeed the silences, as Colleen Brown, Alan Dyson and Alan Millward have highlighted – that exist in the discourses of inclusion and have provided us with some provocation to take the debate forward.

J. Allan (ed.), Inclusion, Participation and Democracy: What is the Purpose?, 225-230.
© 2003 *Kluwer Academic Publishers. Printed in the Netherlands.*

What are the goals/ambitions for inclusion and what forms of participation are
necessary to achieve these? What changes in culture and politics are implied?

In considering the goals of inclusion alongside participation and democracy, several
of the contributors have stressed the need to challenge the narrow understandings
of inclusion that exist at present. Roger Slee reminds us that these are set within
highly technicist discourses, and while Colleen Brown and her colleagues question whether inclusion has outlived its usefulness, Slee argues that we need to
work with this and other concepts which have had troubled histories (including,
he suggests, democracy) and to shape their meaning in more acceptable ways. In
their separate analyses of the Norwegian context, Marit Strømstad and Kari Nes
both concluded that inclusion for 'all' did not always mean for 'all.' Strømstad
went further to suggest that attempts to invoke children's participation in school
were tantamount to a 'fake democracy,' in which children could not be expected
to learn how to understand, and learn from, diversity. Dora Bjarnason's study of
young people in Iceland underlined the importance of inclusion in enabling young
people to reach adulthood and demonstrated how fragile adult status was for young
disabled people.

Several authors drew attention to the negative conditions which they saw
as undermining any ambitions that might be held for inclusion. Keith Ballard's
account from New Zealand, of a dominating ideology of individualism and a low
care environment, which is bereft of trust, and in which teachers are reduced to
managing their learners' outcomes, will be depressingly familiar to us all. The
damaging effects of the 'standards agenda' on inclusion within England and Wales,
documented by Mel Ainscow and Dave Tweddle, and by Colleen Brown and her
colleagues, will also be recognisable in many contexts across the world. Nevertheless, on the basis of their successful work within Local Education Authorities,
Ainscow and Tweddle remind us of our dual responsibilities to promote inclusion
and raise standards.

War perhaps presents the most damaging threat to inclusion, as Alison
Closs's harrowing account of former Yugoslavia illustrates. The exhaustion of whole
populations and slow economic recovery create a dependency on international aid
and Closs documents how 'special education' can thrive in this context, sustained
by professionals' vested interests. In spite of this, Closs reports evidence of 'great
good,' in which citizens showed humanity to others 'across the divide' and remains
optimistic that inclusion can be an important vehicle for fostering citizenship and
democracy.

What is the nature of the interaction between inclusion and identity (both
individual and collective)?

> This is a free country, madam. We have the right to share your privacy (Peter
> Ustinov, cited in Bauman, 2001, p. 205).

Several of the authors in this volume, not only testify to the increasing intrusion into individuals' private spaces, but also suggest that identity itself is under threat. 'Special' identities continue to be nurtured, ensuring inclusion remains elusive at least for some individuals. Dora Bjarnason's study of young adults illustrates vividly how these individuals who were somewhere in between mainstream and special schooling suffered from a lack of identity and place in society. Kari Nes suggests that individuals may be helped to cultivate a kind of 'double qualification,' which could place them at an advantage compared with their mainstream peers and while she is speaking specifically about individuals from minority ethnic cultures, her argument could apply to a multitude of 'others.' Roger Slee leaves us in no doubt about the professionals' culpability in continuing to advocate 'tolerance of difference,' and the response to this by a disabled colleague underlines what impact this has. The new rhetoric of 'celebrating diversity' seems equally vacuous and offensive.

Keith Ballard's searing analysis of the impact on professionals of having to operate in an environment which is stripped of relationships, care and trust. Citing Locke (2000), he contends that 'it takes away your soul' (p. 22). Almeida Diniz, looking back on his years as the only senior black academic in Scotland, recalls his sense of isolation, pain and sense of being under attack. In spite of this, he has sought to mobilise his own sense of 'rage' to push for change within the system.

Is it possible to specify an ethical framework for inclusion?

The contributors have been clear that the project of inclusion is both a political and an ethical one and, as Linda Ware, Keith Ballard and Roger Slee emphasise, must begin with a 'suspicion of ourselves' (MacIntyre, 1999, p. 4) and of our knowledge, understanding and values. Whilst the authors have avoided anything that might amount to a blueprint or a template, they have given some clear steers as to what the responsibilities with regard to inclusion are. As Derrida (1992) reminds us, we cannot avoid the language of responsibility and identity, although we must submit this to critique.

If inclusion starts with ourselves, what should we be doing? Mel Ainscow and Dave Tweddle affirm the important role which academics occupy as 'outsiders,' and appear to have mobilised inclusion within Local Education Authorities in ways which allow officers to respond simultaneously to the 'standards' imperative. Roger Slee's 'insider' role as a not so civil servant (in spite of what he claims) within the Queensland Government appears to have achieved so much in reframing the discourse on inclusion. He achieved this, partly by 'closing the special needs chapter,' but more fundamentally, he has drawn the politicians' and policymakers' attention to the fact that they are asking the wrong questions. That is no small achievement. My own work in the Scottish Parliament left me with some hope that if the politicians could get the point about inclusion and recognise the ways in which contradictory policies created impossibilities for teachers and schools, then so might the Government officials. I remain hopeful, but impatient. Fernando

Almeida Diniz has been more patient and has tenaciously pushed 'race' onto the inclusion agenda in both policy and research. His efforts appear to have been rewarded by the greater awareness of the silencing of 'race,' which has been a feature of inclusion discourses and the general acceptance of a code of practice for the conduct of research on 'race.' Yet, he makes it clear that the exclusion of black academics from senior positions in higher education, and the general absence of minority ethnic role models in schools continue to form the basis of institutional racism. Alison Closs reminds us to keep questioning the role of Westerners in promoting inclusion in other countries and Kari Nes contends that any attempt to pursue the inclusion agenda should involve a cultural analysis of the local context, urging us to make greater use of social anthropology in our activities. Perhaps, as we reframe the debate as cultural politics, as Slee urges us to do, we also need to formulate, in Levinas' (1998) terms, an ethics of the encounter with the other.

The 'suspicion of ourselves' has to be accompanied by extreme vigilance, in which we are on the look out for what is likely to undermine or interrupt inclusion. Gwynned Lloyd warns us against the seductive powers of diagnosis – in this instance of ADHD – which lures parents and professionals by promising them certainty, treatment and – most probably not – inclusion. Roger Slee highlights the dangers of the domestication and taming of inclusion, which threatens to rid it of its complexity and calls for exercises in cultural politics for teachers so that they too can anticipate these dangers. Linda Ware echoes this call and her unquestionable success in engaging teachers with disability studies allows us to imagine possibilities for reframing inclusion practice in schools.

Inter-dependency is clearly a necessary component of inclusion, both in relation to professionals and young people, as Ainscow and Tweddle's work in LEAs and Dora Bjarnason's study illustrate. The authors in each case urged us to view inter-dependency as a positive, rather than pejorative, concept. Yet, given the absence of trust in our systems, underlined by Keith Ballard, it is difficult to envisage how people can be encouraged to 'let go.' Marit Strømstad is clear that this has to be learnt in schools and that schools have to be reconfigured as democratic spaces, in which children gain 'real' experience of being citizens.

What kinds of consequences can be specified in relation to inclusion?

The consequences we are concerned with here are those which are meaningful and acceptable to individuals and their families and contrast with the narrow and highly specific 'outcomes' or 'indicators,' required within frameworks of accountability.

The contributors are in no doubt that this is where there is considerable work to do. Dora Bjarnason suggests that one important consequence of inclusion is the achievement of adult status, with the scope to make choices about work, leisure and relationships and have dreams for the future. Beyond that, however, as Colleen and colleagues point out, we still do not know whether educational attainments convert into improved life chances. More generally, we have little sense of what the consequences of 'good' inclusion might be to those most directly concerned – the failure to engage with young people and their families in this regard is unacceptable. It is only when we start to take seriously what they regard as meaningful inclusion for their lives and selves, that we will begin to get some answers to the question: 'What is the purpose.'

INCLUSION, PARTICIPATION AND DEMOCRACY: AN EPIC GESTURE?

In the introduction to this book, I suggested that asking questions about the purpose of inclusion, participation and democracy amounted, in Derrida's (1992) terms, to an 'epic gesture,' in which both the possibilities and contradictions would be acknowledged. The contributors, in offering their 'visions,' have also underlined the way in which policy, practice and research are characterised by impossibilities, contradictions and uncertainities, within systems and frameworks of accountability which require the enactment of confidence, certainty and transparancy.

Thinking about inclusion, participation and democracy, we might recognise our responsibilities as pulling in different directions, but as having equal importance. For example, Derrida (1992) asks how we might respect and respond to, on the one hand, differences and minorities and, on the other hand, the 'universality of formal law, the desire for translation, agreement and univocity, the law of the majority, opposition to racism, nationalism and xenophobia' (ibid, p. 78). Rather than seeking to reduce these double-edged responsibilities to a single set of 'recommendations,' with the inevitable erasure this will generate, it is perhaps more responsible to acknowledge the divergent nature of these obligations.

Derrida argues that, while daunting, this acknowledgement of impossibility could take us closer to justice. It is a responsible form of education which requires us to ignore some of the haunting voices in the choices that we make (Levinas, 1979) and to resist the temptation to neutralise educational processes 'through a translating medium which would claim to be transparent, metalinguistic and universal' (Derrida, 1992, p. 58). It requires educators to take risks, but if, as Arendt (1968) says, education is where 'we decide whether we love our children enough ... not to strike from their hands the chance of undertaking something new, something unforseen by us' (p. 198) then we need to constantly re-examine what this means for us today (Biesta, 2001).

REFERENCES

Arendt, H. (1968). *Between past and future: Eight exercises in political thought.* Harmondsworth: Penguin.
Bauman, Z. (2001). The individualised society. Cambridge: Polity.
Biesta, G. (2001) Preparing for the incalculable. In G. Biesta & D. Egéa-Kuehne (Eds.), *Derrida & education.* London: Routledge.
Derrida, J (1992) The other heading: Reflections on today's Europe. trans P-A. Brault & M. B. Naas. Bloomington & Indianapolis: Indiana University.
Hobsbawm, E. (1994). The age of extremes. London: Michael Joseph.

Levinas, E. (1979) *Totality and infinity*. Trans. A Lingis. Pittsburgh: Duquesne University Press.

Levinas, R. (1998). On thinking of the other: Entre nous (M. Smith & B. Harshaw, Trans.). London: Athalone.

Locke, T. (2000). *Curriculum, assessment and the erosion of professionalism*. Paper presented to the 18th World Congress of Reading, July, Auckland (NZ).

MacIntyre, A. (1999). *Dependent rational animals: Why human beings need the virtues*. Chicago: Open Court Press.